Industrialization of U.S. Agriculture

Industrialization of U.S. Agriculture
An Interpretive Atlas
Howard F. Gregor

NEW YORK AND LONDON

First published 1982 by Westview Press, Inc.

Published 2021 by Routledge
605 Third Avenue, New York, NY 10017
2 Park Square, Milton Park, Abingdon, Oxon OX14 4RN

Routledge is an imprint of the Taylor & Francis Group, an informa business

Copyright © 1982 by Taylor & Francis

All rights reserved. No part of this book may be reprinted or reproduced or utilised in any form or by any electronic, mechanical, or other means, now known or hereafter invented, including photocopying and recording, or in any information storage or retrieval system, without permission in writing from the publishers.

Notice:
Product or corporate names may be trademarks or registered trademarks, and are used only for identification and explanation without intent to infringe.

Library of Congress Catalog Card Number: 82-050180

ISBN13: 978-0-3670-1889-4 (hbk)
ISBN13: 978-0-3671-6876-6 (pbk)
DOI: 10.4324/9780429048753

Printed in the United Kingdom
by Henry Ling Limited

Contents

List of Figures and Tables ix
Preface xii

1 THE CONCEPTUALIZATION OF AGRICULTURAL
  INDUSTRIALIZATION 1

  The Large Farm as an Industrialization Indicator . 2
  Capitalization as an Industrialization Indicator . 8
  The Research Design 10

2 THE INTENSITY OF AGRICULTURAL INDUSTRIALIZATION . 13

  Intensity of Land and Building Capitalization . . 13
    Concentration on the Better Farmland 13
    Concentration Nearer the Cities 21
  Intensity of Labor Capitalization 24
  Intensity of Capitalization in Mechanization . .   31
    Machinery and Equipment Investments 31
    Operational Expenditures 38
    Higher-Order Mechanization Patterns 44
  Intensity of Capitalization in Cropping 46
    Crop Investments 47
    Cropping Expenditures and Higher-Order
      Cropping Patterns 65
  Intensity of Capitalization in Livestock and
    Poultry Raising 72
    Livestock and Poultry Investments 72
    Higher-Order Patterns of Crop and
      Livestock-Poultry Investments 88
    Livestock and Poultry Expenditures   89
    A Summary Pattern of Crop and Livestock-Poultry
      Capitalization Intensity   96

3 THE SCALE OF AGRICULTURAL INDUSTRIALIZATION . . . 105

  Scale of Land and Building Capitalization 106

    Scale of Labor Capitalization 111
    Scale of Capitalization in Mechanization. 116
       Machinery and Equipment Investments 116
       Operational Expenditures. 124
       Higher-Order Mechanization Patterns 128
    Scale of Capitalization in Cropping 132
       Crop Investments. 132
       Cropping Expenditures and Higher-Order Cropping
         Patterns. 138
    Scale of Capitalization in Livestock and Poultry
      Raising 142
       Livestock and Poultry Investments 142
       Higher-Order Patterns of Crop and Livestock-
         Poultry Investments 149
       Livestock and Poultry Expenditures and Higher-
         Order Patterns. 151
       A Summary Pattern of Total Crop and Livestock-
         Poultry Capitalization. 154

4 THE STRUCTURE OF AGRICULTURAL INDUSTRIALIZATION . 159

    The General Intensity Structure 159
    The Intensity Substructures 166
    The General Scale Structure 173
    The Scale Substructures 177

5 THE TYPES OF AGRICULTURAL INDUSTRIALIZATION . . . 189

    Types of General Agricultural Industrialization . 189
    Types of Industrialization in Cropping and in
      Livestock-Poultry Raising. 192
    Types of Limited Industrialized Agriculture . . . 204

6 THE PERFORMANCE OF AGRICULTURAL INDUSTRIALIZATION 215

    Productivity and Industrialization. 215
    Profitability and Industrialization 221
    The Future Spatial Pattern. 232

Index. 237

Figures and Tables

<u>Figures</u>

1.1	Percentage of Farms 260 Acres or Larger	4
1.2	Percentage of Farms with 100 or More Acres of Harvested Cropland.	5
2.1	Land and Building Investments per Farm Acre . .	15
2.2	Labor Expenditures per Farm Acre.	27
2.3	Machinery and Equipment Investments per Farm Acre.	32
2.4	Machine Hire, Customwork, and Fuel Expenditures per Farm Acre	40
2.5	Crop Investments per Farm Acre.	49
2.6	Crop Expenditures per Farm Acre	67
2.7	Livestock and Poultry Investments per Farm Acre	74
2.8	Livestock and Poultry Expenditures per Farm Acre.	90
3.1	Land and Building Investments per Farm.	107
3.2	Labor Expenditures per Farm	113
3.3	Machinery and Equipment Investments per Farm. .	117
3.4	Machine Hire, Customwork, and Fuel Expenditures per Farm.	125
3.5	Crop Investments per Farm	133
3.6	Crop Expenditures per Farm.	139
3.7	Livestock and Poultry Investments per Farm. . .	143
3.8	Livestock and Poultry Expenditures per Farm . .	152
4.1	Intensity of General Agricultural Industrialization.	163
4.2	Intensity of Industrialization in Cropping. . .	168
4.3	Intensity of Industrialization in Livestock and Poultry Raising	172
4.4	Scale of General Agricultural Industrialization	178
4.5	Scale of Industrialization in Cropping.	182
4.6	Scale of Industrialization in Livestock and Poultry Raising	185
5.1	Types and Levels of General Agricultural Industrialization	190
5.2	Type 1 Levels of General Agricultural Industrialization	193

5.3 Types and Levels of Industrialization in
     Cropping. 195
5.4 Type 1 Levels of Industrialization in Cropping. 197
5.5 Types and Levels of Industrialization in
     Livestock and Poultry Raising 200
5.6 Type 1 Levels of Industrialization in Livestock
     and Poultry Raising 202
5.7 Types and Levels of Limited Industrialized
     Agriculture 205
5.8 Types and Levels of Limited Industrialized
     Cropping. 208
5.9 Types and Levels of Limited Industrialized
     Livestock and Poultry Raising 211
6.1 Value Added per Farm Acre 217
6.2 Value Added per Farm. 218
6.3 Net Value of Farm Products Sold per Farm Acre . 225
6.4 Net Value of Farm Products Sold per Farm. . . 227
6.5 Net Farm Income per Operator-Equivalent . . . 231

Tables

4.1 Correlations Between Capital-Input Criteria
     for the Intensity of Agricultural
     Industrialization 160
4.2 The Intensity Structure of General Agricultural
     Industrialization 162
4.3 The Twenty Leading Counties in Intensity of
     General Agricultural Industrialization. . . . 165
4.4 The Intensity Structure of Industrialization in
     Cropping. 167
4.5 The Twenty Leading Counties in Intensity of
     Industrialization in Cropping 170
4.6 The Intensity Structure of Industrialization in
     Livestock and Poultry Raising 171
4.7 The Twenty Leading Counties in Intensity of
     Industrialization in Livestock and Poultry
     Raising 174
4.8 Correlations Between Capital-Input Criteria for
     the Scale of Agricultural Industrialization . 175
4.9 The Scale Structure of General Agricultural
     Industrialization 176
4.10 The Twenty Leading Counties in Scale of General
     Agricultural Industrialization. 179
4.11 The Scale Structure of Industrialization in
     Cropping. 181
4.12 The Twenty Leading Counties in Scale of
     Industrialization in Cropping 183
4.13 The Scale Structure of Industrialization in
     Livestock and Poultry Raising 184
4.14 The Twenty Leading Counties in Scale of
     Industrialization in Livestock and Poultry
     Raising 186

5.1	The Twenty Leading Counties in Both Intensity and Scale of General Agricultural Industrialization (over 1.64 Standard Deviations)	194
5.2	The Twenty Leading Counties in Both Intensity and Scale of Industrialization in Cropping (over 2.05 Standard Deviations)	199
5.3	The Twenty Leading Counties in Both Intensity and Scale of Industrialization in Livestock and Poultry Raising (over 1.47 Standard Deviations)	203
5.4	The Twenty Lowest Ranking Counties in Both Intensity and Scale of General Agricultural Industrialization (over -1.15 Standard Deviations)	206
5.5	The Twenty-one Lowest Ranking Counties in Both Intensity and Scale of Industrialization in Cropping (over -1.32 Standard Deviations)	210
5.6	The Twenty Lowest Ranking Counties in Both Intensity and Scale of Industrialization in Livestock and Poultry Raising (over -2.15 Standard Deviations)	212
6.1	Correlations of Productivity and Profitability Indicators with Agricultural Industrialization Variables	219
6.2	The Twenty Leading Counties in Value Added per Farm Acre	222
6.3	The Twenty Leading Counties in Value Added per Farm	223
6.4	The Twenty Leading Counties in Net Value of Farm Products Sold per Farm Acre	226
6.5	The Twenty Leading Counties in Net Value of Farm Products Sold per Farm	228
6.6	The Twenty Leading Counties in Net Farm Income per Operator-Equivalent	233

Preface

This book offers a geographic view of what many consider the ultimate revolution in American agriculture: industrialization. The major technological advances and production increases associated with the process have become a significant event in world agricultural history, and for a long time the great majority of Americans accepted them as natural outcomes of economic and even cultural goals. But for the past thirty to forty years agricultural industrialization has proceeded from "a brisk walk to a dash," and the increased pressure on smaller farmers and farm workers, as well as on natural resources, has become serious enough to evoke demands from many quarters for regulatory action. Yet compared to the magnitude of the event and the increasing concern, much is still unknown about its regional character and extent. Certainly this information ought to be at hand before any major conclusions or policy decisions are taken. For those interested in the spatial aspects of American agriculture, I can think of no greater challenge.

For the production of the maps, I am especially indebted to Floyd Hickok for writing the computer programs and making many helpful suggestions, to Mike Gerardo for coding the data, and to the Division of Environmental Sciences and the University of California, Davis, Computer Center for providing the processing facilities. Funds were generously provided by the Committee on Research, the Institute of Governmental Affairs, and the University Computer Center. Hal Grade and Susan Wilcox of the Social Sciences Data Service deserve no less recognition for their always cheerful and patient counseling of an "old retread" in the intricacies of data processing. Finally, I must thank Judy Riddle and Sarah Ann Blair of the Geography Department for typing what I am sure to them seemed at times an unending manuscript.

H.F.G.

1
The Conceptualization of Agricultural Industrialization

To suggest the need for a spatial assessment of the extent and character of the industrialization of American agriculture may seem superfluous in light of the magnitude of the process and the widespread attention it has generated. Indeed, the changes accompanying this process have been so numerous, so rapid, and so far-reaching that for many it represents an economic event second in importance only to the earlier, and more traditional, industrial revolution. Collectively, these changes have been described as the development of advanced management systems, rapidly advancing technology that places a premium on change and further mechanized processes, and changes in the relative prices of labor and capital.[1] Most significant, perhaps, in all of this transformation is the weakening of the production link between the farm and its immediate environment and a strengthening of connections with outside resources through the increasing use of nonfarm inputs, which comprise machinery, fuel, fertilizer, pesticides, feed supplements and mixing, and many other goods and services, including nonfarm hired labor.[2] The result of all this is a well-established record of revolutionary increase in agricultural production, in both volume and labor productivity.

But both of these achievements are now being criticized by an increasing number of observers. Food surpluses have become almost a perennial burden and the byproducts of intensified production now range from increasing drains on water and soil and energy resources to environmental pollution by soil sediment, animal wastes, wastes from industrial processing of raw agricultural products, plant nutrients, forest and crop residues, inorganic salts and minerals, pesticides, and certain kinds of air pollution.[3] Most serious, though, has been the lot of the farmer. Being in a market so large that he can have no perceptive influence on it, the farmer's only alternative for survival is to cut costs. Thus he has eagerly availed himself of the new technologies that increase his output per unit of input. Yet

1

the resulting expansion of production is confronted by the inelastic nature of the aggregate demand for food, so that prices are driven down and the resulting reduction of farm income sets the stage for still another vain effort by operators to preserve their farms. In the past, a rapidly growing industrial sector absorbed most of the millions of people who were both "pushed" and "pulled" from the countryside, but now that outlet appears much less viable in the face of a mature economy and worsening living conditions in the cities.[4]

The reaction to these disturbing effects of agricultural industrialization has been a wide range of recommendations proposed by a variety of individuals and organizations.[5] Yet little is really known about the true areal extent and regional character of agricultural industrialization, as the most recent federal government investigation shows,[6] and most of what is known has been obtained from studies dealing with the subject only indirectly, i.e., writings on a commonly accepted product of agricultural industrialization, the large and rationalized farm, and not the process itself. An associated complication has been the continuing divergence of opinion as to what the principal characteristics of such a farm are and even as to what it should be called. The popular tendency to view the large industrialized farm and agricultural industrialization as one and the same thing is thus, in my estimation, an error in conceptualization and a hindrance to the determination of the true character and extent of the industrialization process.

THE LARGE FARM AS AN INDUSTRIALIZATION INDICATOR

With the problems of food surplus, resource exploitation, and particularly farmer survival turning increasingly around the expanding scale of farming, it is perhaps no surprise that attempts to uncover the spatial patterns of agricultural industrialization have concentrated on the comparative fortunes of the small and large farm. But definitions of farm size vary, and as farming technology has progressed the problem of determining the true scale of the farm unit has become, if anything, even more complex. Advancing technology, primarily through increased economies of scale, has put an ever greater premium on the amount of farmland available to the operator ("Get big or get out"), whereas contrarily that same advance, through more purchased inputs, has reduced the acreage need of the farmer for maintaining the same level of production. The problem of inferring farm scale from acreage alone can easily be illustrated by a look at the national patterns of farm size, patterns that later in this discussion will acquire more pertinence when related to other farm scale criteria.

Figure 1.1 shows the distribution of farms, by county, of 260 acres or more as a percentage of all farms, the proportional form being used instead of average acreage in order to reduce the exaggerating effects of farms that are unusually large in relation to the majority of units. Also, like all the other maps in this book, the number of units (farms) represented are divided equally among the six classes to ensure maximum spatial differentiation. Yet despite these refinements, it is still the West, with its many farms and ranches characterized by an extremely extensive agriculture, that dominates. The same disparity between size and intensity is evident in certain parts of the East and often in areas that popular belief characterizes generally as small-farm, such as the Upper Peninsula of Michigan and the Appalachian Highlands of northern New England and West Virginia. At the extreme opposite end of the size scale, much of the Central Valley of California, considered by many as an archetypal region of the "industrial farm," is included with areas whose farms are judged to be the least representative of such a farm type, in particular the dairy and crop specialty farms of the Great Lakes area and the mid-Atlantic Seaboard, the tobacco farms of Kentucky and the South Atlantic states, and the many subsistence farms of Appalachia. Here the use of a proportion instead of an absolute figure rightly corrects the common impression that highly productive and rationalized farm operations are invariably a function of the biggest farms; on the other hand, this misrepresents the relative economic importance of the largest farms, for although the smaller farms are numerically and socially the most important, it is often the larger ones that control the greatest share of the acreage, something that even the criterion of average farm size fails to show.

If the farm size indicator is further refined by substituting cropland for total farmland, the distribution picture becomes considerably more realistic, although again the grossness of the single criterion poses problems. Farm size categories in Fig. 1.2 are based on the proportion of farms having 100 acres or more of harvested cropland, and it is obvious that the inclusion of this criterion excludes many areas whose farms have little claim as major agricultural producers. All of Alaska except a small patch on the Kenai Peninsula is now consigned to size categories below the national median, and the majority of the counties in the dry Southwest, with the exception of certain irrigated areas like southern Arizona, suffer the same rank reduction. Farther east, the unfavorable terrain and soil conditions of the Ozark region and parts of the Gulf Coastal Plain now show up quite prominently in the very low size classifications. In contrast, the better-producing farms

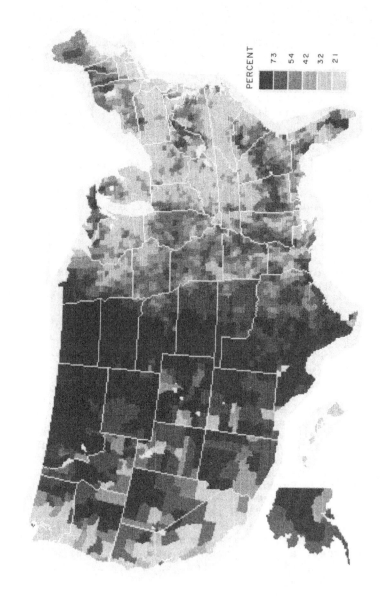

Figure 1.1. Percentage of farms 260 acres or larger

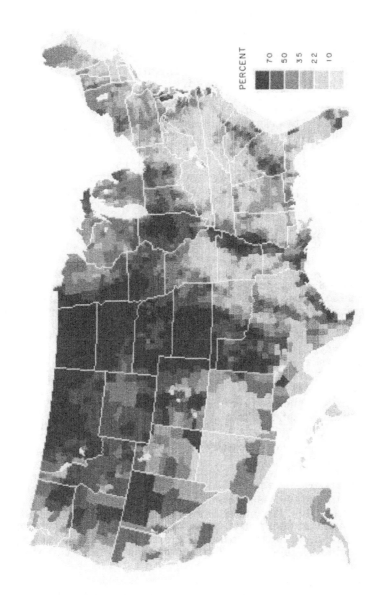

Figure 1.2. Percentage of farms with 100 or more acres of harvested cropland

of the Great Plains now stand out more sharply, as well
as the rich farms of the Midwest, particularly in the
Corn Belt. In the South, the truer picture of the more
important categories of farms shows itself in the now
clearly outlined prominence of the lower Mississippi
Valley, the Texas Blackland Prairie, the western Gulf
Coast, and most impressively in the shift of farm size
leadership in the Southeast, from the Piedmont to the
Inner Coastal Plain. Even the Central Valley of
California is somewhat improved.

However, cropland varies widely in quality and
climatic environment, and it takes a supreme effort of
imagination to view large farming units in still much of
the drier and more rugged parts of the West as the
economic equivalents of farms in such premium agricultural areas as Illinois, or even of farms in the less
intensively cropped wheat areas of the Plains. And, as
with the distribution patterns based on total farm size,
problems of areal comparison also occur on the small-size
end of the classification scale, as evidenced by a comparison of important farming areas like California and
Florida with problem rural areas like the Ozarks and
southern Appalachia, with smaller farms being the most
numerous in all of these regions. Areal comparisons
become no less distorted in the eyes of those searching
for more meaningful size designations when places with
farms of widely contrasting cropland size are matched, to
name as just one example the comparative situations of
the northern Michigan Cutover and the central Florida
citrus fruit area.

Detailed mapping efforts toward a more meaningful
representative of farm scale than size alone have generally concentrated on one of two criteria: The gross
farm product or the type of business organization. The
first has been used for several decades now by the Bureau
of the Census in the maps published in the quinquennial
census of agriculture. Most recently, the bureau has
published a map showing the distribution of farms with
annual sales of $100,000 or more, but with no illustra-
tion of their importance relative to all other farms in
the respective counties, although the proportions may be
obtained by consulting census statistics.[7] The argument
for the value criterion is that it reflects the combined
effect of all inputs, purchased and nonpurchased, that
enter into the size of the farm business. The use of
gross sales has been criticized, however, for a variety
of inadequacies, one of the most serious (from the
standpoint of determining comparative levels of industrialization) being the failure to take into account
differences in purchased inputs. Small farms tend to
import a larger proportion of their inputs than large
farms; livestock farms in particular have this tendency,
so that such units will be favored in a comparison of

gross outputs.[8] A further distortion, but in the opposite direction, is the failure of the gross value criterion to recognize the increased industrialization of small farms that is being effected by combining them in one managerial operation through vertical integration. At least a partial answer to the first objection has been provided by the Census Bureau in a map of net farm income, although census users have been warned to regard the statistics with caution because of the large share of total expenses that are subject to misinterpretations or other failings of the respondents.[9] More to the point of the same problem, but of older vintage, is the detailed U.S. map by Olmstead and Manley of "value produced by farming," obtained by subtracting livestock, feed, and seed expenditures from the mean value of all products.[10]

The other approach in the effort to gain a clearer picture of the national extent of large-scale farming has been concerned with the changing form of business organization. Management has become increasingly more critical as financial stakes and risks grow; it is also becoming more separated from labor as decision making demands more time and inputs from outside the agricultural operation. Here the focus is on the division between the family farm and larger operating units, the latter having become closely associated in the public mind with corporate organization. But the transition zone between these two farm types is a broad one, so despite a wealth of research on the subject, there is still no general agreement by researchers on a precise definition of these and other operational types.[11] On the family farm side, development of a formula based on the proportion of farm work and management performed by the family (a clear statistical indicator of the spread between management demands and family capabilities) has been one of the more inviting possibilities for use in a detailed areal evaluation. Unfortunately, even the comprehensive statistics of the census of agriculture do not provide the precise knowledge of the total labor use on farms that is required, although the Census Bureau did present maps for 1968 and 1974 showing, on a county basis, the distribution of "farms operated by individuals or families," thus indicating proprietorship.[12]

It is on the other side of farm organization, though, that attempts to assess the extent of agricultural industrialization have concentrated most. Here attention has focused on what is generally considered the ultimate product of the industrialization process: the corporate farm. In reaction to public concern over the increasing number and acreage of corporate farms, the Census Bureau published in 1973 the first map showing the nationwide distribution, by counties, of the percentage of land in farms operated by corporations in 1969, and in

1974 offered two maps showing both actual distribution and importance relative to total farmland.[13] However, a comparison of the 1969 and 1974 maps of acreage importance and of the 1974 maps of distribution and acreage proportion, as well as a review of census statistics and other governmental reports, shows that there is little correlation between the vast majority of incorporated farms and the widespread view of what such units are like, i.e., truly "factory farms" with large acreages, massive production, extensive and specialized labor forces, large amounts of machinery, usually absentee ownership with well-organized managerial staffs, and so forth. The greatest number of incorporated farms prove to be operated by families, who are concerned less with increasing their profits than with protecting their investments, and particularly with easing the transfer of farm assets from one generation to the next.[14] This kind of negative pressure to incorporate naturally shows itself prominently in the farm population hearth of the country, the Middle West, although the sizable concentrations of corporate farms in areas like California and Florida are much more important relative to the total number of farms and farmland acreage. Legal restrictions and subterfuge on the part of entrepreneurs reduce still more the usefulness of the corporate farm as evidence of agricultural industrialization. Many states have laws of varying severity that restrict incorporation, and the restrictions themselves often do not so much discourage the industrialization process as encourage it through already widespread practices such as dividing a farming operation among several business associates or relatives or using innocuous or misleading business fronts.

The means of assessing the spatial situation of agricultural industrialization that have so far been noted certainly do not exhaust the formulas proposed for such work. Many of them are quite detailed, but this aspect alone has doomed their use because far too little of the data required for the computations exist on a detailed national basis. Is there an approach, then, that allows one to obtain a clearer distributional picture of the agricultural industrialization process from the standpoints of both conceptual clarity and sufficient statistical detail? I suggest that there is; it would be a concentration on the extent of capital expenditure and investment in farming. The perspective, of course, remains preliminary because no claims are made for a complete definition; the social aspects, in particular, can only be inferred.

CAPITALIZATION AS AN INDUSTRIALIZATION INDICATOR

There is no dispute over the importance of capital in agricultural industrialization. The shifts that accompany its expanding application, from durable to expendable inputs, from farm-produced to nonfarm-produced inputs, from labor-using to labor-saving inputs, to land substitutes, and generally to input-supply specialization, have made agriculture increasingly similar to traditional industrialization.[15] These changes have been so extensive and pervasive in the industrialized countries that numerous scholars see them as representing a natural and ultimate stage in the historical development of agriculture.[16] For the United States, the unique convergence of a sparsely populated but resource-rich environment and an economically motivated and technologically oriented European population has helped to produce undoubtedly the most advanced example of this stage.[17] From 1810, when nonland capital inputs amounted to as little as 5 percent of the aggregate inputs in American agriculture, the share had burgeoned to 70 percent by 1960 and was expected to reach 80 percent (90 percent, including land capital inputs) by 1980.[18]

There is also little debate or confusion over the meaning of the monetary unit used to represent capital expenditures and investments, i.e., money capital as opposed to real capital (physical goods). A problem does arise when the various types of real capital are discussed in terms of money capital inputs, for there is still some difference of opinion over what should be included in these types, particularly in the matter of land. Here I follow the more common and extended definition of the principal forms of farm capital: land and buildings, labor, machinery and equipment, crops, and livestock.

Finally, the agricultural census volumes offer basic statistics on a variety of capital inputs for the nation at the detailed county level, particularly for those farms selling at least $2,500 worth of products annually, the data for which are used here. Also selected as most suitable for this study was the information provided by the 1969 census.[19] It was the first in which all county information was made available on computer tape, thereby enormously simplifying data manipulation and mapping. It was also more accurate than previous censuses because the enumeration was conducted at the end of the year rather than in the fall, thus eliminating the need for estimating production, expenditures, and sales for the remainder of the year. The unavailability of several volumes of the 1974 census during the critical stage of variable formulation precluded the use of the most recently published returns at this writing. This was just as well, because severe weather conditions in 1974 distorted the regional agricultural picture by drastically reducing yields of feed grains in the Middle West and cotton in the South. No such widespread decimations occurred during 1969, although the South did suffer some weather-

inflicted losses in cotton and corn in the late summer
and fall, and western irrigated areas suffered some
insect damage. Distortions of the monetary picture
through inflation, particularly in land values, were also
much more severe in 1974 than in 1969.

THE RESEARCH DESIGN

Neither concepts nor statistics make a research
design, of course, but they obviously greatly influence
it. The emphasis on the process of industrialization
rather than the product puts special emphasis on the need
for knowing the structural makeup, while the data facili-
tate and encourage the search for the variables that best
reveal that inner framework. Eight comprehensive input
variables, covering the capital investments and expenditures for the principal forms of farm capital, have been
created. They are related first to farmland and then to
farms to determine the level and areal distribution of
the various inputs making up what are posited as the two
basic dimensions of agricultural industrialization,
intensity and scale. The structural composition of the
inputs in their contribution to these dimensions is next
analyzed through application of a multivariate (components) analysis, which, through its summation process,
furnishes the basis for several industrialization typologies. Finally, the distributions of the principal types
of industrialization are compared with those of variables
representing several aspects of operational performance
to see how well industrialization justifies the major
argument for its promotion and to determine the areas in
which it might continue to increase significantly.

NOTES

1. A. Gordon Ball and Earl O. Heady (eds.), Size,
Structure, and Future of Farms (Ames, Iowa.: Iowa State
University Press, 1972), p. vii.
2. Harold F. Breimyer, "The Three Economies of
Agriculture," Journal of Farm Economics, Vol. 44 (1962),
p. 686.
3. U.S. Department of Agriculture, Control of
Agriculture-Related Pollution, A Report to the President
of the United States. Submitted by the Secretary of
Agriculture and the Director of the Office of Science and
Technology (Washington, D.C.: Government Printing
Office, 1969).
4. The most comprehensive collection of recent
articles, particularly those of a critical nature, that
cover the human problems stemming from agricultural
industrialization appears to be that of Richard D.
Rodefeld et al. (eds.), Change in Rural America: Causes,

Consequences, and Alternatives (Saint Louis: C.V. Mosby Company, 1978), 551 pp.

5. Richard G. Milk reviews some of the more interesting proposals in "The New Agriculture in the United States: A Dissenter's View," Land Economics, Vol. 48 (1972), pp. 228-235.

6. U.S. Senate, Subcommittee on Monopoly of the Select Committee on Small Business. Hearings on the Role of Giant Corporations in the American and World Economies. Part 3. Corporate Secrecy: Agribusiness. 92nd Cong., 1st and 2nd Sess., 1973.

7. U.S., Bureau of the Census, 1974 Census of Agriculture. Vol. IV, Special Reports. Part 1, Graphic Summary, p. 23. In 1980, Everett G. Smith, Jr., produced a national map showing by dots the location of the headquarters of farms with "an indicated or inferred annual sales of one million dollars." Data were extracted from the Dun and Bradstreet, Inc., directories. "America's Richest Farms and Ranches," Annals, Association of American Geographers, Vol. 70 (1980), p. 530.

8. Angela Edwards and Alan Rogers (eds.), Agricultural Resources (London: Faber and Faber, 1974), p. 254, and Radoje Nikolitch and Dean E. McKee, "The Contribution of the Economic Classification of Farms to the Understanding of American Agriculture," Journal of Farm Economics, Vol. 47 (1965), pp. 1550-1551.

9. The map is to be found in U.S., Bureau of the Census, 1974 Census of Agriculture, Vol. IV, Part 1, p. 59. The warning to users is in U.S., Bureau of the Census, 1974 Census of Agriculture. Vol. IV, Special Reports. Part 5, Corporations in Agricultural Production, p. 4.

10. Clarence W. Olmstead and Vaughn P. Manley, "The Geography of Input, Output, and Scale of Operation in American Agriculture," Agricultural Geography I.G.U. Symposium, ed. E. S. Simpson. Department of Geography, University of Liverpool, Research Paper No. 3 (Liverpool: L. Cocker & Co., 1965), p. 44.

11. Richard D. Rodefeld provides a succinct review of the various conceptions of family and corporate farms and how the many disagreements hinder progress in the assessment of the extent of agricultural industrialization, particularly from the sociological point of view. See "The Changing Organizational and Occupational Structure of Farming and the Implications for Farm Work Force Individuals, Families and Communities," Ph.D. dissertation, Michigan State University, 1974, two parts (Ann Arbor, Mich.: University Microfilms International, 1977), pp. 15-34. An annotated and more comprehensive account of the many views of the nature of the American farm, and more from the economics side, is offered by Richard J. Foote. See his Concepts Involved in Defining and Identifying Farms (U.S. Dept. of Agriculture,

Economic Research Service) (Washington, D.C.: Government Printing Office, 1970), pp. 16-38. I have given a summary of the terminology problem as it applies to the plantation in "Terminology in Typology--The Problem of 'Plantations,'" Agricultural Typology and Land Use, ed. Lloyd G. Reeds, Proceedings in the Agricultural Typology Commission Meeting, McMaster University, Hamilton, Ontario, 1973, pp. 60-68.

12. U.S., Bureau of the Census, 1969 Census of Agriculture. Vol. V, Special Reports. Part 1, Graphic Summary, p. 43, and U.S., Bureau of the Census, 1974 Census of Agriculture. Vol. IV, Special Reports. Part 1, Graphic Summary, pp. 38-39.

13. U.S., Bureau of the Census, 1969, p. 44, and U.S., Bureau of the Census, 1974, p. 41.

14. John Fraser Hart, "The Middle West," Annals, Association of American Geographers, Vol. 62 (1972), p. 275.

15. C. Leroy Quance, "Capital," The Overproduction Trap in U.S. Agriculture, eds. Glenn L. Johnson and C. Leroy Quance (Baltimore and London: Johns Hopkins University Press, 1972), Chapter 7, p. 112.

16. I have summarized the work of several geographers and agricultural economists in discussing the possibilities of an eventual convergence of the American family farm and the industrialized plantation in "The Changing Plantation," Annals, Association of American Geographers, Vol. 55 (1965), p. 236. The extreme version of this "evolutionary determinism" is probably that represented by the conclusion of Jacques Ellul, that only two choices are available in the continuing advance of technology in agriculture: expropriate the land in favor of capitalist corporations or unite the farmers in state collective farms. See The Technological Society, trans. Robert K. Morton (New York: Vintage Books, 1967), p. 310. Objections to the evolutionary view are concisely noted in Rodefeld, Changes in Rural America..., particularly on pp. 197, 232, and 277-281.

17. John T. Schlebecker, Whereby We Thrive--A History of American Farming, 1607-1972 (Ames, Iowa: Iowa State University Press, 1975), pp. 319-320. That most American farmers have always been basically entrepreneurial and not agrarian in spirit appears to be the opinion of the majority of scholars, a view well presented by Richard Hofstadter, The Age of Reform (New York: Vintage Books, 1955), pp. 23-59, and particularly so for the Middle Western farmer by Hart, op. cit., pp. 271-273.

18. Earl O. Heady and Luther G. Tweeten, Resource Demand and Structures of the Agricultural Industry (Ames, Iowa: Iowa State University Press, 1963), p. 9.

19. U.S., Bureau of the Census, 1969 Census of Agriculture. Vol. I, Area Reports. Section 2. County Data.

2
The Intensity of Agricultural Industrialization

INTENSITY OF LAND AND BUILDING CAPITALIZATION

We begin with the capitalization of agriculture as it contributes to the intensity of industrialization through its effect on land. Because of its essential and fixed character, land has proved less amenable to manipulation than other forms of farm capital. The result has been a compensatory shift to other inputs, so that land now constitutes only about 15 percent of the total annual inputs in agricultural production, in contrast to 30 percent for labor and about 50 percent for capital.[1] But this shift has also fostered an increasing selectivity in the choice of farmland, generally in favor of the best but always suited to the particular demands of farming technology. Agricultural industrialization has also put an increasing premium on land near large urban centers.

Concentration on the Better Farmland

The steadily growing attraction of agricultural industrialization to the best farmlands is quite logical. Because of the inelasticity of the market, the way to profitability lies not so much in expanding the scale of production as in reducing its costs. This can be achieved, insofar as land is concerned, by increasing production per acre. Part of this increase is achieved by shifting to more intensive enterprises on the best farmland. The other part is obtained by adding more inputs such as fertilizers, improved seeds, and higher quality animals, which by their own costs reinforce the areal shift, for only the land most receptive to these inputs will suffice. Eventually, as more farmers attain these land economies, the profit advantage is lost as the spread between agricultural prices and the costs of inputs diminishes, so that the pressure for intensification is renewed. For farmers with smaller properties this pressure becomes especially imperative and for those with poorer land as well it becomes increasingly insuperable.

The urge to concentrate land use does not lack inducements from other quarters. The increasing income expectations of farmers and the attraction of the higher incomes of urban jobs are powerful stimulants in their own right. Federal programs supporting farm prices have had even a more direct, though unintended, effect. By requiring reductions in crop acreage while guaranteeing the price for all of the particular crop a farmer can produce on the acreage allotted, the government has simply encouraged the farmer to apply more fertilizer and other production inputs to the reduced, and now the most fertile, acreage. This sets in motion a vicious cycle much like that of the struggle to lessen production costs; in this case the resulting crop surpluses invite further government restrictions on acreage and additional areal concentration and intensification. Thus, political measures have increased the pressures of industrialization on the very group they were designed to help. The Soil Bank Program, which sought to conserve soil by paying farmers to withdraw land from cultivation for certain periods, may also have contributed to the areal concentration, although the long-term evidence is not too clear.[2] The program was terminated in 1971, but a less vigorous "Cropland Adjustment Program," with many similarities to the Soil Bank Program, continues.

The concentration of land inputs in the better-endowed areas of the United States is clearly evident in Fig. 2.1. That the correlations appear so clearly is a further indication of how sharply concentrated inputs are, for the indicator used, although the best available for extensive and uniform coverage, has several significant deficiencies. First, to determine the value of the land input it was necessary to fall back on the farmer's estimate of the value of the land and buildings, an appraisal that is influenced by a variety of biases, not all of which are oriented to production. The real estate values reported by the Census Bureau may well be biased toward the owner's acquisition value, even though farmers were asked to estimate current market value. Buildings are seldom sold separately from the land, so their value is not separated from that of the land in the census questionnaire. Also, there is no way of determining from the census statistics what proportion of the inputs is applied to cropland, thus requiring that the values be related to farmland instead. This has caused an understatement of the intensity of the inputs, particularly in areas like the South and West where the share of farmland in pasture and marginal land is large. It is especially a problem in cartographic representation of the West, where fairly large counties often embrace both irrigated lands and extensive pasture and rangelands. On the other

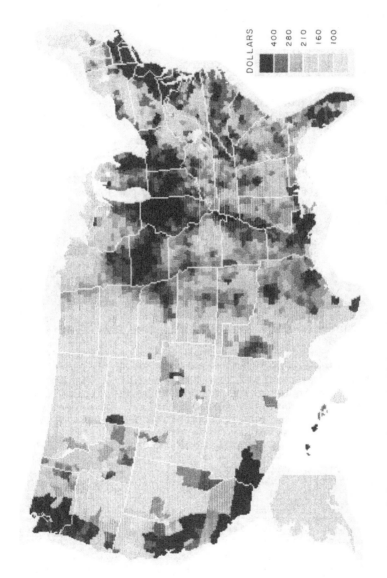

Figure 2.1. Land and building investments per farm acre

hand, in situations where irrigated farming is particularly intensive and nonirrigated areas are extremely marginal agricultural lands, large counties exaggerate the areal representation of the intensive inputs. Counties in southern Arizona and several in southern California are examples. The problem of county-aggregated data is multifold and one of the heavier prices to be paid for attempting to secure both a detailed and nationwide picture of the more sophisticated characteristics of American agriculture.[3] Finally, the utility of land value as an indicator of agricultural input is severely qualified in the vicinities of cities, where urban demands on the land and associated speculation often push land prices well above those justified by the agricultural potential alone; here the possible gap between acquisition and current land values could be a partially mitigating factor.

The first impression provided by the national distribution of land input intensity is somewhat of a negative one, for the majority of the country, particularly in the West, is represented by the lowest of the six intensity classes. The prominence of the areas with very low intensity of inputs, with less than $100 of investments per farm acre, is a more capitalistic expression of the fact that only a fifth of the national territory includes cropland[4] and that still less than half of the nation is included if grassland pasture and range are added.[5]

Another general aspect of the national pattern of land input intensity that is quite evident is the sharp delimitation of the intensive areas of the West and the many more gradations in the eastern part of the country. It is a pattern that will be repeated in gross outline for the other industrialization intensity inputs, and is largely an expression of the prevailing aridity in much of the West and the greater moisture in the East that allows more of the variegating effects of terrain, soil, and regional climatic differences to show in the input pattern. The sharpness of the pattern is also promoted indirectly by drought in that the only means of successful cropping in much of the West is by irrigation, a practice traditionally associated with forms of farming much more intensive than those dependent on rainfall. Thus, most of the counties in the West with significant land investment (above the U.S. median of $210 per acre) are confined to the moister watersheds of the Pacific margins and the majority of them are also in the very highest investment category, over $400 per acre. The Puget Sound Lowland and the Willamette Valley comprise the main segment to the north, with spillovers to the small coastal valleys on the west, and eastward over the Cascade Mountains to the fruit valleys of Hood River in Oregon and Yakima and Wenatchee in Washington. The other

main portion is the semiarc of irrigated lands in
California and Arizona--the northern part is comprised of
the Central Valley and adjoining central coastal valleys,
and the southern part is the chain of basins extending
from the southern California coast through the Coachella-
Imperial trough to southern Arizona. Some scattered
outliers of major land inputs are to be found along the
Snake River, along the Wasatch Front in Utah and the
Rocky Mountain Front in Colorado, and, at somewhat lower
levels of intensity, in a few areas of Nevada and New
Mexico. Honolulu and Kauai counties in Hawaii may also
be included in the outlier category.

In the eastern part of the nation, all six class
levels of land input intensity presented by the map are
well represented, though regional differences in the
proportions are fully obvious. The most extensive area
of inputs above the national median is the centerpiece of
American agriculture, the Middle West, but even here
noticeable spatial variations can be observed. The Corn
Belt forms an inner core, and within it the two most
important parts, the Iowa Prairie of north-central Iowa
and the Grand Prairie of east-central Illinois, are
easily recognizable. The nearly flat glacial till plain
surfaces and the thick deposits of rich prairie soils
make these two centers prize corn and soybean areas.
More rolling and dissected terrain and often less fertile
soil on much of the edge of these cores-within-a-core
reduce the land suitable for cash cropping and encourage
more emphasis on livestock feeding with pasture. A
cooler climate and less well-drained soils create a
broader transition toward the north in Minnesota,
Wisconsin, and Michigan, although the more leached and
acidic character of the soils in northeastern Iowa and
northwestern Illinois, in combination with the more
dissected and sandy soils of the Driftless Area in
Wisconsin, help to narrow this zone considerably. Eastward from Illinois the change from very high to very low
land input intensity is even more gradual, for many
moderately fertile and climatically favorable areas are
still found in Indiana and Ohio. The approach to the
areas of lowest land investment becomes abrupt, however,
at the rough hill country of the dissected Allegheny
Plateau in eastern Ohio. To the west of the Iowa intensity center, the fertile alluvial and loessial soils and
rolling terrain of the Missouri Valley form a relatively
broad transition zone of land input intensity that is
still significant by national standards and extends into
the drier areas of southeastern Nebraska. To the south
of the Corn Belt cores, the rich alluvial bottomlands of
rivers like the Missouri, Mississippi, and Wabash perform
roughly the same function by allowing highly profitable
farming to invade areas characterized by rougher terrain
and less fertile and commonly thinner soils. Yet it is

interesting that in the transition belt of southern Illinois and southern Indiana, regions traditionally held to be economic backwaters, land costs are still largely above the national median, another indication of the high esteem given midwestern agricultural land.

The Middle West also has a sizable investment in farm buildings, although even here its share of the total land and buildings investment is not impressive enough to affect the general intensity pattern; many dairy farmsteads to the north of the Corn Belt actually have a more impressive collection of buildings. It is possible that the combination of a respectable share of the total value of land and buildings in buildings (roughly a third) with a high farm density may partly account for the northward extension of the highest class of land and building investments from the Corn Belt into southeastern Wisconsin and southern Michigan; the same situation could be contributing to the strong showing of the mid-Atlantic Seaboard in the Northeast. The same combination also could be significantly reinforcing the investment intensity of southern Appalachia and the rest of the South, where building investments average a quarter to a third of the total land and building figure. Yet all these proportions promise to become less important as land values continue their rapid increase. Consolidation of farms has sharply reduced the economic value of buildings by creating a surplus of them, even though on a cost-less-depreciation basis they have the same value as before. This process was already well enough under way several decades ago to be generally observed.[6] Today it is common in many parts of the country, particularly on the most productive lands of the western Corn Belt, for sales prices of farmland without buildings to be nearly as high as those for farms with buildings. Building investments as a proportion of total land and building investments come to less than 20 percent for the nation, and range from 32 to 36 percent for the principal dairy states to less than 10 percent for the fruit-and-vegetable specialty states of California and Florida.[7] These regional differences appear to be diminishing also, as farm buildings become less numerous and more standardized.

Despite the impressive levels of land input intensity in the Midwest, it is the South that most graphically illustrates the highly discriminating nature of land selectivity in the agricultural industrialization process. Here it is impossible to find a large, single core of intensity that dominates the region and merges into a continuous strip of declining input intensity along the peripheries. The more restrictive terrain and soil conditions of the South and their very irregular but widespread distribution put a majority of the area below the national median. Especially conspicuous are the Ozark-Ouachita Highlands, extending from southern

Missouri through Arkansas into southeastern Oklahoma; much of the Coastal Plain, particularly in Mississippi, Alabama, and Georgia; the Highland Rim in western Tennessee and Kentucky; and the complex of Highland Rim and Allegheny-Cumberland Plateau, extending through eastern Tennessee and Kentucky and northeastward through most of West Virginia and beyond. The physical disadvantages of these areas are well known: rough terrain and thin and infertile soils in the highlands, and badly eroded and leached soils on the Coastal Plain, including extensive coastal strips of poorly drained land.

The converse of this spatial pattern of relatively low land inputs is a distribution faintly suggestive of the drier West, one that Hart, in referring to the location of specialty crops in the South, describes in terms of islands.[8] Although "island" may be a slight exaggeration for areas as extensive as southern Florida or the Mississippi bottomlands--the latter being the largest single distribution of intensive land investment in the South--the term is appropriate for most important input centers even though land and building investments are not as specific an indicator as that employed by Hart. Investment intensities above the national median outline such centers as the Blue Grass Basin of Kentucky and the Nashville Basin of Tennessee; the Springfield Prairies, where Missouri, Arkansas, and Oklahoma meet; the Arkansas Valley in Arkansas; and the Corpus Christi Plains and Rio Grande Delta on the south Texas Gulf Coast. Many of these more important centers outline a necklace-like pattern as they reflect particularly favorable local farming and historical conditions within a generally hospitable physical area. The best examples are in the fertile crescent of the Texas Blackland Prairie, which extends from about the Texas-Oklahoma line southward to San Antonio; in the northeast-trending Appalachian valleys of northeastern Alabama, eastern Tennessee, and western Virginia; and in the tobacco areas of eastern North Carolina, extreme eastern South Carolina, and southern Georgia, all on the Coastal Plain. The striking concentration in the upper Chattahoochee Valley of northern Georgia is due in part to both the large Atlanta market and the building investments in the dairy, beef cattle, and poultry farms in the area. But the island pattern is not restricted to centers of major input intensity. The most extensive example shown on the map is the Black Belt, a strip running from northern Mississippi southeastward across central Alabama. Once the cotton production center of the South, its rich soils were so overexploited and its money crop so seriously damaged by the boll weevil that it has never been able to regain its regional supremacy, despite a more recent resurgence through livestock raising and cultivation of soybeans. Land values in the Black Belt are only moderate by national standards, ranking slightly below the U.S. median.

Modified versions of the general land investment patterns of the Middle West and the South are presented by the two remaining regions east of the Rockies, the Northeast and the Great Plains. The Northeast is closely allied to the Middle West in having a single, extensive area of extremely high input intensity, a coastal concentration that ultimately goes back to a unique convergence of early massive settlement and a harbor-rich coastline backed by plains and valleys favorable to cultivation. This area of high intensity does not dominate the region, however, as the Corn Belt does the Middle West, a fact for which inhospitality of terrain and climate in the extensive Appalachian Highlands System is largely responsible. So sharp are the contrasts between the low land input intensities of the interior and the high intensities of the seaboard that they almost match those setting off the intensive Pacific Coast strips from the drier interior.

The fragmented patterns of the South continue into the southern Great Plains. Most evident is a strip of highly valued land extending from central Kansas into central Oklahoma, and a more compact district on the Texas High Plains. The former outlines the subhumid Winter Wheat Belt, which is set off on the east by the more extensive grazing lands of the Flint Hills in Kansas and Crosstimbers in Oklahoma; the latter marks an intensively irrigated center of cotton and grain sorghum. Irrigation is also responsible for the less significant, but still observable, land investment islands that extend northward from central Texas into western Kansas and southwestern Nebraska, all of which are underlain by the same irrigation source, the Ogallala Formation. The northern part of the Great Plains, however, shows few investment input islands, the colder climate and fewer developed irrigation facilities being the most apparent causes. The Red River Valley is the one extensive interruption of this largely blank pattern, but its input intensities are still below the national median.

My description of the increasing correlation of land investments with the best agricultural land must end by emphasizing that the map in Fig. 2.1 is primarily one of investment and not of innate land quality. Flatness has become an increasingly prized characteristic of land as machine use and size have expanded, but flatness does not guarantee fertility or adequate moisture and can even create a problem where it is humid. Sizable parts of the pattern of significant land investment owe their existence to the great efforts made to overcome these difficulties. The best example of this is in the Midwest, where ditch-and-tile drainage was begun on an extensive scale as early as the late 1800s. Some of the most intensive reclamation was made in what are today the most productive agricultural areas of the region, the Grand Prairie of Illinois and the Iowa Prairie in Iowa.[9] By 1969, over half of the drained land of the United States was in the five leading drainage states of Illinois, Iowa, Minnesota, Indiana, and Ohio.[10] More recently, the most impressive expansion of cropland through drainage has been in the South, and as in the Middle West, is reflected by two of the most important areas of high land valuation, the part of the lower Mississippi Valley shared mostly by Arkansas and Mississippi (the Lower Alluvial Valley or "Delta") and central and southern Florida.[11] Between 1950 and 1969, cropland in these three areas increased by 40 percent.[12]

During approximately the same period, irrigation made possible impressive cropland gains in the West, two of the three outstanding areas (the Texas High Plains and the San Joaquin Valley of California) roughly coinciding with high land investments. Irrigated cropland in the United States increased by 90 percent from 1944 to 1969,[13] not all of which was in the West. Irrigation is necessary for rice, the major cash grain in the lower Mississippi Valley. It is also a vital summer partner of the drainage reclamation program in southern Florida, and is being used increasingly in such notable land capitalization areas as New Jersey and the South Atlantic Coastal Plain. At the same time, extensive drainage has been the chief means of preventing salinization of irrigated western soils, as well as making it possible for the rice lands of the Sacramento Valley in northern California to rival those of the lower Mississippi bottomlands and the western Gulf Coast, at least in terms of heavy land investment.

A comment on the severity of withdrawal of agriculture from the poorer lands is that despite the impressive gains in cropland acreage achieved by these various combinations of reclamation methods since World War II, acreage for the nation as a whole has remained relatively constant. With the greatest variety of physical conditions for a region of such a large extent, the South is an outstanding illustration of this acreage standoff. So extreme was the range of change in the South that Hart, in mapping the change in cropland harvested from 1939 to 1974, found it necessary to construct two maps, one showing counties that lost more than half of their cropland for that period and another showing counties that lost less than half, or even gained.[14]

Concentration Nearer the Cities

As impressive as the concentration on the better farmland has become, it has not been the only major spatial result of land capitalization. The increasing use of nonfarm inputs, which have stimulated the shift to land best able to compensate farmers for their expenses, has also encouraged heavier application near the source of input, the cities. Cities have also encouraged greater capital intensification in their vicinities through both their market attraction and their more negative stimulus of increased land costs as a result of competition with agriculture for land. The consequence of this three-fold influence of agricultural industrialization has been that a pattern of urban influence is superimposed on one of land influence, for cities and farmlands have traditionally been tied together in a market-production relationship. Spatially, this correlation is only a general one, for the precise locations of cities were most immediately determined by more site-specific characteristics--access to routes, sufficient local power resources, and other historical circumstances, many of which were at least as noneconomic as they were pecuniary. The distribution of the highest intensity category of land and building investments, over $400 per acre, shows that urban areas both expand the high-intensity pattern beyond the margins of the best land and raise the intensity levels within them.

The most visible evidence of the extension through urban influence of investment intensity beyond the choicest farmlands is in the Middle West and Northeast.[15] Along the Great Lakes, it is the heavily urbanized strips that extend the highest category of investment intensity from the Corn Belt to the north. On the southern and southwestern shores of Lake Michigan, the attractions are the cities stretching from Milwaukee southward to Chicago and east to Benton harbor, Michigan. On the southern and southwestern shores of Lake Erie, the urban agglomeration extends more or less from metropolitan Detroit southward to Toledo and east to Cleveland. The northernmost part of this major thrust of land investment intensity to the Great Lakes, however, is reserved for the Saginaw Plain on Lake Huron, which connects to the Detroit area at the Class I level via the force zones of Saginaw and Flint. In the Corn Belt itself, but again beyond the best soils, areas with the highest category of land investment intensity also show the influence of urban concentrations. Most evident is the showing in the southwestern corner of Ohio, stretching from Dayton southward to Cincinnati. No less visible are the metropolitan islands fringing the Middle West: Minneapolis-St. Paul, Omaha, Kansas City, St. Louis, and Louisville.

Urban influence reserves its greatest areal impact for the several tiers of counties that fringe the Atlantic Coast from southern New England to Virginia, which encompass the greatest single concentration of urban population in the country. Although this area is commonly called "Megalopolis" because of the many cities,[16] it contains much agricultural land, but overall its quality and extent are no match for the best farmland of the Middle West. Yet the extent of area that is in the highest class of land investment intensity is at least the match of that in the best of the Corn Belt. Moreover, on an individual county basis, the investment intensity figures are even higher, reaching the highest levels in the nation. How much of this high investment value can actually be ascribed to agricultural demand is problematical. In counties nearest metropolitan centers, land investments usually reflect agricultural demands in only a minor way. But to the extent that high land values can also imply a growing market for farm products and stimulate farming intensity through the pressure of higher taxes, land investment becomes a useful, though diluted, indicator. Idling of farmland apparently is still usually localized in even the most metropolitan counties, if one can judge by the results of recent field research in counties surrounding Philadelphia,[17] and many farmers who give up their farms contribute to the increasing value of land in more removed counties by reestablishing themselves there.

In the South, the centers with the highest class of land investment value duplicate the island-like pattern of the more prominent agricultural areas. But although most such concentrations nestle more or less within prominent farming areas, the correlation between the high investment value of the urban-influenced area and the physical extent and quality of the surrounding agricultural concentration is much less apparent than in the Middle West and Northeast. This weaker pairing may reflect, among other things, the lesser agricultural development of the South and the more recent rapid growth of its cities, so that urban-agricultural functional connections have not been able to develop as thoroughly as in the North.[18] The emphatic land investment concentrations surrounding the Fort Worth-Dallas area in the Grand-Blackland prairies, Houston on the Coastal Prairie, New Orleans on the lower Mississippi Delta, and Atlanta on the Georgia Piedmont, are the major examples of urban centers with overwhelming superiority over their agricultural hinterlands, several of which are only moderately endowed with high quality soils. If the climatic advantages of the Florida Peninsula are overlooked, then the investment value superiority of the Orlando-Tampa-St. Petersburg and Miami complexes over the generally low quality of the soils is even more striking, although the divergence between the high land values ringing Atlanta and the much better soils of Georgia's coastal plain is also noteworthy. There is only one possible major example of the reverse aspect of a disproportionate relationship between urban-influenced land investment

values and the surrounding agricultural region, that
between Memphis and the Lower Alluvial Valley of the
Mississippi. Here the island of high land investment
value is but a small fraction of the valley, much of
which has a moderately good share of prime soils and is
in the second highest category of investment value (from
$280 to $400 per farm acre).

More proportionate relationships between urban
centers and the resources of the surrounding agricultural
regions are offered by smaller cities: Nashville in the
Nashville Basin, Lexington in the Blue Grass Basin, and
the several cities dispersed through the Piedmont Urban
Crescent in North and South Carolina, to name some of the
best examples. Smaller cities also repeat the "island-
within-island" pattern of the South on the southern
plains, but with only two cities--Oklahoma City and
Tulsa--putting their counties into the leading land
investment value category. Also, like many of the city-
agricultural land relationships in the South, Oklahoma
City and particularly Tulsa stand sharply apart from most
surrounding counties. In this case, the great importance
of the petroleum industry in the economy of the two
cities may be the primary reason.

Close mutual proximity of city and agricultural area
in the Far West creates areas that are almost as exclusively in the top class of land investment value as is
Megalopolis. Indeed, it has been estimated that 72
percent of the Class I and II land in California, Oregon,
and Washington lies in metropolitan counties and
counties adjacent to them, versus 42 percent for the
Middle Atlantic and New England states and 33 percent for
the Corn Belt and Great Lakes states.[19] If much of the
poorer farmland in many of the western counties, particularly the larger ones, could be eliminated, the Western
proportion would undoubtedly be even more impressive and
the showing on the variable of land and building investments per farm acre would also be improved. The areal
representation of the high value areas, especially in
southern California and southwestern Arizona, also would
come closer to the actual land situation by being
reduced. Small Honolulu County with its dominating
metropolis offers an idea of what such a corrected
picture might be for some Pacific Coast counties. The
same political-statistical problem applies to many of the
counties of the interior oases, few of which (outside of
Imperial County in California and those in Arizona) now
attain a top class ranking in land investment value.

INTENSITY OF LABOR CAPITALIZATION

Labor, even more than land, has been the target of
expense reduction in agricultural industrialization. It
has been a traditional theme in U.S. agriculture, earlier

in the effort to cultivate a continent with a
comparatively sparse population, and now increasingly in
the areal intensification of production simply to maintain an existence in the face of technological, urban,
and political pressures. As production increases,
however, labor costs also rise, if not proportionately to
production, at least in absolute terms. This is true, of
course, whether we are speaking of a farm operation that
effects labor economies largely through the purchase of
labor-reducing inputs, or of a farm that accomplishes the
same thing by using industrial inputs to increase the
productivity of a labor supply that is relatively inflexible and is the cheapest production factor in the farming
system.

The census figures for "hired farm labor" and
"contract labor" come closest to informing us of the
extent of national and county expenditures for farm
labor. Contract labor is considered crew-type hand
labor, such as berry and fruit picking, or vegetable
harvesting performed by a crew of workers under a contract with a labor contractor, cooperative, processor, or
dealer. The capital input for operator labor is not
given in the census, and this I have attempted to supply
by first determining the number of "worker-equivalents"[20]
and then multiplying it by an annual income based on a
composite hourly wage rate projected to a six-day week
and a fifty-two-week year. Unfortunately for the county
format used in this study, the wage rate furnished by the
U.S. Statistical Reporting Service was only for states,
and the weekly hour rate for labor provided by Sellers
was only for ten state regions.[21] The result, therefore,
may well be the concealment of intrastate differences
where imputed capital input for operator labor is high
relative to total labor input.

The addition of operator labor input to the rest of
the labor investment also raises theoretical problems.
To emphasize the labor input of the farm operator is to
focus on the one means the smaller farmer has of resisting the primary thrust of agricultural industrialization,
which is to increase the productivity of labor by using
more of the other production factors and thus reduce the
importance of labor relative to overall operating costs.
Yet to exclude the operator's share of the labor input
would, in my estimation, distort the picture even more.
Small operators have always reacted to pressures from
larger operators by using their own labor prodigally to
intensify production per acre in order to save the
scarcest resource, land; they have also achieved this
intensification by purchasing production-increasing
inputs like fertilizers, better seeds, pesticides, and
even machinery, which facilitates the application of such
inputs and accelerates and improves the reliability of
cultivation and harvesting procedures. Family labor

inputs are thus indirect contributors to agricultural industrialization. Acre-yield intensification by farmers dependent largely on family labor also tends to bring about a spatial congruence with farms less dependent on their own labor, for many of the high value specialty crops like vegetables and fruits, which provide a good profit per acre for the small farmer, naturally do the same for the operator who has greater flexibility in selecting an enterprise and has more land for planting. More advanced industrialized operations are also being attracted to the labor-intensive family farms where labor is cheap enough, as it often is where labor is the dominant resource; contract farming among poultry farmers in the South is a prime example.

No information was available on 1969 farm labor expenditures for all of Alaska or Hawaii, and this was approximated by determining the 1959 ratios of the composite hourly wage rate of California to those of Hawaii and Alaska[22] and basing the hourly work week on the Pacific Coast average for California, Oregon, and Washington.

Not to recognize the affinities of labor intensity to agricultural industrialization that have just been described is not to be prepared for the national pattern shown in Fig. 2.2, for the majority of the leading areas displayed do not coincide with the popular view of where most of the nation's agricultural industrialization (read "industrial farms") locate. By far the largest single area with an intensity of labor expenditures above the national median of $14 per farm acre is the northeast quadrant. Here is the largest concentration of farmers who best typify the small to moderately-sized family operators upon whom the American rural ethic is so strongly based. This good correlation of labor intensity and family farm becomes even better as one proceeds northward and eastward from the Corn Belt into the Dairy Belt, where in most counties labor intensity reaches a level of $18 or more per farm acre. Noticeable, too, is that despite the northward decline of labor intensity on the poorer farms of the Great Lakes Cutover and parts of extreme northern Appalachia, the high values carry through in several areas right to the Canadian border.

That these extensions go some distance beyond the major marketing zones is an indication of a basic requirement of the commercial dairy enterprise, regardless of location: capitalizing on a labor supply that is cheaper relative to the amount of capital and, even more so, to the amount of land. The use of animals also ensures the fullest use of that labor, a particular asset in a region where long and cold winters allow only seasonal cropping opportunities. The yearly steadiness of the dairy work pattern and its daily, uninterrupted regime have been commented upon frequently. In this

27

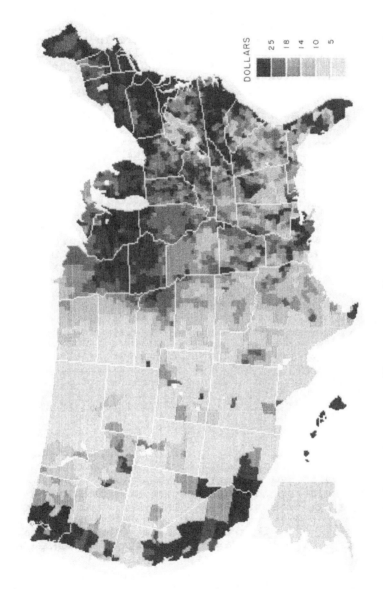

Figure 2.2. Labor expenditures per farm acre

schedule sense, modern dairy farmers come closest to the work routine of the industrial or factory worker, and with their other inputs an agricultural version of a small industrial enterprise is suggested. This similarity is increasing as dairy farms become fewer and larger in the battle to maintain sufficient income. Korb has observed that the large-scale dairy farm in eastern Wisconsin engages a minimum of two full-time male farm workers, supplemented by the contributions of the wife, any children of high school age, and possible additional part-time summer workers during the busy harvest periods.[23] It is also noteworthy that dairy farmers commonly pay a partial or even full wage to their sons, often marking a preliminary stage in the transfer of farm control. Such transfers are becoming less common as farming costs accelerate and wage levels in the cities continue to improve over realizable income on the farms.

Many dairy and other commercial farmers in this part of the country try to capitalize on their labor supply and gain the maximum yield from land by raising vegetables, fruits, or poultry. All of these commodities produce more income per acre than dairying, thus favoring them even more than dairying as candidates for the better agricultural areas, particularly those closest to the cities. This can be seen clearly by comparing the distribution of the highest class of labor expenditure intensity (over $25 per farm acre) with the pattern exhibited by the combined two highest classes. In the Great Lakes region, the distribution of high labor expenditure intensity is now principally confined on the west to the most productive dairylands of eastern Wisconsin, the Milwaukee and Chicago metropolitan counties, and the Western Michigan Fruit Belt along the Lake Michigan shore; on the east there is a close concentration along the southern shores of Lakes Erie and Ontario, stretching almost unbroken from Detroit through Buffalo to Rochester and beyond. This eastern portion, with its populous and agriculturally productive connectors to the mid-Atlantic Seaboard via the Mohawk Gap-Hudson Valley in New York and the interconnecting valleys in Pennsylvania, encompasses an intricate intermixture of crop specialty areas and major urban-industrial centers. By the time the Megalopolis counties are reached, an almost unbroken band of Class I labor intensity counties from southern Maine to the tip of the Delmarva Peninsula is encountered. By this time, too, one finds many more farms that use the large amounts of labor associated in the public eye with "factory farms." Where greater supplies of capital are available, the problem of paying labor costs for the more intensive farming and of matching the strong wage competition of the nearby cities is relatively easier.

On the other side of the continent, the trans-Cascade part of the Pacific Northwest stretching from the Canadian border to the lower Willamette Valley displays much the same labor-enterprise intensity complex in miniature. Unfortunately, the gradations in labor expenditure intensity from the less intensive and more specifically dairy enterprises on the immediate coast to the more intensive operations next to the Puget Sound cities and Portland are obscured on the map by the many large counties.

The South is no less a region of contrasts in the intensity of labor expenditures than it is in the intensity of land and building investments. Large sections fall below the national median of $14 per farm acre, and much of the area is well below that figure. Yet there are several sections where intensities match those of the Class I counties in the Midwest and Northeast and which, like the Northeast, numerically dominate the counties of the region ranking above the median. In certain respects these centers are even more notable. They occur in a region that has the lowest farm wages in the country and has no large urban agglomerations close by to furnish a market stimulus. Also, the values would be even higher if cropland could have been used instead of farmland in the intensity variable, a more serious deflator in the South than in the North, where the cropland-to-farmland ratio is much more favorable. The largest of these leading areas are the flue-cured tobacco "belts" of eastern North Carolina. There probably is no other major agricultural area in the United States in which such a dense farm population is matched with such a labor-intensive crop. Much of the hired labor is former share-cropper labor, the switch caused by farmers shifting to cash wages. If poultry is also considered, then the more fragmented but equally prominent patterns in central and western North Carolina and northern Georgia and Alabama must also be noted, for farm populations are almost as dense and poultry make the least agricultural demands on land of any major farming enterprise. Although both tobacco and poultry farms are generally small and employ mostly family labor, this is not true of the larger farms. At least as early as the 1950s, they were using almost four times as many worker-equivalents as the more numerous and smaller units,[24] and their proportion of the total farms continues to grow.

Central and southern Florida and the Mississippi Delta are additional centers of very high labor expenditure intensity. Unlike the tobacco and poultry areas farther north, these are areas where farms generally operate on a much larger scale, and capital rather than labor is usually the cheapest production resource. Large packing companies and growers' cooperatives provide the production crews and equipment for the small citrus farms in Florida's Central Lake District, and the large packing concerns figure even more in the operations of the vegetable farms located in particularly large numbers farther south. Extensive labor capitalization is also practiced on the large sugarcane farms just south of Lake Okeechobee and in the Mississippi Delta. Large-scale operations are also much more prevalent in the locally important dairy and poultry enterprises of the Tampa-St. Petersburg and Miami environs than they are in similar farm economies farther north.

Toward the drier West, both labor and capital become increasingly scarce production items and land becomes the cheapest resource. This change to a more extensive type of agriculture can already be observed on the eastern margins of the region in the below-median labor expenditure intensities of the most important agricultural areas: Red River Valley in Minnesota and the Dakotas, subhumid Winter Wheat Belt in Kansas and Oklahoma, Blackland Prairie in eastern Texas, and the Texas High Plains. Only irrigation, with its great demands on labor, raises labor intensity levels well above the national median; places with this good fortune are few and far between. The Wenatchee and Yakima valleys of central Washington, lower Snake Plain oases in southern Idaho, Scotts Bluff area in western Nebraska, San Luis Valley in southern Colorado, and lower Rio Grande Plain in southernmost Texas are the only areas in this vast stretch of sparsely used territory that have counties in the highest class of labor expenditure intensity.

In southwestern Arizona, Hawaii, and especially California, the story is quite different. Better water supplies and a mild climate have combined to encourage an intensive specialty crop economy, while increasing urbanization has superimposed on this pressure its own demands for more vegetables and fruits, more poultry and livestock products, and more space for growth. The conjunction of all these land demands on an extremely small agricultural space--California's irrigated acreage is not much more than the area of Maryland--brings land values back up to the level of the Great Lakes/mid-Atlantic Seaboard area so that labor is again comparatively cheaper in the production factor combination. Farm wage rates, however, are also the highest in the nation, not just because of the great labor demands by an agriculture that is very intensive and has numerous work peaks, but also because the labor supply is not as plentiful as in the humid East.[25] Heavy recourse has long been made to hired labor, both sedentary and migratory, and despite continuing mechanization and ending of the "bracero program," it still is vital to the needs of crop farmers. Migratory workers, moving with the crop seasons, are a striking geographic feature of the agriculture in this area, although similar movements contribute significantly to the very high labor expenditure levels represented on our map for many eastern areas, in particular Florida, Michigan, and the North Atlantic Seaboard. California, however, is the most active scene among the states in both movements and numbers of migrants.[26] Extensive use of hired labor on livestock farms, especially the numerous large and more concentrated drylot, feedlot, and poultry operations, also adds considerably to the labor expenditure intensity of the Pacific Southwest, particularly in the metropolitan counties. When this intensity is combined with that generated by the crop farms, the overall value puts practically all important agricultural counties in Arizona, California, and Hawaii in the highest class of labor expenditure intensity, much the same as the situation in the Megalopolitan counties on the Seaboard.

INTENSITY OF CAPITALIZATION IN MECHANIZATION

Certainly no one can dispute the major role of mechanization in the increasing industrialization of agriculture, and for many its extent is a sufficient indicator of the process. But if we accept the corollary that where mechanization is most advanced, dependence on labor is least, then strong qualifications must be made. This is especially true for the intensity of mechanization investment and expenditures, for it generally correlates with that of labor intensity. Census data allow us to distinguish two patterns of mechanization intensity, one based on the value of machinery and equipment as estimated by the operator--a capitalization input possibly referring more to acquisition cost than to current market value--and the other based on operational costs, represented by expenditures on machine hire, customwork, and fuel expenditures.

Machinery and Equipment Investments

High intensity of machinery and equipment investments easily has its most impressive distribution in the northeastern quarter of the country, thus precisely the area of greatest labor expenditures (Fig. 2.3). Furthermore, the same hierarchy of intraregional importance can be observed in the machinery and equipment pattern that is found in the labor pattern; the dairy area is generally superior to the Corn Belt, and the dairy-specialty crop complex of Megalopolis leads them all. This similarity between two supposedly opposing forces, labor intensification and mechanization, can be explained by the fact that although labor may be the cheapest production factor for the family farmer, the charge for real capital is still reasonable. More than any other intensity pattern of capitalization, that of

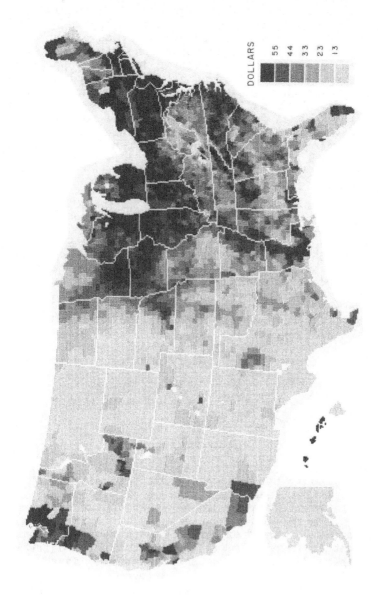

Figure 2.3. Machinery and equipment investments per farm acre

machinery and equipment investments reflects the
preeiminence of this part of the country as a source of
capital.

Up to a point, most farms can profitably employ
additional capital for nonfarm inputs, including machinery, to increase labor productivity. On a per-acre basis,
livestock enterprises are notably prominent in their
demands for machinery and equipment, both in their
distributional density and in their nature as a confinement operation, the latter reflected in heavy capital
investments in specialized buildings, feeding equipment,
and waste-handling facilities. Korb, in an interview
survey of dairy farms in eastern Wisconsin, found that
the average complement of equipment was two tractors,
pickup baler or forage harvester, an extensive range of
tillage-cultivation implements, grain drill, corn
planter, two wagons, manure spreader, conveyor, milking
machine, and variety of small power tools. Most farms
also had a truck or combine, and many had bulk milk
tanks, barn cleaners, and silo unloaders. On the larger
dairy farms, the inventories were even more prodigious,
the majority employing three or more tractors, four
harvesting machines, mechanical barn-cleaning systems (if
required), and silo unloaders; several used milking
parlors or pipeline-in-barn milking systems.[27]

The close correspondence of labor and mechanization
intensity patterns is not without its implied diseconomies. Farms with more need for multiple-type operations
in order to employ fully the family labor supply are not
as capable as the larger and more flexible units to
accommodate the specialization demands of machinery.
Moreover, smaller machinery does not provide the same
labor productivity as the larger equipment, so more
machine capital must be invested per acre to achieve the
same productivity obtained by the larger and more mechanized farms. To assume such parity, however, is to
assume that the machines would be working with higher
acre-yields than obtained on the larger farms, and this
is often not the case. In those situations, the smaller
operator must either reduce consumptive income in order
to invest, or use the machinery longer than the larger
operator so as to lower the annual rate of machine write-off costs to the level of the larger operations. The
latter alternative, though, prevents the smaller operator
from capitalizing on technological improvements as
readily as the larger operator--another handicap in the
ever-tightening competition for profits and survival.[28]

All of these disadvantages are magnified for the
small livestock or dairy farmer because of labor demands
and a regime that are less susceptible to the economizing
effects of mechanization than those of the farmer emphasizing crops. Some of the diseconomies associated with
mechanization among smaller farms may also be traced to

more psychological than economic stimuli, or as Lier puts it, "a tendency towards consumer spending as opposed to capital spending."[29] Is the farmer any more immune to the blandishments of machinery advertisers or the allure of a new piece of equipment bought by a neighbor than is the urbanite to the deluge of appeals to buy cars? Certainly the desire to "keep up" is just as strong in many rural areas as it is in urban neighborhoods. And one cannot deny the very real desire to buy equipment simply because it "makes things easier." Although it may prove to be impossible to determine to what extent these motivations contribute to overmechanization, there is increasing evidence that the phenomenon is widespread. The possibility that dairy farms are particularly susceptible is suggested by Monmonier and Schnell, who found that counties in New York and Pennsylvania with larger farms also had fewer tractors for the same unit of cropland.[30] Although this finding implies greater mechanization inefficiencies in the more urbanized areas, where farms are smaller, there is no doubt that mechanization intensity has also noticeably increased there, reaching its peak in areal extent in Megalopolis. Vegetable raising, the single most important farm enterprise in much of this area, and traditionally labor-intensive, has been affected in many ways. Tractors and tractor-drawn equipment such as plows, harrows, listers, bedders, precision planters, cultivators, and high concentration sprayers and dusters, have materially reduced labor inputs. Harvesting requirements have also been reduced, particularly through flash freezing. Thus, in the shift from fresh to frozen peas, for example, growers no longer plant in rows, cultivate, weed, hoe, and then handpick several times; now they drill the seed and harvest mechanically. The impetus to mechanize specialty-crop operations is even stronger on farms where other income sources are more important, because otherwise it would be difficult to make the necessary labor available. This additional capability adds significantly to the mechanization intensity of many dairy farms in both the Northeast and Middle West.

In impressive increases in mechanization intensity like these, it is possible to overlook the still powerful influence of land quality. The most extensive areas of favorable terrain and fertile soil are still in the Corn Belt, which ranks with the Great Lakes States and Megalopolis in having a majority of its counties in the highest category of intensity presented on the map, over $55 per farm acre. This more restrictive areal aspect of mechanization can also be noted in the drop-off to below-median values in the peripheries, such as the Great Lakes Cutover to the north and the hillier surfaces of northern Missouri and southeastern Ohio to the south.

As in the Middle West and Northeast, the intensity patterns for machinery and equipment investments in the South reinforce the showings of the areas that also excel in labor intensity. And, as with the most productive area in the North, the Corn Belt, so is the relative standing of the premier southern center, the lower Mississippi Valley, improved considerably over that represented in the distribution of labor intensity. Highest levels of mechanization and equipment intensity are actually achieved in the Louisiana portion of the valley, the smaller farms accentuating the intensity of application of respectable machine inventories. Rice, sugarcane, cotton, corn, and increasingly, soybeans all make sizable demands on machinery, the most critical items also being some of the most expensive machines employed in agriculture: combines, corn pickers, and cotton pickers.

Even more surprising is the continued premier position of the highly labor-intensive poultry-tobacco "belt" extending through North Carolina and the Appalachian sections of eastern Tennessee, and the big poultry areas of the upper Chattahoochee Valley of northern Georgia and the limestone valleys of northern Alabama. Although the distribution of counties in the highest intensity class is spottier than that of labor intensity, the largest number of counties in the South with that rank are still in this area. For the newer poultry enterprise, an important part of the explanation is the increasing use of automatic feeding and watering equipment, the costs of which are usually borne by outside sources, commonly the dealer who furnishes the feed. Also, poultry farm employment has not been regarded as a preferred occupation, and this has helped to hasten mechanization.

For the much older tobacco enterprise, the combination of high mechanization and labor intensities is due to greater success in mechanizing operations other than harvesting, which still takes almost half the labor. But even in the preharvest stages, mechanization has not been all-conquering. The machines that greatly reduced the chore of transplanting the seedlings to the field, earlier performed by crews of thirty to fifty workers, still require two workers for each row, and a dozen people are needed to operate and service a modern tractor-drawn two-row transplanter. Even the latest four-row machine carries eight workers.[31] Prior to the introduction of the mechanical harvester in the late 1960s, the machine used required a crew of seven and did not reduce labor needs as much as it modified them. By transporting the harvesters over the fields, the "taxi rig" allowed the farmer to employ women, children, and older men who were not considered sturdy enough for the backbreaking labor of picking the leaves while walking.

The mechanical harvester, which uses only the operator, now is spreading rapidly among the larger tobacco farms in North Carolina. Already, great numbers of blacks, the predominant farm labor force, have left the fields. Fortunately, most have found jobs in nearby new industries, which have also indirectly contributed to the mechanization process by offering better wages.[32] The job prospects for field workers and small operators in many other tobacco areas appear much less promising, however, as mechanization continues to gain ground.

The high intensity of machinery and equipment inputs in poultry and tobacco raising can also be traced to other enterprises, some with which they are combined and others that are pursued independently. Cotton, soybeans, and corn are especially favored by larger operators because they are more receptive to mechanization. Poultry, cattle, and dairy operations are also becoming favorites on the larger farms.

Although the distribution of advanced machinery and equipment investment intensity exceeds that of high labor intensity in the South, this is not exemplified just by the lower Mississippi Valley and the poultry-tobacco-mixed crop area. These regions are connected through northern Alabama and Mississippi and western Tennessee by above-median areas, where cotton, soybean, and corn farmers are heavy users of machinery. Most of central and western Kentucky is also above the national median, with tobacco, soybeans, and corn furnishing the principal bases for cropping mechanization. Significant parts of the Coastal Plain also show up in Virginia, South Carolina, and Georgia. By 1960, farms in Georgia concentrating on peanuts, cotton, and corn already had an investment in machinery per one hundred acres of harvested cropland that was nearly as high as farms in the Corn Belt.[33] Another island of important intensity concentrates in the Mobile Bay area of Alabama and the adjoining end of the Florida Panhandle, soybeans being the principal mechanization stimulant.

The peninsula of Florida, particularly the central part, is the only significant regional exception to the superiority of mechanization intensity to labor intensity in the South. Only the extreme southeastern coastal counties maintain a mechanization intensity equal to that of labor; most of the others on the peninsula rank well below the U.S. median. The fewer mechanization requirements of orchardists, combined with a marked seasonality in peak labor demands and generally smaller farms, are most areally evident in the very low rankings of many of the counties in the central area. When more machinery is needed, as in the harvest season, it is commonly hired from larger farms or contracted for through the services of specialized machinery-operating firms. Such arrangements are also common among smaller vegetable farmers,

whereas among the larger vegetable growers, who often
hire engineers to design their own machinery, the low
mechanization intensity may be ascribed at least partly
to the fewer growers in an area. This last condition
applies particularly to the southern part of the
peninsula.

    The diminished position of intensity of machinery
and equipment inputs relative to that of labor inputs
characterizes an even larger area: the Pacific Southwest. Especially notable is the position of the most
important segment of the region, the San Joaquin Valley,
with the majority of its counties not even in the first
two intensity classes of the map. Yet here, perhaps, is
the greatest variety of agricultural machines in the
nation: mechanical onion planters and toppers, digging
machines for potatoes and other root crops, spinach
cutters and loaders, apple graders, bean threshers, pea
harvesters, nut harvesting and hulling equipment, mechanical hop pickers, portable field graders and sackers for
onions, and one of the most expensive pieces of farm
machinery, the tomato picker, to name just a few.

    Why such a great amount of machinery does not
translate into an equally high position of intensity can
be at least partially explained by the similar situation
in the fruit and vegetable areas of Florida. Most farms
are smaller and specialize in raising fruit, and do not
require sizable year-round complements of machinery.
Usually only a tractor, a plow or disk, and some kind of
furrowing implement are used. But machine hire, principally during harvest time, is significant. Vegetable
farms are generally much larger and less numerous, and
although operators own sizable amounts of machinery, they
contract out for still more. Undoubtedly, too, there is
some statistical dilution of mechanization intensity in
the larger counties. In Fresno County, the leading
agricultural county of the nation, larger farms, especially those concentrating on cotton, are probably
unsurpassed in value of machinery both owned and hired,
but their statistics are combined with those of many
smaller farms and ranches.[34] Only in the northern
extremity of the San Joaquin Valley, where vegetable and
dairy farms with larger machine inventories become more
important, and still farther north in the Sacramento
Valley, where rice farms with extensive repertoires of
machinery and equipment dominate the acreage, do mechanization investment intensities achieve the highest class
ranking. Comparatively tiny Santa Cruz County just south
of San Francisco is the only county on the entire
California coast in the number one class, probably
because of its emphasis on fruit and vegetables and its
much greater homogeneity in farming enterprises than
exists in most San Joaquin Valley counties. Data aggregation within counties may again be one of the reasons

why mechanization intensity is so much lower in the metropolitan counties of California than in those of Megalopolis.

Even Hawaii suffers in the comparison of mechanization intensity with labor intensity, with the "Big Island" county of Hawaii dropping almost to the lowest class. Apparently the widely distributed cattle ranches and the many small coffee farms, whose location on the steep slopes overlooking the Kona Coast make even a tractor impractical, are enough to cancel out the effects of the heavy machinery investments of the sugar plantations on the eastern side of the island.

The Pacific Northwest west of the Cascades again displays marked similarities to the midwestern dairy specialty areas and thus contrasts sharply with the Pacific Southwest. Correlation between the input intensities of labor and of machinery and equipment is close. The extensive distribution of difficult terrain for mechanization restricts the counties with highest intensity rankings to the developed and well-populated lowlands rimming Puget Sound on the south and east and to those locating in the Willamette Valley.

It is difficult to make a single generalization in comparing labor and mechanization intensity patterns for the rest of the West. Southeastern Idaho, with larger farms and an emphasis on potatoes, sugar beets, wheat, and hay, definitely has a better national showing in the intensity of machinery and equipment inputs than it has for labor intensity. So do the Red River and middle Platte valleys, the subhumid Winter Wheat Belt, and the southern Texas High Plains, where cotton, grain crops, and large farms make sizable machine inventories an integral part of operations. There is less mechanization intensity, however, in areas like the upper Platte Valley in western Nebraska and northeastern Colorado, where smaller farms appear to be at least one cause; and in areas like the Yakima Valley, Wasatch Oasis, Colorado's Western Slope, and the middle and lower Rio Grande Valley, where both small farms and specialization in orchard crops discourage extensive mechanization. Comparatively the same in labor and mechanization intensities, though, are notable areas such as the middle and lower Snake River Plain oases in Idaho, the San Luis Valley in southern Colorado, and the southern Texas High Plains.

Operational Expenditures

Operational costs, the other dimension of mechanization intensity, are best covered on a national and county basis by the census statistics on expenditures for machine hire, customwork, and fuel. The combination of these indicators into one variable, however, conceals several major regional differences that must be kept in mind. Machine hire and customwork are a combined category in the census, so that regions like the Middle West and Northeast, where farmers carry on such job activities as grinding and mixing feed, plowing, combining, corn picking, and silo filling are not distinguished from the West and increasingly the South, where nonfarm operators perform such tasks as airplane spraying for weeds, airplane seeding of rice, mass-combining of wheat, and leveling of land for irrigation. In this case, then, it may be argued that the more industrialized organization of many farm jobs in the South and West is being ignored. Fuel expenditures, in the words of the census, cover "total gasoline and other petroleum fuel and oil for the farm business," but the poultry and tobacco areas of the South, where fuel is used heavily for heating chicken houses and curing tobacco, are not differentiated from other areas where fuel is used mainly for farm machinery. Somewhat the same qualification applies to irrigation areas, particularly on the Great Plains, where fuel for pumping is a heavy charge and is not differentiated from that used in operating agricultural machinery. From this standpoint, the importance of many places in the West is being exaggerated.

Machine repair costs and depreciation charges were not provided by the census except as a part of "all other production expenses." If one can assume that these two items of expense are directly proportional to the amount of machinery and equipment used, then their omission in our spatial review would appear to benefit the less mechanized areas more than they deserve.

Two broad distributional changes can be noted when the intensity pattern of operational expenditures is compared with that of machinery and equipment inputs: increased emphasis on the better farmland and a pronounced southward shift (Fig. 2.4). The net result is the increased importance of the Middle West in the northeast quarter of the nation and the powerful reinforcement of intensities in all major agricultural regions in the southern half of the country, i.e., the South, southern Plains, and Pacific Southwest.

In the northeastern quarter, the rough outlines of the Great Lakes Cutover and northern Appalachia that were observed in the intensity patterns for machinery and equipment inputs now become clear-cut, with practically all counties in the two areas registering values below the national median ($3.50 per farm acre). Farther south in the Middle West, the retreat from the poorer agricultural lands is revealed principally by the contractions of the areas with counties in the highest class of input intensity (over $6.00 per farm acre). Most exemplary are the closer focuses on the rich soils of southern Minnesota and the prime farmlands of southeastern

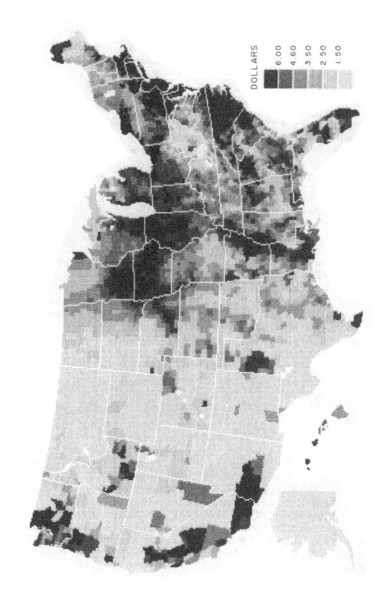

Figure 2.4. Machine hire, customwork, and fuel expenditures per farm acre

Wisconsin, accompanied by lessening of intensity in the intervening Driftless Area. In Michigan, only the peripheries of the Lower Peninsula now remain in the top category: part of the Lake Michigan Fruit Belt and the lands along the eastern shore where specialty crops (potatoes, beans, sugar beets--Saginaw Plain) and adjacency of large urban markets (Detroit) are important intensity incentives. This pattern continues along the lakes and into western New York. In the western Corn Belt (Illinois, Iowa), expansion of the top intensity class is the rule, and this area now becomes the concentration center of the Middle West. A counterbalance of this spread of the highest intensity class, however, is its drastic reduction in the eastern part of the belt, a result no doubt of the comparatively fewer mechanization demands of the smaller farms there.

Although fuel expenditures are the greater part of operational inputs in the Middle West, customwork is rapidly increasing in importance because it affords farmers an opportunity to maximize use of their machinery and thus to reduce costs per unit to the minimum in the battle with the "cost-price squeeze." The popularity of custom farming is closely related to the expansion of the fragmented farm, a growing phenomenon in a region where farmers are under increasing pressure to expand their properties but cannot add contiguous units because of the comparatively high farm density. As more distant and scattered units are accrued, it becomes increasingly advantageous for both expanding operators and those adjacent to these tracts to enter into contracts for working the land. Neighboring farmers can then secure supplemental employment and spread costs of machinery over more land, thus ensuring the benefits that come with larger landholdings for the expanding operator. That this practice is growing vigorously may be inferred from the fact that in the Corn Belt states the percentage of land transactions for farming purposes made to enlarge the farm rose from 28 percent in 1950-1954 to 62 percent at the end of 1971, an increase even greater than that for the nation as a whole.[35]

The strong effect of cities on the intensity of operational expenditures in adjacent areas is even more evident than it is for machinery and equipment inputs, for despite the increasing use of machines, many must still be hired because of the lower production of the smaller farms and the marked labor peaks of the vegetable crops. Practically all Megalopolitan counties hold firm to the first-class ratings in defiance of the now much lower values in the Appalachian hinterlands. Urban areas also help extend the large Class I intensity areas in Illinois northward and eastward to Chicago, in Wisconsin eastward to both Milwaukee and Chicago, and in Minnesota northeastward to Minneapolis-St. Paul.

The best illustration of the influence of urban centers on intensity patterns for operational expenditures (except for Megalopolis) is the almost uninterrupted strip of very high intensity along the shores of the eastern Great Lakes, as already described. This area has also been the traditional center of the American greenhouse industry, with its high fuel demands, although newer greenhouses are now being built in the Southwest.

Fuel expenditures have their greatest effect on operational intensity in the poultry-tobacco-mixed crop area of North Carolina and its spillover in Virginia and South Carolina. As both a large and compact distribution pattern, the area has no equal in the nation. Although this showing is an impressive improvement over the already appreciably high intensity values for machinery and equipment inputs, it is but one of several that occur in the South. The Lower Alluvial Valley north of Louisiana now becomes the second largest area of top-class intensity, reversing its position relative to that state's share of the Mississippi bottomlands. The equally high intensities of central and much of southern Florida confirm our earlier reference to the great demand for hired labor and customwork. Fuel expenditures for curing tobacco and drying peanuts, and to a smaller but not inconsequential degree for powering machinery on peanut-cotton farms, now also make the Coastal Plain in Georgia a serious competitor of the intensity concentration in the northern part of the state. Fuel for pumping irrigation water is also becoming a significant expenditure in all of these areas. Irrigation of rice in the lower Mississippi Valley has long been established, but by 1964 it had spread to all southern states. Some of the reasons given for this upsurge are decreasing profits in agriculture, increasing shift to specialty crops, growing contract farming with the resultant need for dependable production and uniform quality, and past federal government policies subsidizing farm pond construction for irrigation.[36]

Fuel expenditures are the principal explanation for the expansion of the high-intensity centers of poultry raising in northern Georgia and Alabama and for the improved ranking of the other poultry specialty areas already depicted in the pattern for machinery and equipment inputs, such as the northwestern and southwestern corners of Arkansas, extreme eastern Texas, and in the Pine Hills of southern Mississippi. High operational intensity for poultry, as just noted, also buttresses the advanced intensity rank of North Carolina.

Machine hire and customwork expenditures, though definitely the minority share of operational inputs, are not insignificant in any of the major U.S. cropping areas. Also, except for poultry, their distribution is generally similar to that of fuel expenditures, despite a widely varying ratio between the two across the nation.[37] In these two characteristics, the South is like the other principal farming regions of the country.

Farther west, operational intensity makes its presence evident in the outlines of the subhumid part of the Winter Wheat Belt in Kansas and Oklahoma and on the High Plains, particularly in Kansas and Texas. Among these sectors, intensity is more prominent on the High Plains than in the subhumid part of the Wheat Belt, and on the High Plains it is more extensive in the south than in the north. Larger farms and irrigation, both of which favor heavy production, mechanization, and pumping on a large scale, help to cause the higher intensities in the West than in the East. A longer growing season has stimulated both production and irrigation efforts farther to the south, on the Texas High Plains. But here, too, the additional well drilling has created a serious water shortage and, as implied by our map, a worsening pumping charge. In the present period of increasing energy shortages, the latter development now threatens to become in some respects as serious a problem as water shortage. The natural gas that is used as a source of power for pumping is now five times as expensive as it was in the early 1970s.[38] Both water and power resources are also being subjected to further drains through a new type of sprinkler irrigation that began to gain popularity in the late 1960s, center pivot irrigation. An individual center pivot system consists of a long pipe that is surmounted by sprinkler heads and rotates on wheels around a fixed center in a large field. It has allowed land heretofore considered unirrigable, at least economically, to be watered and has drastically cut much of the high labor costs associated with irrigation. It has also greatly increased pumping costs. One study has estimated that the system consumes ten times the fuel needed to till, plant, cultivate, and harvest a crop like corn.[39] Center pivot systems are now extensively distributed throughout the southern Plains, especially in Nebraska and Kansas.[40]

Machine hire, customwork, and fuel expenditures reach their maximum in the Pacific Southwest, with an intensity that exceptionally improves the showing of all major agricultural areas: Sacramento and San Joaquin valleys, southern coastal California, and the interior oases of southeastern California and southwestern Arizona. Almost all counties in those areas are now in the highest intensity class. Hawaii generally maintains the high position it already had in the intensity of machinery and equipment inputs. More is also spent in this region on machine hire and customwork than on fuel, a consequence of excellent growing conditions, pronounced emphasis on specialty crops, numerous large farms, and highly advanced management systems. Small farms are definitely in the majority, but it is the larger units that control the majority of the land, and they are able to use machinery most extensively and economically. Larger and more specialized machines also have their price for full utilization, however, and larger operators, even among the huge and highly mechanized cotton farms, find it more profitable to rent the machinery or to contract with a firm specializing in mechanized work. It is also no longer unusual for farm corporations to subcontract all the steps in the growing process to management firms and specialized operators. Smaller growers also avail themselves of these services in varying degrees, a practice that contributes to the high-intensity rankings of the metropolitan counties, despite the smallness of the farms and the sharp seasonality of many of the crops on the city margins.

The trans-Cascade Pacific Northwest again shows its greater affinity to mechanization intensity standards of northeastern United States by contrasting sharply with the Pacific Southwest. The eastern Puget Sound rimlands and the lower Willamette Valley stand out even more clearly as prime intensity centers for operational inputs as the values for the areas less adapted to mechanized farming fall still lower, some counties even slipping below the national median.

Other western agricultural areas, almost without exception, share with the Pacific Southwest and regions farther east the distinction of having an operational intensity higher than machinery and equipment input intensity. Every Intermountain state except New Mexico has at least one county above the U.S. median. Most prominent on the map are the county agglomerations on the Idaho Snake River Plains and in central and eastern Washington, embracing the Wenatchee and Yakima valleys, the Columbia Basin Project area (appearing for the first time as an above-median area), and the Walla Walla Valley. Also quite visible on the map, but east of the continental divide, are the Scotts Bluff, Colorado Piedmont/South Platte, and lower Rio Grande areas.

Higher-Order Mechanization Patterns

With distribution patterns for two aspects of mechanization intensity now before us, it seems logical to conclude by considering what the overall pattern comes to. Combining patterns to arrive at a summary distribution of agricultural industrialization becomes the main business in Chapter 4, but here and in the next chapter I shall note briefly the more obvious intermediate distributions as they are suggested during consideration of the individual intensity and scale variables. They should also give us a better background for understanding the more comprehensive but therefore more general areal orderings.

Comparing the two mechanization intensity patterns (Figs. 2.3 and 2.4) leaves one in no doubt as to the regional leader: the northeast quarter of the country, with the highest class rankings in both intensity categories outlining the western Corn Belt (Iowa and Illinois), and the more intensive dairy and crop specialty areas, with a pronounced urban influence, in the lower Great Lakes and Northeast. Next in areal extent come the southeastern areas emphasizing poultry, tobacco, and other specialty crops. Then follow many areas that are smaller but of equally high rank: the sugarcane-rice-soybean-cotton areas in the lower Mississippi Valley in Louisiana, the vegetable-cane area of southeastern Florida, the fruit-dairy-poultry area in the extreme northern end of the San Joaquin Valley, the rice "core" in the Sacramento Valley, the dairy-fruit-vegetable area of the lower Willamette Valley, the dairy-vegetable lowlands on the eastern shore of Puget Sound, and the sugarcane-pineapple lands of Oahu and Kauai in Hawaii.

Another, but more conjectural, facet of the relationship between the two distribution patterns of mechanization intensity is the possibility of a ratio that might give us a clue to the areal arrangement of mechanization efficiency. Assuming that machinery is used more fully if it is rented rather than owned and more fuel is consumed rather than less, then a high ratio of operational intensities to machinery and equipment investment intensities should indicate superior performance (Fig. 2.4 : Fig. 2.3). On this basis, it is the major cropping areas in the southern half of the United States that are most efficient in the use of machinery (i.e., lower Mississippi Valley; peninsular Florida; southern Plains, particularly the High Plains portion; and the Pacific Southwest). Whether to include, as the ratio indicates, the northern Piedmont and the Inner Coastal Plain in the South is debatable because of the large amount of fuel used for curing tobacco and not powering machinery. Nevertheless, expenditures for the latter are considerable in many counties, particularly in southern South Carolina and southern Georgia, where farms become larger and crops other than tobacco become more important. The cultivation and harvesting needs of corn and soybeans also make high demands on machinery fuel in the tobacco areas of the Carolinas, but principally on the Coastal Plain.

In contrast are the Middle West and Northeast, where counties with a reverse ratio dominate, particularly in the predominantly dairy areas with poorer physical resources and, though somewhat less pronounced, in the eastern Corn Belt (Indiana, Ohio). Megalopolis, the western Corn Belt, and western Washington and Oregon maintain an efficiency equal to operational costs, although counties with superior efficiency are liberally sprinkled through Iowa and Illinois.

A third pattern combination may be made by reason of a partial but definite relationship between the operational input variable for mechanization intensity (Fig. 2.4) and the labor expenditure intensity variable (Fig. 2.2). If it is remembered that labor is also provided by the operators of the machines that are hired and are used for customwork (i.e. mechanized labor), then joining the two variables should give a more comprehensive picture of the distribution of labor intensity. Both hand and mechanized labor intensities rank high (Class I) in the more intensive farming areas of the Lower Lakes and Northeast regions, the same places already noted as leaders in the combined mechanization input (Fig. 2.3 + Fig. 2.4); in the poultry-tobacco-mixed crop belt, middle and southern Florida, and southern Louisiana in the South; and on the Pacific Coast and in most of the principal oases in the West. The heavy use of fuel for purposes other than operating machinery in the poultry and tobacco areas undoubtedly inflates the contribution of high labor inputs there, whereas the ratio of machine hire and customwork inputs to fuel expenditures in the Pacific Southwest, though now reversed, understates the situation somewhat.

Manual labor intensities fail to match those of mechanized labor in the Corn Belt, all of the lower Mississippi Valley except southern Louisiana, and the Coastal Plain in southern South Carolina and southern Georgia. Divergence between the two types of labor intensities is at its greatest in Illinois.

INTENSITY OF CAPITALIZATION IN CROPPING

From mechanization, it is logical that we next go to cropping, because crops have been especially favored by the technological advances associated with agricultural industrialization. Most of the new machines that have been developed, such as tractors, combines, corn pickers, hay balers, and cotton pickers, have been designed for use in crop production. In turn, increasing emphasis on crops, both in amount and quality, continues to challenge machinery manufacturers to expand and improve their offerings. This mutual stimulation of technology and production inputs is not lacking in livestock raising, for many improvements have been made by animal scientists in feeding, breeding, parasite and disease control, and the like, although results of these improvements in increasing production have come more slowly. Crops also bring a faster return on an operational basis and thus attract greater capitalization. Long-term investments, such as in beef production, require substantial inputs before significant profits can be expected.

As with mechanization, we shall consider two spatial patterns, in this case one of crop investments as estimated by the value of crops harvested, and another of costs of cropping, here confined to the payments for commercial fertilizers, chemicals, and seeds.

Crop Investments

Despite its comprehensiveness as an indicator of the importance of crops in the farm enterprise, the value of crops harvested must be largely inferred when considering detailed areal distributions. Census data are available only at the state level,[41] and those are for farms in general; it is specifically the "1-5" farms, which sell at least $2,500 worth of farm products, whose statistics form the basis of this study. To isolate the values for these "real" farms, the ratio of value of crops sold to those harvested for all farms was applied to the value of crops sold by the "1-5" farms. I justify the assumption of similar proportions by the very minor contribution of the smaller farms to the total value of crops sold and harvested, though the smaller units may often sell less of their crops than do the "1-5" farms (e.g. more livestock or poultry raising, more subsistence farming). The possibility of areal distortion does increase where the very small farms form a sizable percentage of all units, particularly in the South, although even here the proportion of the value of crops sold and harvested by the "1-5" farms is overwhelming.

The next step in the data approximation procedure, apportioning among the counties the estimated state total of value of crops harvested on "1-5" farms, requires an even more liberal assumption of "1-5" values and their spatial distribution. County figures were computed by applying the county proportion of the state value of crops sold to the state value of crops harvested. Significant intrastate areal contrasts could well be concealed this way, especially in states where both livestock raising and cash cropping are important. Although a general examination of the distribution pattern seems to show no obvious misrepresentations, the definite possibility of their occurrence, particularly for small county groupings, must be accepted.

Another possibility of local skewing of data exists in the omission by the census of the value of unharvested crops. Fortunately, the percentage of cropland planted to cover crops not harvested or crops that failed is generally minor, although some drought damage to cotton and corn in the lower Mississippi Valley and in Texas and Oklahoma may have increased the proportions there slightly.

The pattern computed for the value of crops harvested is well dispersed, despite the extensive empty spaces in the West and Alaska (Fig. 2.5). But there is no doubt as to where the most impressive area is, the Middle West, and what is its core, the Corn Belt. Not only does it encompass the largest single stretch of national territory with counties that have a crop investment intensity above the median of $21 per farm acre; its counties with even higher intensities (classes I and II) extend well away from the Corn Belt to the eastern end of the lower lakes, into the Cutover of Wisconsin and Michigan and, via the Red River Valley, to the Canadian border in the northwest. The overall extent of this impressive intensity is certainly not something new; rather, it is the dramatic reinforcement of an already well-established intensity that makes this region so illustrative of certain aspects of the agricultural industrialization process.

The increasing emphasis on specialization, the addition of more intensive crops and crop varieties, a growing shift from livestock to crop enterprises, and the raising of yields have all contributed to strengthening the agricultural preeminence of the Middle West. The pressures to specialize have been particularly strong in this heartland of the family farmer, who cannot, as the big operator can, organize large machinery aggregates into a diversified, yet fully mechanized, operation. Because most machines serve only one purpose and thus put a premium on an acreage that can fully exploit its capacity, the smaller operator must specialize even more. But there are other incentives to specialize, through the force of mechanization, and these have encouraged large as well as small operators to concentrate on fewer enterprises and products. The worsening of an historic farm labor shortage with the competition of nearby industrial centers, the equally traditional high regard for the latest and most modern machines and techniques, and the price attractiveness of crops that are both basic commodities and eminently suited to machinery application are some of the more important of these additional agents that have indirectly encouraged crop specialization. Specialization has also been encouraged by the buying and selling economies available to the larger producers of the commodity. A political stimulus also exists in the form of the various federal farm programs and agricultural subsidies, which have in effect reduced the danger of dependence by the farmer on only one crop; no such aids are available for mixed farming.

Indicative of the extent of specialization is the continuing increase in the production of corn, the traditional specialty crop of the Middle West, and the particular prominence of this augmentation in the subregion long famed for its specialization, the Corn Belt. With

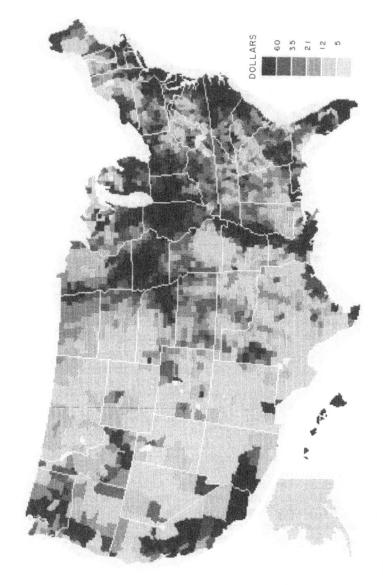

Figure 2.5. Crop investments per farm acre

its already existing advantages of larger farms, better terrain for machinery operation, and lower freight rates to nearby cities, it was logical that this area benefited more than most other midwestern sections of comparable size from the introduction of hybrid corn. Hybridization increased the expected yields of corn by 20 to 30 percent, but its impact was even greater because of the possibilities it provided for combining other technologies such as fertilizer, increased plant populations, narrow row spacing, and chemical herbicides. As late as World War II, corn typically was grown in a three-year rotation of corn-oats-hay, without fertilizer, in 40-inch rows, and planted 10,000 seeds to the acre. Yield was about thirty-eight bushels per acre.[42] Today corn is seldom rotated, and when it is done, its partner is another burgeoning money crop, soybeans. In areas outside the Illinois Grand Prairie, the hayfield may also be left for a second year to be used for pasture, and perhaps it is this rotation system that some have in mind when referring to the new crop prosperity of the bigger Corn Belt farmers ("corn-corn-Miami"). Leading growers also now typically fertilize with 150 pounds of nitrogen, plant 25,000 seeds to the acre in 20-inch rows, control weeds with herbicides, and get yields of 130 to 150 bushels per acre. The average Corn Belt yield is now about 90 to 100 bushels.[43] Increases in corn have thus been multidimensional.

    The drive for ever greater specialization has not prevented the search for more intensive crops and varieties. The "soybean revolution" is certainly the best illustration of this quest, and, if one accepts the commercial inclusion of the bean with the grains, then this event can also be said to have contributed to specialization in the form of cash grain cropping. Soybeans first became prominent during World War II and now rival corn to the extent that "Corn-Soy Belt" has become a respectable alternate to the traditional regional term. The Corn Belt is now the principal soybean area in the country, with the heaviest concentrations of the crop in the two leading cash grain areas of east-central Illinois and north-central Iowa.

    With all their attractions, it is hard to see how the fortunes of soybeans could have been any different. Their greatest value is in the seed, which yields an oil rich in protein and minerals, one that is a vital ingredient in a host of the most diverse food and industrial products. The whole soybean--oil and all--is also prized as a food product in a wide range of forms. Ironically, one of its most promising commercial possibilities is as a substitute for beef, bacon, and pork, the end products of corn. For a growing number of people who are concerned about the possible disadvantages of a diet too rich in meat, this use of the soybean comes as a godsend.

Corn is also supplemented by soybeans as a feed crop in the harvest of its vines. However, just as with corn, soybeans also owe a good part of their success to political regulations despite their great economic value. Restrictions on corn acreage have encouraged farmers to turn to soybeans, which, though supported in price, are not controlled in acreage.

Soybeans have also appealed to farmers with their hardiness. The crop grows well on soils of limited fertility (in part because they are a legume) and it is more resistant to drought. It can also be harvested earlier than corn, and in areas where winter wheat is planted, this advantage has enabled farmers to add soybeans as a second cash crop. The move has been especially strong in southern Illinois, where soybean acreage now even exceeds that of corn. The ultimate effect of this crop addition, however, may well be a reversal of the corn-soybean acreage ratio as the presently greater income from soybeans allows farmers to apply more fertilizers to the land to prepare it for higher-yielding but more soil-demanding corn.[44]

The huge expansion of corn and soybeans is also a part of a shift from livestock to cash-crop enterprises occurring in many parts of the Middle West. It is taking place both through crop exchanges within the livestock farming system and through outright conversion of livestock systems to cropping systems. With the rapid demise of older rotation systems, corn has made major inroads into the acreages of hay crops and small grains. Soybeans have made their biggest gains in Illinois, Indiana, and Ohio, chiefly at the expense of oats. Field crops in Illinois, a state that accounts for over one-third of all farm product sales in the Corn Belt, expanded their share of sales from 37 percent in 1945 to over half in 1964,[45] and that proportion has continued to increase. Cash grain corn, and, to a much smaller extent, soybeans, are also making gains on the warmer southern margins of the Dairy Belt, most notable in southern Minnesota, southeastern Wisconsin and northeastern Illinois, and southern Michigan. The average acre-yield for grain corn in Wisconsin has doubled since 1935, from thirty-five to seventy bushels.[46] A mirror image of the expansion of corn into this cooler area is the already noticeable edging of grain sorghum ("milo") into the corn-soy areas along the warmer southwestern edge of the Corn Belt. This expansion is an extension from the southern Plains, where the resistance of the crop to heat and drought has made it a regional favorite.

As both pressures and attractions for shifting to cash grain production continue to grow, the farmer eventually has to make the decision as to whether it is still possible to carry on by simply engaging in more cropping activity within the livestock farming system, or to abandon livestock raising as the ultimate objective. During the 1949-1964 period alone, the proportion of Corn Belt operators opting for cash grain sales as their principal income source increased from 20 to 33 percent; for Dairy Belt farmers, the share grew from 14 to 22 percent.[47] These shifts are also evidence of the continuance of an already well-established spatial trend in American agriculture: specialization by regions. Although less favorable terrain and climatic conditions help to explain why cash grain farming is not as popular in the Dairy Belt as it is farther south, this does not mean that the stress on cropping has been any less vigorous where dairying systems predominate. More and more cropland pasture is being sown for feed crops, with cattle confined to the barnyard. The feed crop mix is also being intensified; alfalfa, a heavy and more dependable yielder, now achieves acreage superiority over clover-timothy. Alfalfa now ranks with soybeans and grain sorghum as major transformers of the American crop landscape in the last half century.

A more important qualification of the various generalizations that can be made on midwestern cropping is offered by the areas concentrating on fruits, vegetables, and other specialty crops. Acre-yields have also been boosted in these places, to be sure, but specialization, crop variety, and emphasis on cropping are nothing new to the growers. These more intensive money crops are raised in many areas of the Middle West, but their principal concentration is in the Dairy Belt. Here the lower returns of dairying, greater amount of farm labor, and larger markets make such auxiliary income sources especially attractive. Contracts are made with processors, who usually provide the equipment and labor needed to harvest the crop, much as the companies in the Florida orange areas do. Harvesting expenses are charged to the grower, minus any contributions he may have made.

On the average, only about 5 to 10 percent of crop acreage on a farm is planted to truck crops, but collectively the area is impressive. Wisconsin, for example, has for some time been second to California in vegetable acreage for sale. Where climatic conditions and markets become especially favorable for specialty crops, as they do particularly along the shores of the lower Great Lakes, specialization increases to the point where dairying often takes second place among the enterprises. Fruit also now vies with vegetables and other specialty crops so that crop investment intensities rise to some of the highest levels in the nation. On our map, these intensities are clearly outlined by most of the counties in the Class I category (over $60 per acre).

There are important outliers in southeastern, central, and extreme northern Wisconsin; northern Illinois; central Michigan; and extreme southern

Minnesota. Truck farming and market gardening in the
Dairy Belt thus become noteworthy counterparts of cash
grain farming in the Corn Belt, where the latter is
equally well represented in intensity by the Class I
group of counties. But the high-intensity areas of cash
grain farming do not share another distinction of the
Class I intensity areas of specialty crop operations: a
scattering of counties with a significant amount of farm
incorporation.

 Another aspect of the Class I intensity pattern for
the Middle West may be seen when its areal extent is
compared with that of Class I agricultural areas elsewhere. This is the much smaller margin of its regional
superiority, particularly over the South and the Far
West. Even the Megalopolitan counties stretching from
southern New England to Maryland and the Delmarva
Peninsula exhibit a more impressive ratio of Class I
territory to remaining area, particularly in light of its
much smaller amount and generally poorer quality of land.
Restricted arable acreage naturally has also indirectly
contributed to this higher crop investment intensity as
the majority of operators strive to maintain a profit
while the many expanding cities continue to take over
more land and to force land costs upward. The result is
an exaggerated version of the midwestern dairy-specialty
crop complex, in which intensity levels are so uniformly
high and enterprises so spatially intermixed that it is
impossible to discern the two broad and distinct regional
levels of intensity as observed in the Middle West. A
higher proportion of dairy farms on the Appalachian
fringes have fruit enterprises than do midwestern dairy
farms, while on the lower Piedmont in southeastern
Pennsylvania, tobacco, grain corn, soybeans, and potatoes
are further additions to the dairying system. On the
Coastal Plain, vegetables dominate the returns, but grain
corn and soybeans have begun to come in on the Delmarva
Peninsula, and the most intensive and massive horticultural operations in the country continue to expand nearer
the cities. The expansion of horticulture has become as
much a defensive measure as an opportunistic one as
California and Florida continue to assert their environmental advantages on the fresh vegetable market.

 There is no difficulty distinguishing between the
several intensity levels of our map when viewing the
distribution pattern for the South. As already
described, the better farmlands of the region are much
fragmented and the range between their intensities and
those of adjacent areas is wide, in many places running
through the entire six classes portrayed on the map (from
less than $5 to more than $60 per farm acre). And though
the South does have a respectable number of counties
surpassing the national median, a much larger proportion
than is the case for the Middle West and Megalopolis only

barely do so (between $21 and $35 per farm acre). There are enough counties left over, however, to form three large clusters in the highest intensity class that compare favorably in size with those to the north. Several secondary but almost as intensive agglomerations can also be seen. Yet unlike the clusters in the two northern regions, many and particularly the most important of them in the South are set off from each other by distinctive crop or crop group specializations.

Tobacco quickly comes to mind when the largest of the Class I intensity centers is viewed, for the boundaries of much of the area that occupies all of eastern North Carolina and spills over into neighboring Virginia and northeastern South Carolina encompass the counties in which brightleaf, flue-cured tobacco has its greatest concentration. Like the tobacco outlier of the Maryland Peninsula, west of Chesapeake Bay and outlined on the map by equally high intensity, the North Carolina center was already well established in the seventeenth century. Since 1930, North Carolina has been the leading tobacco state. The immense labor inputs associated with tobacco raising are the main reasons for the high value of the crop, so the mechanization-crop linkage is one of the weakest of any of the principal cropping centers in the country. Still, mechanization in eastern North Carolina is the most advanced of any of the tobacco areas, and the consolidation of farms into more favorably sized units is proceeding rapidly. This development has been furthered considerably by the more recent action of the federal government in allowing holders of tobacco allotments to rent or sell them beyond the boundaries of their own county, but still within the state. Another consequence of this move has been a further focus of tobacco on the Coastal Plain (where most of the high intensity area of North Carolina already is), as more and more Piedmont farmers with their smaller acreages and rougher land transfer their allotments to the more favored and better-equipped operators to the east. Yields per acre doubled between 1954 and 1974, although this was not enough to prevent a production drop of 12 percent for the same period.[48] The decline was a result of increasing concern over the discovery of a link between tobacco and some forms of cancer and the stiffening competition on world markets.

Not all of the high investment intensity in this concentration can be attributed to tobacco. Because it is both a high-yielding crop and one traditionally demanding abundant labor, tobacco takes up only a minority of the cropland on the farm. Corn, wheat, cotton, vegetables, peanuts, and soybeans can all be found in varying amounts in these counties. Soybeans are especially expanding and are pushing the intensity boundary into the Tidewater, where land is being reclaimed through drainage. Peanuts add the extreme northeastern corner of this large high-intensity center, straddling the easternmost part of the Virginia-North Carolina boundary. This area, like the tobacco area, has a long record of production; it was also the first of the major peanut centers to mechanize harvesting operations.

A triumvirate of cotton, soybeans, and rice dominates the cropping scheme of the Mississippi Lower Alluvial Valley, the second largest concentration of counties in the South ranking in the first class of crop investment intensity, and which for most observers is one of the best examples anywhere of large production scale and factory-type operations. Almost flat terrain, rich alluvial soils, and a fruitful subtropical climate have provided an ideal physical base for cropping, and help to account for this region easily being the most productive agricultural part of the South. Cotton is the traditional crop and today its yield preserves the decades-long supremacy of the region in spite of the disintegration of most of the southern Cotton Belt and the shift of over half of the national production to the Southwest. How intensive this contraction of cotton to the Mississippi Valley lowlands has been may be noted by comparing the high investment intensity of the area with the below-median ratings of formerly important cotton areas like the Georgia-South Carolina Piedmont, the Alabama Black Belt, and the Texas Blackland Prairie. Cotton in the Lower Alluvial Valley is especially concentrated in the Yazoo Basin of Mississippi, the St. Francis Basin of northeastern Arkansas, and the "Boot Heel" of southeastern Missouri.

Rice production makes the Lower Alluvial Valley one of the three major rice areas in the country (the others are the Louisiana-Texas Coastal Prairies and the Sacramento Valley in California). Rice is grown most extensively on the Grand Prairie of southeastern Arkansas, but has been gradually extended northward into the St. Francis Basin and eastward across the Mississippi River into the Yazoo Basin. Rice farms are the most mechanized of any type in these areas.

Soybeans, however, offer the best example of recent and major cropping intensification in the Lower Alluvial Valley. Its progress in several ways parallels and even caricatures the details of its rise in the Middle West. Here, too, it was not until World War II that soybeans first became a major crop, but its expansion has been truly stormy since then. By 1947, it had already exceeded cotton in acreage and it now accounts for over half of the cropland; in this acreage push, it has been both a stimulator and the major beneficiary of extensive drainage reclamation of the more poorly drained soils of the region, a continuing effort that increased cropland by 37 percent during the 1950-1969 period[49] and thus made the area one of the few notable exceptions to the general postwar U.S. situation of crop acreage stability or even decline. Soybean expansion has also been much more impressive than in the Middle West on an acre-yield basis, though the greater part of the national soybean plantings still lies to the north. Arkansas, which has the greatest state share of soybean acreage harvested in the Delta, was already in the late 1960s second only to Iowa and Illinois as a soybean producer. Unlike the process of overall spatial contraction that has accompanied the increasing relative importance of the Lower Alluvial Valley in southern cotton production, the change in soybean distribution has been one of rapid expansion in many other important southern farming areas as well, and in enough volume to contribute importantly to the above-median crop investment intensities of those areas.

Most other major crops in the farming systems of the Delta have had to yield to soybeans in various degrees. The fluctuating supply-demand fortunes of cotton and rice contrast markedly with the meteoric growth of markets, both national and international, for soybeans. This situation, in turn, has at least partly helped in providing soybeans with a more favorable position within the complex of federal agricultural programs; all three crops are price-supported, but only rice and cotton are acreage-controlled as well. Corn, a long-time favorite of southern farmers, has declined most drastically in the face of the soybean advance in the Mississippi lowlands, and has now ceded field crop leadership to the bean both here and in the rest of the South. A notable exception to this general picture of retreat is the recent expansion of wheat, though it too owes a significant part of this change to the fortune of the soybean. Growers have found, as did farmers in the winter wheat areas of the Corn Belt, that the crop could be double-cropped with soybeans (as it often is with cotton and rice), thus bringing an income from two cash crops. Given continuing good wheat markets, this practice seems bound to continue its spread as farmers capitalize on a growing season even more conducive to the combination than in southern Illinois.

Citrus fruit, vegetables, sugarcane, and horticultural products are the main objectives of crop investment intensification on the Florida Peninsula, the third of the three most important southern areas shown on the map. It is hard to overestimate the role of a mild winter climate in explaining the successful and intensive character of agriculture in this region, although large markets in northern United States have been a critical prerequisite, and local terrain and soil conditions have significantly influenced distribution patterns within the Peninsula. After several severe freezes in the past, citrus plantings have found their main area well south of the northern boundary of the state but still in the north central part of the peninsula, the Central Lake District, where gently rolling terrain and numerous lakes reduce frost hazard and much of the best drained soil of the peninsula is found. Another area, the Indian River District, observable on our intensity map as a northern extension along the east coast from southern Florida, is poorly drained but produces the highest quality of fresh fruit raised in the state. Oranges are the main citrus fruit raised and now constitute almost 80 percent of U.S. production. Grapefruit is also an important product. Citrus production continues to augment, and additional plantings have been made in the Flatwoods between the Interior and Indian River districts; yet for some experts the increasing loss of citrus land to urbanization in the main crop area, the Interior District, points to a possible serious reduction of Florida citrus production in the long run.

Vegetable production is concentrated on the southern tip of the Peninsula--on the better-drained limestone ridge of the southeast coast and sandy soils in the southwest, and on the rich peat and muck soils of the Everglades by Lake Okeechobee.

Sugarcane and horticultural products are not new entries on the Florida agricultural scene, but they have experienced their greatest prosperity in the last few decades. New and more liberal crop quotas, as well as an embargo on Cuban production, have spurred cane farming in both the Everglades around Lake Okeechobee and the Mississippi Delta in Louisiana, but a longer growing season and more industrialized operations have now made Florida the leading cane producer in the nation. Nonetheless, the serious and continuing erosion of the organic soils of the Everglades by sugarcane operations is raising doubts about the future. The rapid rise in horticultural production since World War II is especially the expression of massive growth in Florida's population. Shrubbery, flowers, and other nursery products have found ready markets in the mass building of homes complete with landscaped yards. With big markets in the rest of the eastern United States as well, Florida accounts for almost half of the total value of horticultural sales in the South.

Smaller concentrations of high crop investment intensities also occur in sections of the South, though only a minority of the counties in each center achieve the highest class rank of more than $60 investment per farm acre. The best showing in this respect is southern Louisiana, where the top-class counties run from the truck farming areas around New Orleans and the sugarcane lands of the bayous on the east to the rice and soybean areas of the Acadian Prairies on the west. Several counties in the second-highest intensity group connect the southern Louisiana group to the larger Delta region in the north. Peanuts, fruit, cotton, and tobacco all help to make southwestern Georgia another important secondary intensity center. One might even argue for a higher rating of this area because it is connected to both the tobacco center of North Carolina on the north and the specialty crop center of Florida on the south, with large numbers of Coastal Plain counties still averaging above the U.S. median in intensity. In kinds of crops, the southwest Georgia area is in many ways only a more intensive version of the production variety of the area between it and eastern South Carolina. A similar generalization may be made for the hub of the burley tobacco belt, the Blue Grass Basin of Kentucky, which marks the highest investment intensity of a crop that is primarily responsible for the above-median showing of much of Kentucky, neighboring areas in north central and northeastern Tennessee, and a bordering strip in North Carolina.

High-intensity islands of a third order are even more widely scattered in the South, ranging from the lower Rio Grande Valley on the west, to the Mobile Bay-Florida Panhandle on the east and the several Appalachian "fruit counties" on the north.

Few counties on the Great Plains make the premier crop-investment intensity class, but the overall showing of the region is nevertheless the best presented so far in our review of individual intensity inputs in agricultural industrialization. For the first time, the Red River Valley on the northern Plains is well represented throughout its length by above-median values, although there is still no representation in the top intensity class. The strong showing of south-central and southeastern Nebraska now points out even more the difficulty of drawing a sharp line between the Corn Belt and the Plains in this part of the state; indeed, the irrigated counties along the lower middle Platte manage even more intensity than the more eastern and humid counties abutting Iowa. To the southwest, the High Plains from Amarillo northward become as prominent in above-median counties as the subhumid Winter Wheat Belt in the east, although neither area matches the class ranks of eastern Nebraska and the Red River Valley. That distinction is approximated by the southern end of the Texas High Plains, in the vicinity of Lubbock. There are other areas where less water is available that also show up in this intensity pattern. The extensive grainlands of the northern Plains now show up, as do more of the riverine strips with their irrigation supplies, such as those along the upper Platte in Nebraska and Colorado, the Arkansas in Colorado, and the tributaries of the upper Missouri in Montana and Wyoming; however, only along the Colorado Rocky Mountain Front and the upper Platte and in the Big Horn Basin are intensities sufficient to surpass the national median.

The almost exclusive focus of very high intensity values in the northern Plains on the Red River Valley is explained by the wide range of crops raised there. Production of barley, flax, oats, wheat, dry beans, sugar beets, and potatoes make the valley an important national center of all of these commodities. Barley, flax, and oats, in fact, are centered here, though sugar beets and potatoes are the most valuable crops; potatoes closely correspond to the distribution of counties having the highest intensity-class, and sugar beets do the same for the combined Class I-Class II intensity pattern. Yields of all these crops continue to increase, and soybeans have begun to make a serious entrance into the southern end of the valley from the Corn Belt. The increasingly northward expansion of winter wheat into Wyoming and Montana from the Winter Wheat Belt has not had enough impact on the overall investment intensity of the region to make itself visible in any form of distribution pattern on the map.

Contrarily, the crop changes that have been occurring on the southern Plains have strongly affected the intensity patterns. Intraregional relationships have been altered and an already important regional contribution to the national crop economy has been augmented, but both at the price of what is rapidly becoming one of the most serious resource depletion problems of the Plains to date. Grain sorghum and irrigation have been the principal actors in this event. The rise of grain sorghum (popularly called "milo") and its far-reaching effects on southern Plains agriculture quickly bring to mind the surge of the soybean in the Corn Belt. The crop did not begin to acquire important acreages until just after World War II, but as its advantages became apparent, the gains became prodigious. Grain sorghum acreage is now about equal to that of wheat in Texas and Nebraska, and is second only to wheat in Kansas, the heart of the Winter Wheat Belt. Acre-yield increases have also been notable, with hybridization and fertilization now commonly tripling returns of the 1950s. Grain sorghum has proved an excellent livestock feed and is considered to have as much as 90 percent of the nutritive value of corn.

Irrigation has been indispensable to this impressive progress, for it has greatly increased yields, ensured reliability, and made it possible to raise other crops profitably as well. The extremely high intensities of south central Nebraska are now a focal point of significant production of grain sorghum, corn, soybeans, alfalfa, and potatoes, to name the most important irrigation beneficiaries. On the High Plains, artificial watering has enabled grain sorghum to achieve its greatest acreages and a crop leadership in the driest areas, yet other crops have also benefited. Corn has made remarkable progress on the part of the High Plains extending from southwestern Nebraska to Amarillo in the Texas Panhandle, and in Kansas the center of production has now shifted from the humid east to the west. South of Amarillo, cotton and truck crops join with grain sorghum to make that part of the High Plains the high-intensity counterpoise of the Nebraska center in the north. Both cotton and sorghum were dry farmed before extensive irrigation was established, but their production increases since then have been enough to make this one of the few areas in the country where cropland has significantly expanded since World War II; practically a third of the total national increase in irrigated area from 1944 to 1964 was accounted for by Texas.[50]

The cropping intensification made possible by irrigation has also had its price, and precisely in the places where the intensification has been greatest. Most of the added supplies of irrigation water have been pumped from underground deposits, some of the richest of which lie under the High Plains in the Ogallala Formation. Nevertheless, reservoir levels continue to fall faster than the water can be naturally recharged, although research is under way to develop ways of recharging the aquifer with surface water that is available in surplus intermittently from rainfall or melting snow. South of the Canadian River, the situation is even more serious, for there the Ogallala Formation is isolated by erosion from connection with water-bearing formations outside of the region. A critical shortage of irrigation water is now being predicted by the end of the next decade, and many fields have already reverted to the original dryland farming.

Agriculture has even greater stakes in irrigation in the Pacific Southwest, for there is no other region of similar size where both handicaps and opportunities have joined on so vast a scale to encourage the supplementation of rainfall. It is an unfortunate fact that good agricultural land takes up only a small part of this area and that much of that is in the driest part of the country; the grower must thus accept the high costs of irrigation farming as a necessary price for survival. The rewards of irrigation have been great, however, allowing the operator to capitalize on the beneficial climatic characteristics of abundant heat and sunshine and a year-round growing season. Extremely high acre-yields have become the norm, and agricultural technologies like fertilization and hybridization have generated even greater returns. The same combined positive-negative stimulation of intensification in crop investment is now being exerted more strongly than ever by the burgeoning cities and towns, through both their market attractions and their competition for land and water. The consequence of all this for our map is the juxtaposition of areas with almost universally very high intensities with extensive territories of very low intensities.

The need for and attraction of extensive cropping intensification is expressed on the landscape in several ways. Fruits, nuts, and vegetables dominate the cropland no less than corn and soybeans in the Middle West and cotton, corn, soybeans, and tobacco in parts of the South. A detailed and minute adjustment of these crops to particular locations to ensure the best possible yields is more evidence. Fruit growers, the leading operator group, have sorted out their crop areas to an unusual extent, with production emphases ranging from apples (cool, temperate climates) to avocados (subtropical climates) to pineapples (tropical climates) to dates (hot desert climates). Deciduous stone fruits dominate the fruit acreage in central California, citrus fruits give their special stamp to the agricultural areas of southern California and southwestern Arizona, and sugarcane and pineapple prevail in the tropical croplands of Hawaii.

Even patterns like these are generalizations, for local climatic and soil variations have been strictly observed wherever possible. Vertical zonation of crops on alluvial fan slopes furnishes widespread evidence of the effort of growers to seek lands least susceptible to frost damage. Experience, often disastrous, has shown that the middle and higher slopes of the fans are least affected by frost, since the heavier, colder air settles at lower elevations. Oranges are commonly succeeded at higher levels by the more cold-sensitive lemons, and where the overall regional climate provides more plant opportunities, the zonation pattern can become much more extended. In southern California, for example, the sequence may range from vegetables and walnuts in the lowlands, through oranges and lemons on the middle slopes, to avocados, the most frost-sensitive, on the fan apex. Although frost is no problem in Hawaiian fruit areas, altitude still appears to influence the planting of sugarcane usually at lower elevations and pineapple in low uplands.

Areal specialization by variety as well as genus has been still another way fruit growers have expanded and intensified their acreages. Valencias are the principal orange along the southern California coast, but interior expansions of citrus to the east and especially to the north into the San Joaquin Valley have been made possible by the better adaptability of Navel oranges to hotter summers and cooler winters. Grape growers heavily favor the middle of the San Joaquin Valley, but they have also found the benchlands and hillside slopes rimming the central coastal valleys to be exceptionally favorable to the dry-wine varieties. Varietal specialization as a spatial disseminator of intensification also finds a good example in the activities of California plum growers, who raise fifteen to twenty widely differing varieties and in the process have created a widespread distribution of the fruit.

Relative to their total acreage, vegetables have been an even better agent for the expansion and further deepening of crop investment patterns in the Pacific Southwest. They are more elastic than fruits and nuts in the farming system, and as a group they thrive in a much greater variety of physical environments. Significant quantities of both warm- and cool-season vegetable crops are raised, and the shifting of principal production centers from place to place in the course of the year surpasses even the important seasonal movements of the East in complexity. The extensive distribution of mild-winter climates, close proximity of interior growing areas to those along the coast, microclimatic influences of mountains, great areal intricacies of crop patterns, and seasonal dictates of Eastern market demands all make for a wide variety of migration patterns. Some crops range from the Mexican border to Oregon and take the whole year in the process, thus ensuring a year-round supply. Other crops make the same journey in much less time. Others take a shorter latitudinal trip but repeat it several times. Still others display a spatial pattern that expands and contracts around a single, major producing area, whereas other types, particularly those raised for processing of some kind, simply concentrate in one area. Much of this areal movement is effected by incorporating vegetables into a rotation with other vegetables or field crops. Intensification of this kind reaches its peak in many southern areas; in the Imperial Valley vegetables such as tomatoes, carrots, celery, and melons are commonly combined with cotton, sugar beets, alfalfa, flax, and barley in the same operation.

Although areal specialization and seasonal shifts are marks of fine adjustments, and thus presumably of stability in land use, changes continue to be made in the same direction as before: toward greater cropping intensification. This is nothing new in the region, particularly in California, for crops have not so much been eliminated by the competition of more valuable ones as they have been shunted to less favorable sites or given less place in the farming enterprise; the buildup to the great variety of crops raised in California is essentially such a history. These shifts also continue to affect crops at all intensity levels, such as avocados taking over from oranges and lemons; oranges replacing olives; olives, grapes, and almonds substituting for grains; and Mexican wheat varieties eliminating barley and the common California wheats. Safflower and kiwi are two of the more interesting examples of new additions to the crop diversity.

All of these changes have taken place within the context of irrigation, both through the increased application of water and its introduction. Irrigated land, in contrast to cropland in the eastern United States, has continued to increase in much of the Pacific Southwest. The most impressive addition since World War II has been on the western side of the San Joaquin Valley, where deep-well irrigation made it possible to increase cotton acreage almost seven times between 1945 and 1951. Although it has been the principal money crop in California for much of the time since then, cotton, in turn, brought with it still other crops because of its heavy irrigation costs. The costs of pumping installations and of pumping water make up well over half of the cost of farming, and even the high returns from cotton are not enough to compensate growers; only by planting and irrigating additional crops like barley, alfalfa, corn, and grain sorghum has the operator been able to bring those charges down to an economical rate. Because cotton in the Southwest has not had as long an "acreage history" as that of the South, it has often been subjected to sizable acreage cuts by the federal cotton control program. At these times, the acreage of other crops, particularly the more profitable ones, increases. The recent planting of more fruits and vegetables in this area, as new water supplies begin to come in from the northern mountains via the California Water Project, is partly the result of these governmental limitations.

The most extensive current land use intensifications, however, are those taking place in response to the rapid spread of urban areas. Increased cost of land on the urban margins is forcing a change to more intensive crops, and the displaced crops in turn are forcing out less intensive uses still farther out. These effects are particularly noticeable on the edges of the two largest metropolitan centers, the San Francisco Bay Area and the Greater Los Angeles Area.[51] Tree crops have been affected the most because the areas best suited to their growth in terms of terrain, drainage, and fertility are most accessible to the urban areas. Prunes, pears, cherries, and grapes have figured in some of the more important migrations from the valleys of the San Francisco Bay Area to the Central Valley and neighboring coastal valleys, whereas oranges and lemons have been the most noticeable tree crop shifts from the Los Angeles Basin to the surrounding coastal valleys and the San Joaquin Valley to the north and the desert to the east. Vegetables and horticultural products have correspondingly increased their acreages in the areas closest to the urban centers. Their special ability to provide high returns from small acreages and fragmented plots, not to mention their large local and national markets, has made them ideal "defensive" crops.[52] So extensive has been the spread of horticultural crops, in fact, that Kern County, the nearest Central Valley county to Los Angeles, recorded for the 1959-1969 period the largest increase in horticultural sales in the nation.[53]

Underlying this continuing productive and spatial intensification is a nagging and worsening problem, the high cost of water. As cities keep growing, their demands on water bring closer the time when agriculture can no longer compete. In Arizona, where both urban and agriculture pressures on water supplies are particularly acute, need priorities are already being extensively revised. The increasing competitive inferiority of agriculture in the struggle for water is also strengthening the arguments of those who question the wisdom of using expensive irrigation to raise crops that are often in surplus or can be grown in more humid parts of the country.

Crop investment intensity that is above the national median clearly outlines all major cropping areas of the Pacific Northwest, although there is not the near-unanimous representation in the highest intensity class that is typical of the Pacific Southwest. Class I counties include the entire Willamette Valley, several of the lowlands rimming the eastern shore of Puget Sound, the Yakima and Wenatchee valleys on the western margins of the Columbia Plateau, and the cores of the middle and lower oases of the Snake River Plains. Most important of these groups is the Willamette Valley. Although 80 percent of its acreage is in field crops, which support the production of livestock and livestock products, it is the increasing yields of small fruits, nuts, mint, and vegetables that has characterized the significant intensification of cropping in Oregon since World War II. Both local and national markets have expanded, and supplemental irrigation has been a major technological boost. The crop intensification process along Puget Sound suggests the situation of the areas bordering the metropolitan centers of coastal California: a growing coalescence of urbanized areas at the expense of agricultural land and a corresponding emphasis on vegetables and horticultural products. Another similarity to the Pacific Southwest is found in the Class I counties east of the Cascades, where irrigation has been vital to the production of fruits and other crops.

Both irrigation and dry-farming rotations have expanded the above-median area beyond the Class I counties to encompass much of the cropland in central and southeastern Washington, and to outline all of the Idaho croplands on the Snake River Plains. Especially visible is the Class II representation of the lands benefiting

from the expanding irrigated area of the Columbia Basin
Project, in the Big Bend area of central Washington.
Alfalfa, sugar beets, grapes, potatoes, beans, and other
vegetables are the principal products. The principal
wheat areas of the Palouse country in eastern Washington
fail to achieve above-median status, but the addition of
peas in a rotation improves the ranking of counties in
the southeastern portion. Irrigated potatoes, sugar
beets, and beans are most responsible for the overall
intensity pattern of the Snake River Plains. More powerful pumps, sprinkler irrigation, and large-scale corporate farming are now spearheading irrigation expansion
onto the higher and drier benchlands, paralleling the
older irrigated lands of the plain.[54]

South of Idaho and Oregon, irrigated areas become
much smaller, though most of the established oases rank
above the U.S. median in intensity. The San Luis Valley
is the only one achieving first rank, and it is followed
by the Salt Lake Oasis, the middle Rio Grande Valley in
the vicinity of El Paso, and the Virgin Valley in
southern Nevada. The Grand Valley on Colorado's Western
Slope is also visible, though its intensity class is the
lowest of the group.

Cropping Expenditures and Higher-Order Cropping Patterns

A fuller view of the cropping intensity pattern for
the nation can be obtained by comparing the distribution
of crop investments with that of expenditures bearing
most immediately on crop productivity. These are the
outlays for commercial fertilizers (including lime),
agricultural chemicals (including herbicides, pesticides,
fungicides, growth-control chemicals, defoliants), and
seeds. A strong argument might be made for including
irrigation charges with these expenses, but unfortunately
the Census Bureau has lumped them together with other
outlays under the general heading of "all other production expenses." The omission of irrigation expenditures,
however, is partially compensated by the intimate association of fertilizer and chemical applications with
irrigation. Cropping expenditure variables of a less
direct and agronomic nature--those associated with the
intensity of capitalization in land, labor, and mechani-
zation--are too intertwined with livestock inputs to
allow them to be isolated and combined with the more
direct cropping inputs, and thus cannot give us a
comprehensive picture of the distribution of cropping
intensity. Such disentangling must be reserved for the
application of more powerful statistical techniques in
Chapter 4.

The distribution pattern of expenditures for
fertilizers, chemicals, and seeds corresponds fairly well
with that of crop investments, although as observed many

times earlier, noticeable departures become evident when the individual intensity classes are considered (Fig. 2.6). Of the general regions we have been discussing, the South shows this aspect the best. Most immediately apparent is the extensive improvement of the Coastal Plain, which is now well outlined by the highest intensity class (over $10.50 per farm acre) in an almost uninterrupted belt extending from Virginia to the Gulf Coast of Alabama. No less areally extensive are large sections of the Piedmont, Appalachia, the loess bluffs east of the Mississippi floodplain, and the Coastal Plain in southern Mississippi, all of which, though not in the top intensity class, are now above the national median (over $4.70 per farm acre). Even some areas that fail to match the median intensity figure, such as the Texas Blackland Prairie strip, improve their visibility.

Southern farmers spend so much on yield-increasing inputs in relation to their crop investments because of the peculiarly contradictory nature of their physical environment and the kinds of crops they grow. The climate is the most prolific of any in the country and much of the terrain, though not as uniformly gentle as in much of the Middle West, is highly favorable for extensive cropping operations; yet the abundant heat and moisture have accelerated the decomposition of the organic material and the often heavy rains have rapidly leached them out, leaving an infertile soil. Man-made depletion has been no less vigorous, for cotton, corn, and tobacco, all heavy feeders, have been traditional crops of the South. Heavy fertilization was thus a characteristic of southern agriculture even before the current pressures of agricultural industrialization for greater acre-yields began to have their nationwide effect. Today cotton and corn take up less area, and less demanding forage crops are expanding. Nevertheless, the drive to increase yields of both contracting and expanding crops, not to mention the fertilization of newly drained areas on the Coastal Plain and Mississippi bottomlands, keeps the rate of fertilizer application in the South at the highest levels in the nation. Only the Megalopolis area and California apply as much fertilizer to an acre of harvested cropland. The Virginia and North Carolina shares of the Coastal Plain, central and southern Florida, and the lower Mississippi Valley are the major exceptions to the superior ratio of crop expenditure intensity to crop investment intensity so common in the South. Here the high value of the cash crops of the respective areas--tobacco; citrus fruit and vegetables; cotton, rice, soybeans, sugarcane--may be given a good share of the credit, although the richer alluvial soils of the Mississippi bottomlands and the organic soils of southern Florida also play a part.

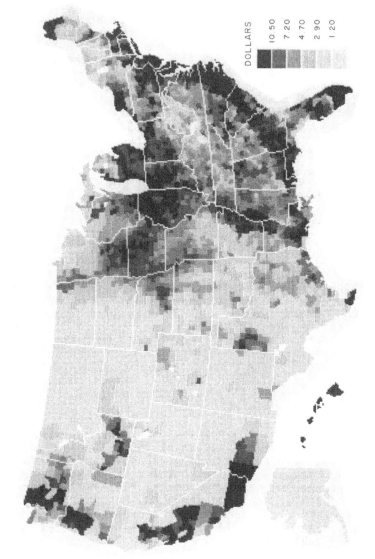

Figure 2.6. Crop expenditures per farm acre

Agricultural chemicals first began to make impressive advances in the South in the 1960s, and as with fertilizers, are used in large amounts in practically all major crop areas. Chemicals used for control of insects, weeds, grass, and defoliation are applied much more liberally than fertilizers in the lower Mississippi Valley, whereas the ratio is more equal and often reversed on the Coastal Plain, where drainage conditions are relatively better but soils are less fertile and cotton is not as important.[55] Chemicals play practically no role in crop expenditure intensification in the air-cured tobacco areas of Tennessee and the Kentucky Blue Grass Basin, and combined with somewhat less fertilizer use than in flue-cured areas, these areas are the only notable examples in the South where expenditure intensities rank below investment intensities. Greater emphasis on farming systems incorporating dairying or livestock and less dependence on cash crops like tobacco contribute a good part of the explanation for this one-sided emphasis on fertilizer inputs.

As in other areas of the country where fertilizers and chemicals are now being used in large amounts, there is an increasing undercurrent of concern over their ultimate effects on the soil and other aspects of the environment. General opinion holds that where good management has prevailed, the poorer Coastal Plain soils have improved since they were first cultivated. But the increasing rate of nitrogen application, for example, is increasing acidity, which demands much more lime than is presently being used. Far too much phosphorus is being used on tobacco, in terms of both yield increases and soil improvement; tobacco is probably the most heavily fertilized crop in the country. Accumulating fertilizer residues are also posing a potential threat through eutrophication, especially in coastal sounds next to areas being reclaimed for crops.

Although the South still ranks at the top in intensity of fertilizer application, it is no longer alone, as the intensity pattern of yield-intensifying inputs in Fig. 2.6 shows. Except for a brief interruption on the Maryland Peninsula, the Class I strip that characterizes so much of the Coastal Plain in the South continues northward into southern New England. The same intensity class also encompasses much of the Corn Belt and borders the lower Great Lakes in many counties, while the second-ranking intensity class ($7.20 to $10.50 per farm acre) takes up practically all of the remaining Corn Belt and the great majority of the Dairy Belt, the most impressive showing for that category in the United States. On the Pacific Coast, the agricultural areas in both the Southwest and Northwest are outlined largely by counties in the highest intensity class.

This more extensive distribution is another spatial expression of the increasing adjustment of yield-increasing technologies to the quality of the land, because it is only on the best land that the highest compensation for these expensive technologies can be secured. Good farmland and sufficient capital are available to more farmers in the North and West than in the South, so even the current rapid tempo of increased cropping expenditure intensity in the South has not been able to equal that of the other two areas. The bulk of this growth beyond the South has occurred in the Middle West, for here the attractions and compulsions of yield-increasing inputs-- good land, abundant capital, acreage controls, labor shortages, etc.--have affected more farmers and more land than anywhere else. The Middle West is now the leading area in acreage fertilized and farmers using fertilizers.[56] But the search for the areas most receptive to yield-increasing inputs has been pursued on a microscale as well so definite areal variations in intensity may also be noted within the Middle West and other regions where the general rate of intensity increase has been so impressive. Measured by Class I intensity, cropping expenditure intensities equal those of cropping investment where cash crops dominate because of peculiarly favorable physical environments, as in central Illinois and the Western Michigan Fruit Belt, or where they prevail because of the attractions of large nearby urban markets, as along the southern shores of Lakes Michigan and Erie. Conversely, cropping expenditures often fail to match Class I investment intensities where livestock income is more important than crop income. Most notable is the almost complete lack of Class I representation among the counties of the Iowa Prairie, where even our coarse equal-frequency classification of intensity rank is enough to separate an important cash grain area from the even more crop-specialized Grand Prairie of Illinois. Also important, though having less to do with Class I counties, is the Driftless Area of western and southwestern Wisconsin, where cropping expenditure intensities are not only less than investment intensities, but are also below the national median. Rougher terrain and poorer soils in this part of the Dairy Belt are much less attractive to operators who must apply intensity inputs on a large scale in order to prosper or even survive. Northern Minnesota, with its soil and climatic restraints, also shows less expenditure than investment intensity, even though the great majority of counties there are already below the U.S. median in investment intensity. It is conceivable that expenditure intensities might well equal investment intensities in many dairy and livestock areas if manuring were taken into consideration, although the regional patterning of application intensity also shows a favoritism towards the better agricultural areas.

Much manure is also wasted, but no overall or regional figures on this loss are available. Manure also does not fit in our category of capital inputs because it is a byproduct of farm operations and used on the same farm.

With more commerical fertilizers and other chemical products being used in the Middle West than in any other region, the current wave of concern over possible damaging effects on the environment has special meaning for this region. Many feel that the spectacular production increases, particularly for hybrid corn, have masked an accelerating depletion of organic material, and that diminishing returns are now setting in. Commoner has claimed that the organic content of midwest soils has declined in the last one hundred years by about 50 percent, and that in 1968 it took five times the amount of nitrogen fertilizer than it did in 1949 to produce the same crop yield per acre.[57] The growing worry over the effects of ever-increasing applications of other chemicals, particularly pesticides and fungicides, also has considerable pertinence for the Middle West and other important producing regions. Evidences of a vicious cycle associated with the use of biocides are now coming to the fore. Chemicals are reducing the number of species of soil animals essential to the quality of humus, the reduced soil quality makes crops more vulnerable to attack by pests or disease organisms, and this danger creates a still greater need for chemicals to sustain agricultural production. Ignorance of long-term effects on soils and man, immediate economic motivations, and political considerations, both domestic and international (natural gas and nitrogen), are some of the stiffer obstacles to a quick solution of these problems.[58]

The Megalopolitan area of the Northeast is in some ways intermediate between the Middle West and South in its expenditure-investment ratio for cropping. As in the Midwest, the good supply of capital and shortages of labor have spurred intensification of cropping expenditures to some of the highest levels in the country. Indeed, there is little difference in most areas along the North Atlantic Seaboard between the two distribution patterns of Class I intensity, expenditures and investments. But high intensity of fertilization is a much older story for Megalopolis than for the Middle West, and this aspect puts the region with the South. Land with favorable terrain and good fertility have also been much more limited than in the Middle West, and this too, as in the South, has been a strong impetus for intensification.

Westward into the Plains and the Intermountain oases, we encounter for the first time an almost universal lowering of expenditure intensity relative to investment intensity, and because many areas exhibit only moderately high (Class III) crop investment intensity to begin with, expenditure intensity generally falls below the median. Even regions of high cropping intensity like the Red River Valley, the middle Platte Valley, the South Texas High Plains, and the Snake River Plains show these low levels on their margins, although the largest single regional illustration is the Winter Wheat Belt. The high natural fertility of soils in dryland areas is the main explanation for the low expenditure intensities, though that condition is changing. Increased plantings of crops, many of which are also more productive varieties and thus more demanding of the soil from that aspect alone, have begun to degrade fertility in many areas. Heady claims that the Great Plains have had the greatest percentage increase in fertilizer use since 1940, although the originally low figure must be remembered.[59] Much of this increased application has been associated with irrigation expansion.

On the West Coast, cropping expenditure intensity values in all principal agricultural areas are above the median, and in the majority of counties they equal the Class I ratings for crop investment intensity. The counties that do not quite come up to the investment values are in California and Arizona, a reflection at least in part of the drier conditions that reduce leaching and the threat of pests. Nevertheless, the increasing intensity of production is quickening the consumption of fertilizers and chemicals everywhere. Fruits and vegetables are particularly heavy feeders, and the great variety and density of plant populations provide a wealth of targets for insects and diseases. Irrigation has been the main underlying technological input allowing a high level of expenditure intensity. It has stimulated intensity indirectly through the expansion of both crop acreage and acre yield, thus putting greater demands on soil resources and increasing the potential for biological destruction; it has also stimulated intensity directly through the ease with which fertilizers and other chemicals can be readily applied with the different irrigation systems. Almost three times as much fertilizer is applied to an irrigated acre than to an unirrigated one in the West (418 lbs. vs. 153 lbs.), although the national leadership for intensity of application on irrigated farms belongs to the Northeast and its Megalopolitan counties (1,091 lbs.).[60] Irrigation in the Pacific Southwest is beginning to face constraints as water and project costs escalate and competition from urban areas continues to augment. For areas on the edge of the growing cities these problems are a particular threat to the principal tool of production intensification.

Elsewhere in the Pacific area, Hawaii and the Willamette Valley maintain a perfect correspondence between their Class I ratings for cropping investment and expenditure intensities. In the Puget Sound lowlands, more counties rank in Class I for intensiveness of expenditures than for vigor of investments, probably ultimately due to the greater amount of amendments needed to remedy the leached and acidic character of many of the soils.

INTENSITY OF CAPITALIZATION IN LIVESTOCK AND POULTRY RAISING

We complete our study of the capitalization intensity patterns for the principal forms of farm capital with a look at livestock and poultry raising. One might argue that this should have been done first, for despite being secondary to cropping as an object of capitalization, livestock and poultry raising come closest to industry in several basic respects. Bulky raw materials are converted into less bulky finished or semifinished goods--largely the latter. A great amount of real capital is thus expended relative to the produce, and some feed ingredients, such as urea and aureomycin, do not even originate on the farm. The "machine," the animal or bird, is also less tied to the land than crops, not only by virtue of its mobility but because of its growth characteristics. Biologically determined time intervals between many livestock and poultry operations are much shorter than those between crop operations, and thus they come closer to the modern simultaneous pattern of activities that characterizes the factory system.[61] The result is that certain specialized livestock or poultry enterprises can be reorganized off the farm in an approximate factory pattern: drylot dairies, large feedlots, "egg" or "broiler factories." The greater adaptability of livestock and poultry operations to industrial procedures also has promoted product standardization and thus facilitated a closer integration of the operator into a network of contractual arrangements linking producer to consumer. Vertical integration has proceeded most rapidly among poultry farmers via contract farming, and has resulted in a type of operator many consider to be the rural equivalent of a factory worker.

Livestock and Poultry Investments

As with crops, the county values of livestock and poultry on "1-5" farms had to be approximated. Only the number of animals and birds was available for counties, and this figure was multiplied by the state price per head or bird, as extracted or computed from separate government statistics.[62] Thus, to the extent that significant differences in production and associated contrasts in prices occurred within a state, regional variations have been underestimated. Regional variations beyond state boundaries also may be misrepresented in some places because both inventories and prices refer only to the situation at the end of the census year. In general, though, the maximum seasonal use of feed for cattle, when the most important livestock inventory is at its peak, has for many years been in the October-December quarter; since 1960-1962 it has even approached the yearly average as quarterly feed expenditures have largely evened out.[63]

Despite wide distribution, there is little difficulty recognizing the two largest single concentrations of extremely high livestock investment intensity (over $46 per farm acre): the western parts of the Dairy and Corn belts, and most of the area in the northeastern states (Fig. 2.7). The gap between these two areas is also large enough to show how erroneous it is to equate the premier position of the Middle West as a livestock region with a spatial distribution that is uniformly favorable.

The Middle Western center embraces the productive core of the Dairy Belt, the biggest part in Wisconsin, but also extends into southeastern Minnesota and northern Illinois; to the southwest, it encompasses the heart of the cattle and pig feeder portion of the Corn Belt, centering predominantly in Iowa but also including parts of neighboring states, particularly Illinois, Minnesota, and Nebraska. The Corn Belt, particularly the western part, has long been the epitome of concentrated livestock feeding. Its ability to produce corn, soybeans, and other fodder crops in quantities unmatched by any other area of similar size has also made it the biggest cattle importer. Traditionally, the biggest source of feeders has been the seventeen Western states, but with increasing competition from feedlots supplying the rapidly growing cities in parts of the West, more and more animals are coming from the South. Beef consumption, however, has also dramatically increased in the last thirty years, and breeding herds have had to be greatly expanded in the Corn Belt. How rapid this expansion has been is illustrated by the situation in Illinois, which includes less than one-fifth of the Class I intensity area in the western Corn Belt: between 1951 and 1963, cow herds nearly doubled and the number of cows increased from 404,000 to 730,000.[64] From 1950 to 1970, beef cows in the Corn Belt increased by almost 300 percent.

This great growth of the cattle population has had more of an effect on the areal intensification of livestock investment than simply the large numbers. Livestock have always been confined to a smaller part of the Corn Belt farm, taking second place to cropping demands. The animals are assigned to feedlots that usually hold less than one hundred head, and to land that is rough, poorly drained, or otherwise marginal. Feedlots are being expanded, however, and the farms with small

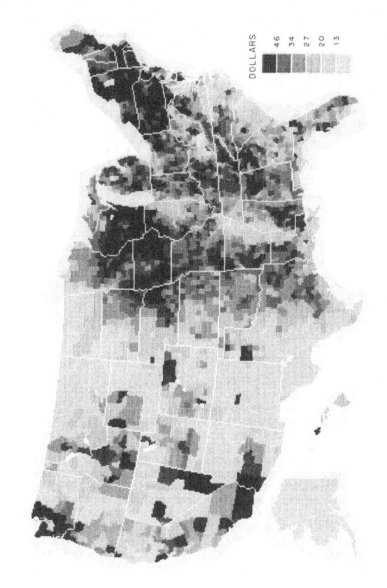

Figure 2.7. Livestock and poultry investments per farm acre

feedlots are now experiencing some of the most rapid declines. Economies of scale play a particularly crucial role in feedlot operations, and the smaller farmer finds it increasingly difficult to keep up with the new technologies and pricing mechanisms. Pastures, long considered primarily exercise yards and seldom fertilized, have also been greatly improved. Sowing them with alfalfa or brome grass and applying liberal amounts of fertilizer and lime have multiplied forage yields several-fold. Again, it has been the larger operator who has been most able to create such improvements.

The greatest concentration of the hog population of the United States practically duplicates the area of strongest concentration of beef cattle. For a large number of farmers, particularly smaller ones, hog raising is the ideal income source. Only chickens require less space and feed, convert feed into meat more efficiently, and breed more rapidly. Since they do not need large quantities of forage during an accelerated feeding program, hogs have been confined more and more to small open yards or buildings, although hogs used for breeding are often kept in pastures. They easily surpass cattle in relative meat yield, storing more than three times as much of what they consume in their bodies and dressing out as much as a quarter more relative to dead weight; their effectiveness in meat production is matched by their efficient eating habits, affirmed by the time-honored practice of pasturing cattle and hogs together in the feedlot: the hogs feed on what has gone through the cattle. Two litters a year also provide financial advantages in more frequent sales and less long-term financing.

Specialization, and therefore increasing intensity of investment, promises to be even more advanced in hog farming in the future. Although most pigs in the Corn Belt are farrowed and raised ("finished") as market hogs on the same farm, there has been an increasing tendency to separate the two operations. By 1969, feeder pig sales already accounted for almost one-fifth of the total number of hogs and pigs sold, and litters were farrowed on almost a third fewer farms.[65] The feeder pigs are sold to hog feeders, who more often than not have a wide range of facilities and equipment for processing large numbers of animals. Inventories of a thousand head or more are common in the larger enterprises in Nebraska, for example, and large feeder-pig corporations, generally owned by small groups of farmers, produce from 7,000 to 15,000 pigs per year.[66] The location of this example, peripheral to the main mass of the high investment intensity area in Iowa, is not atypical; breeders are concentrating increasingly on the margins of the principal feed area.

Specialization is also bringing about a split between hog and cattle raising. As economies of scale bulk ever larger, the urge of the larger farmer to concentrate more on cattle and to deemphasize the hog enterprise grows stronger. More cropland makes it more advantageous to produce the more profitable beef and at the same time makes more disadvantageous the competing labor demands of hog raising. For the operator, it is much cheaper and easier to buy feeder cattle from somebody else in the fall, when the crops are harvested and full attention can be devoted to fattening them. Spatially, this growing separation may be expected to strengthen the already obvious contrast between the operations of the generally larger farmers of the western Corn Belt, and those of the predominantly smaller operators in the eastern part (Figs. 1.1 and 1.2). The same selective processes are, of course, also taking place within the high investment intensity center of the western segment, although the areal sorting is necessarily of a lower order.

New technologies and more specialization have also contributed to increases in livestock investment intensity in the predominantly dairy part of the Class I area. Production increases per animal do not match the spectacular per-acre yields wrought by agricultural science for crops, but they have been considerable. Herd quality has been greatly improved through such measures as substituting breeds (most prominent is the continuing diffusion of the Holstein, the biggest milk producer), artificial insemination, and improved breeding practices. Most evident, perhaps, to one returning to a dairy farm after many years is the increasing practice of feeding cows in a lot next to the barn rather than putting them out to pasture. Farmers have found that they can get more milk per acre of forage by harvesting the crop when it is mature and storing it as hay or silage until the cattle need it. This practice of green feeding, or "green chopping," as it is commonly called, ensures maximum feed production and quality because crops are harvested at the optimum time and losses from trampling and soiling are eliminated. Green chopping is also readily adapted to mechanical feeding systems. Mechanization in both harvesting and feeding roughages also enables the operator to care for a larger dairy herd. The heavier requirements in machinery, feed storage facilities, and additional housing for the larger dairy herd occasioned by this feedlot system have favored the larger farmer, and many operators have compromised by harvesting the forage at various stages of development rather than all at once.

Specialization, both operational and spatial, has also been leaving its mark in the dairy areas. In the heart of the midwestern Dairy Belt, Wisconsin, and particularly in the eastern part of the state, cow populations reach their greatest densities. In this region, there has been a trend for several decades toward mono-enterprise: an emphasis on dairy cows and the elimination of auxiliary livestock enterprises. Poultry and sheep have almost completely disappeared, and now hogs and pigs are declining. In compensation, dairy herds are increasing, not only to take care of the milk needs of the growing urban markets, but also to satisfy the growing demand for dairy herd replacements and beef both within and without the Dairy Belt. It is also no longer unusual to find beef cows raised on dairy farms, often being substituted for hogs. This change, however, only becomes really noticeable as the Corn Belt, with its longer and warmer growing season for feed crops, is approached. Feeder pigs are also becoming a favorite enterprise of more farmers in this transition area as Corn Belt farmers continue their own specialization trend of accentuating feeding at the expense of breeding.

Implicit in the continuing intensification of livestock investment in the Middle West is an outward as well as inner expansion of intensity patterns. This outward expansion has been so forceful that above-median levels of intensity (more than $27 per farm acre) characterize areas of quite low agricultural productivity. Even the Cutover in Wisconsin, a region with a severe climate and generally poor soils, is not able to prevent above-median values from extending northward to the shores of Lake Superior. In Missouri, only the most rugged parts of the Ozark Highlands keep superior intensity values from continuing southward from the Corn Belt to the Gulf coast. Expanding milksheds and the ability of livestock enterprises to support farmers in areas less favorable for cropping are the two most obvious reasons for extension of higher intensities well beyond the Class I areas.

No less apparent, but in the opposing sense, is the much less important showing of the eastern half of the Midwest in investment intensity. The less important position of Michigan, which has only a few counties matching the Class I ranking typical of the great majority of Wisconsin counties, again demonstrates the difficulty of using convenient regional terms without ignoring important intraregional variations. Michigan forms enough of an interruption to the Dairy Belt to make its overall intensity ranking more similar to that of the predominantly Corn Belt sections of Indiana and Ohio. There may be a variety of reasons for this "saddle" in the belt; most can be debated and perhaps the only answer is history. Undoubtedly, the more level terrain and the generally more fertile soils of the Dairy Belt heart in southeastern Wisconsin provide a better forage base than that offered by the more variable topographic and pedologic conditions of the Lower Peninsula of Michigan. Yet there are enough favored sections on the peninsula to allow for a greater distribution of fruit and specialty crops, some so profitable (counties in the Western Michigan Fruit Belt and on the Saginaw Plain) that livestock investment intensity cannot even reach U.S. median levels. One might also be tempted to ascribe the greater intensity of investment in dairy stock west of Lake Michigan to the closer proximity of the large markets of Chicago, Milwaukee, and Minnesota's Twin Cities, a major reason why western Wisconsin, with its poorer soils and rougher topography, is in the same high intensity class as the eastern part of the state; yet there is more population dispersed through the agricultural areas of the Lower Peninsula than through the dairy areas of Wisconsin, and Michigan lies closer to the dense urban concentrations of the Northeast, where market demands have greatly stimulated the production of the valuable cash crops. A less debatable reason for the east-west intensity difference in the Lower Lakes region probably lies in the simple fact of the overwhelming concentration of Class I investment intensity in dairy animals within the boundaries of Wisconsin. Here the efforts of a population ancestrally conditioned and long-trained in dairying, the tremendous influence of scientific research and able leadership, and the early development of an economic infrastructure facilitating the smooth operation of all phases of the dairying industry have contributed to agglomerative tendencies of a scope more suggestive of industry than agriculture.

The same eastward decrease in livestock investment intensity occurs in the Corn Belt, with the most abrupt change in Illinois, immediately on the edge of the Class I core. Here we encounter the largest single area of submedian intensity in the Midwest except for the Cutover in Minnesota and Upper Michigan, and even these areas do not reach the low intensity typical of many of the counties in central and eastern Illinois. The explanation for this large gap in the intensity pattern is much like that implied in the reasons for the similar but smaller interruptions in the pattern in Michigan: the land is simply too productive and expensive to use for forage crops other than corn. However, farms are also some of the largest in the Corn Belt (Figs. 1.1 and 1.2), and this size structure also encouraged cash cropping from the very beginning of settlement. Another prominent, though smaller, example of the effects of comparative advantage is the Maumee Valley of northwestern Ohio with its corn, soybeans, and rich variety of specialty crops.

Elsewhere, investment intensity in the eastern Corn Belt is generally higher; it surpasses the median in the great majority of counties, but only a few of them acquire Class I status. On smaller farms (Fig. 1.1), it is difficult for the farmer to produce enough corn to warrant buying many feeder cattle, whereas enough can be grown to support a profitable swine enterprise. Smaller farm size also gives the farmer more time to fatten pigs. However, even the greater emphasis on hogs in this part of the Corn Belt does not give it the leadership of the region in either numbers or density, and a good part of the explanation is again an illustration of comparative advantage. The greater proximity to a much larger number of markets makes it advantageous in many areas to grow more vegetables and less forage crops. The cities also provide opportunities for jobs, so livestock raising and especially dairying are often abandoned because of their rigorous chore schedules. On city margins, livestock enterprises become even more of a burden because long-term capital investments in such forms as barns and herds make it difficult for the farmer to react quickly enough to swiftly changing tax situations, environmental regulations, and community attitudes. Berry, Leonardo, and Bieri have found that inventories of both beef cattle and dairy cows in the metropolitan counties of the mid-Atlantic area are more sensitive than crops to urban pressures on land,[67] and our map of overall livestock investment intensity appears to bear this out, not only for the seaboard but for the Middle West as well. Counties with very low intensities in the eastern part of the Corn Belt include a wide range of cities: Detroit, Cleveland, Cincinnati, Columbus, Indianapolis, to name the largest. To the west, the fewer metropolitan centers make for fewer interruptions of the intensity pattern, but those of Chicago, Milwaukee, and St. Louis are clearly evident. Even Des Moines, in the heart of the Corn Belt's cattle-hog area, is noticeable, though still having an intensity above the national median. However, in almost all of these areas there is an immediate rise to above-median values in the neighboring counties, reflecting in part the greater viability of dairy and livestock farmers farther from the city.

There are also variations in the general livestock investment intensity pattern that run counter to the west-to-east decrease. Four county clusters reach Class I levels in the eastern part. The largest is that of Allegan-Ottawa-Kent counties on the eastern shore of Lake Michigan, the most important dairy region in Michigan and an important poultry center as well. Poultry, beef and dairy cattle, and hogs combine in varying proportions to highlight three other areas: the more dissected, morainal country of northeastern Indiana, southwestern Ohio, and a part of the hill country of southern Indiana. In the western part, in contrast, is the comparatively lower ranking of the Iowa Prairie, where a greater emphasis on cash corn and soybeans lowers livestock investment intensity to somewhat lower ranks in Iowa and, with increasingly more wheat northward, to below-median levels in the Minnesota Valley.

The second of the two main high intensity centers in the northeastern quarter of the country, that of the northeastern states, rivals the western Midwest center in the extent of its distribution and even surpasses it in the proliferation of industrialization technologies. Only where rougher terrain and poorer soils thoroughly dominate or where competition from more profitable land uses is too strong do livestock investment intensities drop below the Class I threshold, and even there the decline is usually not great enough to lower values below the national median. Thus, superior intensities are maintained in the more difficult physical environments of northern New England, northern New York State, and western Pennsylvania, as well as in favored crop areas like the Finger Lakes Region in western New York and many sections of the Atlantic Coastal Plain near the large markets. Only where the advantages of specialty crops become overwhelming, as in the Maine potato area, or where strong crop competition and high land costs combine, as in parts of the Delmarva Peninsula and New Jersey, do livestock intensities drop lower. All of this indicates the overwhelming influence of the huge market in the Northeast, a region that includes the largest single concentration of urban centers in the Western Hemisphere.

The market demands of these centers, as conditioned by size, rate of growth, and distance from farming areas, have also strongly influenced the choice of enterprise and the manner in which it is carried on. Dairying dominates livestock income in most counties, and the less intensive beef cattle economy only makes a respectable regional showing in southeastern Pennsylvania. Poultry are also more regionally prominent in the Northeast than in the Middle West. The dairy operation in many parts of the Northeast duplicates that in the Dairy Belt farther west, but closer to the heavily settled areas of the Middle Atlantic Seaboard and southern New England it becomes more profitable for the operator to buy feed grains instead of raising them and to use the time saved to take care of more cows. Large volumes of fresh milk are the overriding goal. This greater emphasis on cows at the expense of cropping is further encouraged where soil and climatic conditions are poor for corn and oats but still good for pasture and hay. The ultimate stage in dairy specialization--the spatial and operational separation of milking from the rest of the farming system in the form of drylot dairying--is also beginning to occur. Megalopolis, with its huge markets but high land costs, has been the focus of a variety of drylot enterprises. Contractual arrangements and degree of specialization vary, but the objective remains the same: keep only milking cows and depend on others for all replacements and feed.[68]

Small land requirements and a low proportion of costs represented by rent have made poultry raising a favorite enterprise among many operators in Megalopolis. Centers of concentration string along much of the mid-Atlantic Seaboard: Delmarva Peninsula, southeastern Pennsylvania, the southern and northern ends of New Jersey, eastern Connecticut and Rhode Island, eastern Massachusetts and southeastern New Hampshire, and southwestern Maine. Poultry farming deserves to be mentioned with dairying when explaining how the highest class of livestock investment intensity is able to prevail in the great majority of Megalopolitan counties despite all the problems faced by livestock enterprises in this region of fiercely competitive land use. Hog farming also is a small space consumer, and it too is important in Megalopolis, but particularly in the Delmarva and southeastern Pennsylvania counties.

Yet none of these adaptations to the twin stimulants of market attraction and production costs have guaranteed any permanence, and the position of many presently successful Megalopolitan farmers is no less precarious than that of small-to-medium businessmen in a prosperous but highly volatile manufacturing industry. In general, poultry can be raised more cheaply close to feed sources, and with improved transportation, states like Minnesota and Michigan are now competing successively for the poultry and egg consumer in the Northeast. Many see the same scenario about to begin for dairying, as the Middle Western part of the Dairy Belt enjoys an ever greater comparative advantage with its abundant feed sources. So far, though, the increasing pressures on Megalopolitan dairy farmers appear to be leading to a spatial reorganization within the Northeast rather than a flight from the entire region. Milk sales are declining in the more urbanized areas of the Megalopolitan counties, but they are increasing in adjacent, less urban-impacted counties and more distant but also favorable agricultural areas.[69] Predictions are also becoming more precarious as rising energy costs handicap transportation and pressures for less federal regulation of prices of reconstituted milk increase.

Beyond the Middle West and Northeast, livestock investment intensity falls off rapidly. In the South, the extremely low values in practically all of its major agricultural areas are striking, and where figures are above the median, must less of the distribution is in the highest intensity class. Why should there be such an emphatic rejection of intensive livestock raising on such large acreages? All of the lower Mississippi Valley and the Louisiana-Texas Coastal Prairies, most of the South

Atlantic Coastal Plain, the great majority of Florida's peninsula and panhandle, and a good chunk of the northern Piedmont have intensities well below the median. Undoubtedly the plantation system, with its stress on specialized cash cropping, has played a major part in the early establishment in the Lower Alluvial Valley and on the Coastal Plain of what are now seen as some of the major characteristics of modern industrialized agriculture. On the Gulf Prairies and Florida Peninsula, cattle raising has been traditional in the economy, but poor soil and drainage conditions and the tardy introduction of valuable crops have prevented livestock raising from becoming an areally-intensive operation in most sections. On the northern Piedmont, the depressant has been the high density of small farmers dependent on tobacco, an intensive money crop. The lesser extent of even the highest intensities in the South is due at least in part to far fewer markets there than in the North, a condition that also can be ultimately traced in part to the plantation system.

It would be wrong to infer from all this, however, that the overwhelming concentration of the highest intensities on poorer lands in the South is simply the result of inability to compete with other land uses for the land that can be profitably cultivated. These high-intensity centers are those of poultry raising, an enterprise that has been attracted to the areas with farmers of marginal income, operators who have only small properties and even smaller areas suitable for row cropping. The correlation of the principal poultry areas--northern Georgia, northern Alabama, southern Mississippi, northwestern and southwestern Arkansas, and a strip straddling the Louisiana-Texas border--with the patterns of farm size in the South is marked (Figs. 1.1 and 1.2). The rougher terrain of these areas has been no handicap to an enterprise that only needs space for buildings, can import feed from other areas (especially the Corn Belt), and can ship the product swiftly and cheaply to all parts of the country. But most attractive to outside capital have been the lower labor costs at both farm and processing levels. On the farm, struggling operators have generally been only too glad to enter into contractual agreements that in effect make them employees of feed companies or processors in return for the necessary capital and a guaranteed margin of profit. The processor has benefited from the lower wages of a less unionized labor force, though greater security is sought by tying in with feed companies at the upper end of the production line and retail chains at the lower end. Vertical integration of one kind or another has thus been the way the South has achieved broiler production supremacy. It has also posed more starkly than in any other region the dilemma of the smaller farmer and entrepreneur: how to satisfy the ever-increasing capital demands of agricultural industrialization without sacrificing independence or the operation itself.

Vertical integration also is an important part of the explanation as to why the high-intensity areas for poultry still concentrate in islands rather than in larger and more compact areas, even though there are many places beyond the Class I centers with the same kind of land and economic conditions. For the vertically integrated farm, transfer economies and other types of agglomeration advantages are of utmost importance. In turn, the large investments made in an area to make these economies possible have discouraged movement to new areas because of the cost.[70]

The promotional efforts of local entrepreneurs and agricultural officials must also be given some credit for the fragmentary pattern of the Class I intensity centers, particularly because it is a question of an agricultural enterprise that is so free of environmental bonds. The work of J. D. Jewell, a feed merchant, in encouraging farmers in the vicinity of Gainesville, Georgia, to raise broilers in the 1930s,[71] and the enterprise of a former businessman who set up an experimental poultry house in Duplin County on the North Carolina Coastal Plain (standing out as an island of Class II intensity on our map)[72] in the 1950s, suggest a parallel to the locational influence of industrial pioneers like Ford and Carnegie, whose home areas became the early centers of the automobile and steel industries.

Not all centers of Class I intensity for poultry investment have had the same economic bases. Poultry operators in the neighborhoods of Tampa-St. Petersburg, Jacksonville, and the Florida "Gold Coast" are like their counterparts in Megalopolis who trade off the high costs of land for the advantages of a nearby large market. Farmers in the Shenandoah Valley also have found it profitable and even imperative to shift to poultry as the growth of the greater Washington, D.C., area casts its economic shadow of increasing food demands and rising land prices.

The much greater extent of above-median livestock investment intensities, exclusive of those of Class I, is accounted for by prominent contributions of all three of the most important livestock activities in the South--poultry, livestock, and dairy farming. Especially conspicuous, though, is the poultry representation. The Georgia and Alabama centers almost become one; in Mississippi, most of the southern half of the state is now included; and west of the Mississippi bottomlands, the poultry area now extends practically without interruption from the edges of the Springfield Plateau in southwestern Missouri to the edges of the Louisiana Coastal Prairies. Livestock raising, the second most important animal economy in the South, is largely responsible for the above-median showings of the many counties in southern Alabama, particularly in the Black Belt, and on the inner margins of the Texas Coastal Prairies and in the adjacent Post Oak Strip.

All other sizable areas with intensities above the median represent major overlaps of two or more noncrop enterprises. Most extensive is the belt running through middle Kentucky and Tennessee, where both cattle raising and dairying are important. Cattle raising has been a traditional part of the activities on the small farms of this area, common well before the post-World War II "cattle revolution" of the South. The fine grassland soils in the Nashville and Blue Grass basins and the excellent capability of livestock raising for complementing the tobacco enterprise (lesser labor demands and manure for the crop) have been basic advantages. As beef demands continue to increase and part-time farming keeps spreading (already one of the highest proportions in the nation), cattle raising promises to become even more popular. Dairying is not new to this area, but its greatest increase has been in the last few decades. Its expansion has been greater than in any other part of the South, and today this area is the principal southern dairy region.

Beef and dairy cattle also are plentiful in the Appalachian Valleys of eastern Tennessee and western Virginia, and dense enough in some parts to reach Class I levels. A broad area of the North Carolina Piedmont also stands out, with poultry raising and dairying the most important elements. Poultry intensities rival those of Georgia and Alabama in areal extent. Dairy intensities help raise overall intensities to some of their highest levels in the most rapidly urbanizing part of the North Carolina Piedmont, the "Urban Crescent."

The intensity picture becomes much simpler, in both numbers and distribution, on the Great Plains. Intensity patterns are largely those of beef cattle and most have values much less than the national median. On the edge of the Corn Belt--in southeastern North Dakota, eastern Nebraska, and northeastern Kansas--counties do exceed the median. The most impressive values, however, with several counties in each distribution now ranking in the first intensity class, show up in the middle Platte Valley of Nebraska, the South Platte Valley of northeastern Colorado, and the Texas Panhandle. Their sharp differentiation from the surrounding area and their association with rivers and locally rich underground water supplies are evidences of the almost meteoric success of the feedlot industry in favored spots of the West. Water has been the bottom line in intensive feedlot operations, for only where suffcient irrigation supplies have been available has it been possible to

capitalize fully on the circumstances encouraging a
westward expansion of this kind of enterprise. The great
increase in national beef consumption, the rapid growth
of western population, the development of high-yielding
grain sorghum, the improvement of transportation, and the
westward decentralization of packing operations have been
given as some of the more important of these favorable
events. One might also hypothesize that because feedlot
operators in western areas have generally started in
business later than the smaller, crop farmer-cattle
feeders of the Midwest, they have been less hampered by
capital limits and fixed resource commitments and consequently
freer to select the combination of inputs best
suited to realize the economies of scale possible in
feedlot fattening. Here, too, we begin to see more of a
trend toward vertical integration, such as already
accomplished on a large scale in poultry raising in the
South. Ranch, cow herd, feedlot complex, and packing
plant all become links in the integration chain.

The concentration of cattle in these feedlots now
reaches prodigious proportions. In Nebraska, almost two-thirds
of the feed cattle marketed for slaughter come
from lots of 1,000 or more, with the largest lots holding
as many as 40,000. In the Texas Panhandle, more than one
million cattle can be accommodated at one time in large
feedlots, and in northeastern Colorado, a highly automated
and computer-controlled operation on a single
"farm" allows 200,000 head to be fed simultaneously or
600,000 head for the year. With such operational scales,
it is not surprising that concern for the survival of the
smaller rancher or crop-cattle farmer has been mounting.
The huge accumulation of feedlot manure, with its potential
for serious water, soil, and air pollution, has also
become an issue in these and other areas of large-scale
feedlot operations.[73]

West of the Plains, in the Rocky Mountain and
Intermountain areas, livestock investment intensity
declines still further. Yet more centers of very high
intensity (Classes I and II) are to be found in this vast
region than on the Plains. The explanation for this
paradox lies partly in the explanation of another: the
role of irrigation in much of the West is both a last
resort and a technological bonanza. Irrigation must be
undertaken if something more than the most extensive
livestock economy is to be practiced; yet once initiated,
it allows some of the most intensive livestock production
achieved anywhere. Another prime part of the explanation
is the intimate association of mountain range with river
valley: the animals graze the range in appropriate
seasons, while supplemental feed is grown under irrigation.
Poultry and dairy enterprises are confined to the
irrigated regions, although the irrigation link between
valley basin and mountain watershed is still as vital as

it is for the cattle industry. As demand for beef continues to grow, many ranchers are finding it profitable to expand the carrying capacity of their lands in the higher range country through such measures as irrigating more of the meadows, fertilizing them to increase yields, and doing more rotational grazing. Sheep are also being replaced by beef cattle on some of the ranches, in part because of the generally poor market and the increasing difficulty of obtaining workers for the more labor-demanding sheep operations. In the lowlands of many areas feedlot operations also have been expanded, as has production of forage crops. The same may be said for dairying, where the bigger cities are growing. Although the boundaries of most of the Class I and II counties include much land besides the irrigated portions, the location of the political units still allows one to note the close correlation of higher livestock investment intensity with streams or stream basins: in southern Idaho and northwestern Wyoming, with the Snake; in northern Idaho and western Montana, with the Salmon, Bitterroot, and Flathead Lake lowlands; in Utah, with the Wasatch lowland in the north and the Sevier in the south; in southwestern Colorado, along the Uncompaghre; in New Mexico, on the upper Rio Grande; and in Nevada, in the west along the Truckee, Carson, and Walker rivers in the west and in several other small basins in the southeast.

The high-ranking Yuma and Salt River valleys of southwestern Arizona and the Coachella and Imperial valleys of southeastern California belong to the Intermountain region physically, but the magnitude of livestock investment and closeness of market connections also make these lowlands a part of a highly developed livestock complex, the so-called Feedlot Belt, which begins in the Middle West and loops to the southwest across the southern Plains into southern Arizona and California. The true force of large markets is best illustrated in the Imperial Valley. The valley undoubtedly has the most unfavorable physical environment of any of the major feedlot centers, being located in the hottest and driest part of the continent. Mean daily temperatures from June through September average about 92°F, and frequently do not go below 79°F. Maximums occasionally reach 126°F in the middle of the summer. Air temperatures above the body temperatures of the animals may last as long as eight or nine hours every day. The southern latitude and almost cloudless skies also make solar radiation intense. Good range is nonexistent, with more than one hundred acres needed to support one steer. Yet despite these handicaps, feedlot operators supply one-fourth of all cattle on feed in California, a state that has nearly 10 percent of the cattle feeding business of the nation. Much feed is raised on irrigated land, but it is also imported in large amounts. Of course, it is also true that once irrigation is introduced, the mild winters enable cattle to remain on full feeding rations and to yield high gains, while the sparse precipitation reduces sanitation and storage problems. A smaller version of the Imperial Valley feedlot economy is provided in southern Arizona, and all surplus animals are exported to southern California packing plants.

Drylot dairying and poultry raising on the level of "egg factories" also contribute strongly to the Class I intensity ranking of this southwestern corner of the country. The objective of drylot dairying--to make the greatest use of the smallest amount of land by concentrating on milking cows to the exclusion of all other enterprises--has been most vigorously pursued on the margins of Los Angeles, with cow densities rivaling those of people in some sections. Buildings and corrals are also intricately arranged to ensure maximum compatibility between herd numbers and the smooth and uninterrupted movement of cows between feeding and milking areas; the layout resembles that of factories, where the objective is also the expeditious flow of the product through the plant. Where land costs are not quite so high, corrals and buildings to accommodate the larger herds sometimes become extensive enough to suggest the headquarters of a tropical plantation.[74] Poultry installations in some cases are of the same order of magnitude.

In spite of the market stimulus that has made possible such intensive use of land by livestock operators, livestock enterprises have continued to give way to urban pressures. The combination of rising taxes and competition of the more flexible and areally productive vegetable and specialty crops--all within a context of very limited good agricultural land and an increasing urban-rural competition for water--has been even more formidable than in many areas of Megalopolis. The retreat to the outermost agricultural margins of the metropolitan areas has been a characteristic feature of southern California farming for some decades.[75] Even dairy areas incorporated as cities to thwart urban annexation have not survived, and both drylots and feed-lots have moved out of the region in growing numbers. Tulare County, with the highest intensity in the southern end of the San Joaquin Valley, and several counties with livestock investment intensity well above the median in the northern end of the valley, owe their rankings in good part to this outflow. The pull of the San Francisco Bay Area also has a definite influence on the intensity of the northern part of the San Joaquin Valley.

Western Washington and extreme northwestern Oregon form the northern counterpart of the high-intensity area to the south. Practically all counties from Portland north to the Canadian border attain Class I intensity ranking. Dairy cattle are the principal element in this pattern; a long pasture season along the coast and the dense and growing urban population centers of Portland and the Puget Sound littoral are the favoring agents. Beef cattle are more numerous on the other side of the Cascades, but the feedlot industry is growing noticeably as the urban centers continue their rapid expansion. Lands logged over and even once used to support dairy and sheep inventories are now being pastured by beef cows and heifers.

Higher-Order Patterns of Crop and Livestock-Poultry Investments

At this point, the overall pattern of livestock and poultry investment intensity may be profitably compared with that of crop investment intensity (Fig. 2.5), for we have seen that both enterprise groups have a strong claim to prominence in agricultural industrialization. Cropping has benefited more from capitalization, but advanced livestock and poultry raising come closest to industry in locational flexibility, reproduction timing, and operational organization. This does not mean that areas having a high investment intensity in both groups of activities are necessarily more industrialized than those with an even higher level of intensity in only one group; specialization also has accompanied agricultural industrialization, and this has meant an increasing divorcement of traditionally-combined enterprises, the crop-animal combination being no exception. The combination intensity position does indicate more directly, however, how influential industrialization is on the total enterprise structure.

The first impression from a comparison of the two patterns is their mutual exclusiveness in many areas, cropping being favored in many of the better agricultural regions. Crop investment intensity overwhelmingly dominates great swaths of territory: east-central Illinois, the lower Mississippi Valley, South Atlantic Coastal Plain, and much of the Gulf Coast and the Florida Peninsula. It also holds sway in smaller, but still quite important areas like the Maumee Valley, Red River Valley, much of the Willamette Valley, Palouse country of eastern Washington, Sacramento Valley and parts of the San Joaquin Valley in California, and all of Hawaii except Oahu. This disproportionate relationship also appears to hold true for urban areas closest to large metropolitan centers.

Nonetheless, livestock investment intensity of above-median rank does keep in step with crop investment intensity in several important farming areas. The largest part of the Middle Western livestock intensity core and the Megalopolitan portion of the Northeastern core are the foremost representations. The burley tobacco areas of Kentucky and northeastern Tennessee also correlate with superior livestock intensity. Counties in the Mobile Bay area of southern Alabama and the Tampa Bay-St. Petersburg and Gold Coast areas of Florida also rank high in investment intensities for both enterprise groups. The same distinction is also held on the southern Plains by the South Platte Basin in northeastern Colorado and the Texas High Plains near Amarillo. All principal Intermountain oases are also represented. The showing is also good in the Pacific Coast area: the high-ranking counties encompassing southern California, the San Francisco Bay Area, parts of the San Joaquin Valley, the northern extremity of the Willamette Valley, the eastern shore of Puget Sound, and Oahu in Hawaii.

There is also no lack of areas in which the investment intensities of both crops and livestock and poultry reach the highest levels, as defined by the Class I thresholds. They are naturally also smaller and the strong urban influence is most evident. Much of Megalopolis, extreme southeastern Wisconsin, the Alleghan-Ottawa-Kent county group in western Michigan, and the east Lake Erie littoral stand out in the northeastern quadrant. Southern California and southwestern Arizona, sections of the San Joaquin Valley, and the heavily urbanized counties in the Pacific Northwest are conspicuous in the Pacific states. More restricted areas include scatterings of counties in the western Corn Belt, some counties in the Tampa Bay-St. Petersburg and Gold Coast areas of Florida, the nucleus of the middle and lower oases on the Snake River Plains in Idaho, and Honolulu County in Hawaii.

Livestock and Poultry Expenditures

Expenditures for purchasing cattle, poultry, and feed provide the basis for computing the other facet of livestock and poultry capitalization intensity. These inputs do not comprise all outlays for improving livestock and poultry production, for it is impossible, both statistically and methodologically, to separate them from cropping inputs. Expenditures for livestock, birds, and feed nonetheless are the most directly related inputs and are also the major portion of operational expenses.

The separation between the Northeast and western Middle West, so noticeable in the distribution of livestock and poultry investment intensity, becomes even more conspicuous in the pattern of expenditure intensity (Fig. 2.8). Both beef cattle and poultry raising take a bigger share of total national expenditures for cattle, poultry, and feed than does dairying, and this difference is largely responsible for the now lower--though still above-median--ranking of much of the Dairy Belt (over $14

90

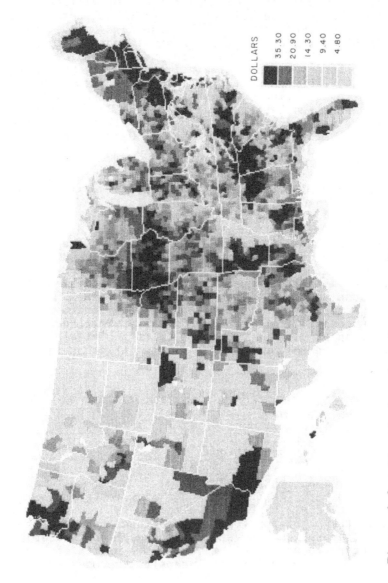

Figure 2.8. Livestock and poultry expenditures per farm acre

per farm acre). The inability of counties in the eastern Corn Belt to improve their position can be attributed in good part to the limitations of smaller farms, greater emphasis on cash cropping, and more part-time farming. Only the western Corn Belt and Megalopolis remain as the two centers of very high intensity in the northeastern quarter (more than $35 per farm acre). Although cattle feeding has developed more rapidly in other regions of the country, it is still a major, growing enterprise in the Corn Belt. Thus, while eight of thirteen regions were showing a higher percentage increase in cattle fed from 1955 to 1968, the Corn Belt surpassed all of them in increase in number of cattle.[76] And, although competition of new feedlot areas on the Plains has reduced the number of feeders going from that region to the Corn Belt, it still remains the principal outside source. To compensate for this reduction, farmers are now going to the Southeast. None of these import flows, though, has become large enough so far to match the volume of the movements within the western Corn Belt itself; the region still remains its own best supplier.

The decline in livestock expenditure intensity northward into the Dairy Belt, though definite, is not abrupt. A significantly wide belt of counties in northeastern Iowa and southern Wisconsin outlines a transitional region whose inputs are varied and voluminous enough to achieve a Class II rating (over $21 per farm acre). Feeder cattle and pigs are still very important here and the expenditures for the dairy enterprise are not unimportant. Feed purchases are now one of the leading operational expenses of dairymen, because most dairy farmers feed better balanced dairy herd rations and more concentrates per milk cow than were fed in the not-too-distant past. In many cases, dairymen also have increased their dairy herds faster than the capacity of the farming operations to supply needed feeds, for this is the only way they can capitalize on their cheapest production factor, labor, in order to satisfy the constant pressure for more productivity. The number of dairy cattle purchased for breeding, replacement, or feeding should not be underestimated as an expenditure item. Korb believes the number of dairy cattle purchased in Wisconsin may approach the number of those shipped out of the state, a considerable amount in itself.[77] Feed and cattle purchases are of sufficient volume to push above-median expenditure intensities still farther northward into Wisconsin and Minnesota in the form of the Class III pattern.

Small farm size (Fig. 1.1), less good cropland, and the nation's biggest market all join to make Megalopolis the eastern counterpart of the Class I expenditure intensity center in the Middle West. Ultimately, though, the explanation of the basic outlines of the intensity

patterns comes down to market distance. The majority of
dairy farmers just beyond the Class I intensity area of
Megalopolis try to grow all the hay and as much as
possible of the grain needed to feed their animals. In
this way they compensate for the lower price they receive
for their milk because the market is farther away. They
also sell surplus hay to Megalopolitan operators. Nevertheless, their milk prices are higher than those in the
western Middle West, so it is expedient for the farmer to
buy a greater share of his feed requirements and spend
more time milking cows than is the case for the Middle
Western farmer. In the densely populated seaboard
counties, the still higher milk prices make it profitable
to increase the emphasis on cows and depend still more on
imported feed supplies. Feed grains are mostly imported
and hay production becomes almost the sole cropping goal.
Still closer to markets (where land costs more), even the
haying enterprise begins to lose favor, in some places to
the point that operators abandon it and shift to drylot
operations where all feed is purchased. As Megalopolitan
population continues to grow, the area of high expenditure intensity can be expected to keep expanding, with
consequent repercussions on many farmers now situated in
the predominantly Class II and Class III areas. Imports
of feed and cows by dairy farmers in Megalopolis come
from suppliers throughout the Northeast, Middle West, and
Canada.

Although it is impossible to isolate costs of
poultry feed purchases from the total livestock and
poultry expenditures, there is no doubt that they add
considerably to the high intensity rating of Megalopolis.
The distribution pattern of Class I intensity also gives
definite evidence of this important role in its northern
and southern extremities. Income from poultry now
exceeds that of dairying in both Maine and New Hampshire,
and the Delmarva Peninsula has long been the leading area
of broiler production on the mid-Atlantic coast. Poultry
feed is purchased in greatest amount from the Middle
West.

It is in the South that poultry has its greatest
effect on the expenditure intensity pattern. This
distribution dominates the region even more than that of
poultry investment intensity. The centers of maximum
intensity become larger and their total extent surpasses
that of all other major regions except possibly the
Pacific Southwest, where coverage is considerably exaggerated by several large counties. Conversely, the areas
in the South that lie beyond the major centers of expenditure intensity are noticeably less prominent than in
the investment intensity distribution, many counties
falling below the median. The severity of the contrast
is a reflection of marked differences between poultry
operations on the one hand and cattle raising and

dairying on the other in the role that feeding plays in the enterprise.

Poultry producers have profited from a number of technological, political, and economic events that have encouraged the widespread diffusion of feed at reasonable prices. Foremost among these influences has been the development of formula feeds, which has loosened the locational bonds of concentrate feeds and made them available everywhere at smaller regional and area price differentials.[78] In the broiler industry, this has meant that concentrates can now flow freely from the principal feed surplus area, the Corn Belt, to locations where other resources are available on the most advantageous terms. In the South, such resources have been initially pools of underemployed labor. Poultry also have benefited more from the innovations that have increased the advantages of concentrate feeds, since they consume more concentrates than do animals feeding on roughage. The increasing yields of corn in the Middle West and its year-round availability, due in part to federal price supports and storage policies, respectively, have also promoted the feed flow to the South. Even transportation has been facilitated through reduction of barge shipping rates.

The failure of dairymen and beef cattle raisers to at least equal their investment rankings is evident in most counties where one or both of these operator groups figure strongly in the economy. In Kentucky and Tennessee, where both are important, only the most favored spots in the Blue Grass and Nashville basins and the eastern Appalachian valleys preserve above-median expenditure classifications. Much of the Black Belt drops below the median. Beef cattle raising in the South, despite the "livestock revolution" beginning after World War II, has never seriously progressed to the feeder stage, as has been the case in other major cattle raising areas. Cattle are marketed primarily as calves, and usually are moved to pastures for raising as "stockers" and to feedlots in the Middle West and Southern Plains for fattening as "feeders." Why this step in the cattle raising process has not been developed more completely has not been fully explained, although the combination of an abundance of cheap grains and roughage in one place has undoubtedly favored the flow of feeders to the Middle West. Corn acreage is also declining in the South at the same time that corn production in the Middle West is accelerating, and the expanding soybean crop of the South is moving into the more profitable cash grain channels. More negative stimulants for moving calves out of the South are such influences as the varied quality of the pastures and the smaller size of many farms. These two handicaps also confront the dairy farmer in the South, although the basic problem is the lack of sizable markets, particularly on the scale of those in the Middle West or Northeast.

The livestock expenditure intensity pattern is not completely one of contrast between poultry raising and the enterprises of dairying and cattle raising, and a few of the exceptions, though small in area, show up in values that are above the median. Some of the more important exceptions are found on the Coastal Plain running from South Carolina to Florida, where drylot and "semidrylot" dairying are expanding and both feed and stock purchases are made from near and far. Another clearly evident exception is the more prominent position of the Texas Blackland Prairie and the southern Post Oak Belt, with both poultry and beef cattle encouraging above-median intensification of feed purchases.

The meaning of the regional term, "Omaha-Amarillo Beef Belt," is well illustrated by the distribution pattern of above-median expenditure intensity on the southern Plains. This strip, from southeastern Nebraska to northwestern Texas, embraces the largest number of Plains counties with superior intensities, though the Flint Hills of eastern Kansas and the South Platte Basin in northeastern Colorado are important outliers. The fragmented pattern of the concentrations of higher intensities reflects the highly favored positions of the counties lying astride the river valleys crossing the plains. It is especially the surge in the grain production of these centers that has transformed the southern Plains from a traditional cattle supplier to the Corn Belt to a net cattle importer. A large number of cattle are still shipped northeastward, particularly from the northern sections, but imports now exceed them, and the southern Plains has become a serious competitor of the Corn Belt for the increasing number of calves being raised in the South.

Nowhere on the Plains has this transformation been so extensive as in the Texas Panhandle. With the introduction of grain sorghum hybrids in 1948 and the application of anhydrous ammonia as a fertilizer, yields increased almost immediately from an average of 2,000 pounds per acre to as much as 10,000 pounds.[79] By the late 1950s, grain surpluses had become serious enough to convince farmers, ranchers, and businessmen that the only solution was to introduce feedlot operations on a large scale, much in the way it had already been done in the Corn Belt and the Pacific Southwest. By 1969, Texas had surpassed all other states in value of livestock purchased, with almost a million head on feed for that year. The state still exports cattle to other areas, but these flows seem destined to diminish as cattle feeding there continues its unparalleled growth.

The high level of livestock and feed expenditure intensity and a wider distribution than that indicated just by the principal livestock concentrations (i.e. investment intensities) are characteristics of the southern Plains that are even more illustrative of the Pacific Southwest. A solid band of counties extending through southern Arizona and southern California and most of the counties in the San Joaquin Valley appear in the top class of expenditure intensity. The addition of Class II counties results in an area that includes practically all of the principal agricultural lands in California, except for the part of the Sacramento Valley where rice farming prevails.

No other major agricultural region displays such a superiority of expenditure over investment patterns in livestock and poultry raising capitalization intensity. There are many more farmers that engage in one or more aspects of animal farming on a smaller scale than those that operate extensive, fully integrated systems. The volume and variety of crop production in the Pacific Southwest, particularly in the San Joaquin Valley, have made it possible to carry on such specializations as feed production and raising replacement stock at these lower levels. Alfalfa, grains, volunteer grain fields, grain stubble, and highly nutritious crop residues like sugar beet tops and cottonseed are all available in abundance.

Economies of scale and market demands nonetheless continue to exert ever greater pressure on operators here as elsewhere and, combined with the efforts of the larger operators, have encouraged heavy purchases of animals and feed outside of the region. Cattle raisers buy feeders from practically all the western states, with Texas as the main source. They also go as far east as Alabama, as far west as the Philippines, and as far south as Mexico and Central America for supplies. Drylot dairymen, especially those operating on a large scale, go to similar operational and geographic extremes; in Los Angeles County they replace almost half of their herds every year with cows from fourteen states and Canada. Feed concentrates are obtained from Texas, the southeastern states, and such far-flung foreign areas as the Philippines, South America, and East Africa. For number of sources and distances covered, however, the dairy farmers on Oahu, the only island in Hawaii with a Class I intensity rating, take the honors. Copra meal is brought in from the Philippines, wheat-mixed feed and milo grain from southern California and the southern Plains, cottonseed meal from California and southeastern United States, corn gluten feed and soybean meal from the Middle West, sugar beet pulp and alfalfa from western United States, barley from California, and liquid molasses from Louisiana. A third of the animals are also imported, the majority from mainland United States.[80]

The magnitude of these operations is not without its problems, particularly for the smaller operators. As feedlot operators continue to increase their imports of feeder cattle in response to growing markets and technological pressures, they lose some of their advantage over more distant operators who produce feed grains more cheaply but have to pay more for transportation of livestock to the Southwest. Competition from dairy, poultry, and sheep farmers for feed grains is also increasing, so for many feedlot operators the future does not appear bright. The same problems are also bearing down on drylot dairymen, although the extraareal competition comes mostly from less populated sections within the Pacific Southwest. Drylot dairying has also come under criticism as an operation that destroys soil, wastes fertilizer, and degrades animal quality. No economic means has yet been found of returning most of the huge accumulations of manure to the outlying croplands and pasturelands. Nor have profit margins been sufficient to encourage drylot dairymen to sell their cattle for at least breeding purposes rather than shipping them to the slaughter house because they can no longer satisfy the high production requirements.

Livestock expenditure intensities in western Washington and Oregon are of the same impressive order as investment intensities. Livestock purchasing and feeding have in fact been expanded enough to add some counties to the above-median group in the feed-rich Willamette Valley. The growing popularity of feeding has also reinforced a more established center in the Yakima Valley on the other side of the Cascades. Still farther in the interior, expenditures for feed and feeders are also intensive enough to outline clearly the middle and lower Snake River Valley in Idaho and the backbone of early Mormon settlement in Utah, the irrigated oases in the tiers of valleys running from north to south along the edge of the Wasatch ranges and Colorado Plateaus. In contrast are the low intensities of livestock expenditures in the counties with mountain pastures in the northern Rockies, where poorer climatic conditions limit the economy mostly to one that supplies but does not fatten feeders.

A Summary Pattern of Crop and Livestock-Poultry Capitalization Intensity

A comparison of the overall distribution of the expenditure intensity of livestock and poultry raising with the pattern of expenditure intensity of cropping (Figs. 2.6 and 2.8) presents much the same spatial relationships noted in the comparison of the investment intensity patterns for the two activities (Figs. 2.5 and 2.7). However, livestock feeding intensity on the southern Plains and in California is strong enough to reverse the ratio presented in the investment intensity patterns, where cropping was superior; now it is livestock raising that leads, although in the total agricultural scheme the superior expenditure intensity of livestock raising is closely linked to the better showing of cropping in investment intensity.

We can now also ask, with the intensity distributions for investments and expenditures in both cropping and livestock-poultry raising now revealed, whether there are any agricultural regions that are prominent in all four categories. Visual comparison allows only the most general conclusions, but it is fairly obvious that few areas are well represented by above-median ratings in all four categories of capitalization. Three areas, at the extremities of the coterminous United States, come closest to having all counties in the Class I group for all categories: Megalopolis, southwestern Arizona and southern California, and the eastern Puget Sound littoral. Only when Class II representation is also considered does the beef-hog-dairy area in the western Middle West, with Iowa as the core, come into prominence. If representation by Class III is included, then most of the San Joaquin Valley, the oases of the Snake River Plain, and the southern Texas Panhandle can be included. On a smaller scale, places like Oahu and the Tampa Bay area and part of the extreme southeast coast of Florida can also be added to the above-median pattern.

NOTES

1. Walter W. Wilcox, Willard W. Cochrane, and Robert W. Herdt, Economics of American Agriculture, 3rd ed. (Englewood Cliffs, N.J.: Prentice-Hall, 1974), p. 464.
2. John Fraser Hart, "Loss and Abandonment of Cleared Farm Land in the Eastern United States," Annals, Association of American Geographers, Vol. 58 (1968), pp. 430-433.
3. Twelve counties were excluded from consideration in this study because they either had fewer than six "1-5" farms (i.e., those with annual sales of at least $2,500) or had information on hired labor expenditures, value of all crops sold, feed expenses, or total expenses that was deleted in the census. The lower limit of six farms was based on the ratio of "1-5" farms to total farms, as applied to the minimum (ten) of all farms required by the census for publication of detailed statistics for a county. These counties appear as blank spaces on the maps in this book. Four of the remaining 3,036 units are in Alaska; they are not counties, but combinations of election districts made by the Census Bureau.

4. Thomas Frey, Major Uses of Land in the United States. Summary for 1969, U.S., Department of Agriculture, Economic Research Service, Agricultural Economic Report No. 247 (Washington, D.C.: Government Printing Office, 1973), p. 1.

5. Ibid.

6. William H. Scofield, "How Do You Put a Value on Land?" in Land--The Yearbook of Agriculture 1958, ed. Alfred Stefferud, U.S., Department of Agriculture, 85th Congress, 2nd Session, House Document No. 280 (Washington, D.C.: Government Printing Office [1958]), p. 187.

7. All of these percentages were computed from information published for states and state regions for the same year (1969) used to collect the agricultural census data analyzed in this study: U.S., Department of Agriculture, Major Statistical Series of the U.S. Department of Agriculture. Vol. 6. Land Values and Farm Finance, U.S. Department of Agriculture Handbook No. 365, April 1971, pp. 11-12.

8. John Fraser Hart, "Cropland Concentrations in the South," Annals, Association of American Geographers, Vol. 68 (1978), p. 507.

9. Leslie Hewes, "The Northern Wet Prairie of the United States: Nature, Sources of Information, and Extent," Annals, Association of American Geographers, Vol. 41 (1951), pp. 307-323, and Leslie Hewes and Phillip E. Frandson, "Occupying the Wet Prairie: The Role of Artificial Drainage in Story County, Iowa," ibid., Vol. 42 (1952), pp. 24-50.

10. U.S., Bureau of the Census, 1969 Census of Agriculture. Vol. VI, Drainage of Agricultural Lands, p. 87.

11. Orville E. Krause, Cropland Trends Since World War II -- Regional Changes in Acreage and Use, U.S., Department of Agriculture, Economic Research Service, Agricultural Economics Report No. 177 (Washington, D.C.: Government Printing Office, 1970), p. 7.

12. H. Thomas Frey and Henry W. Dill, Jr., Land Use Change in the Southern Mississippi Alluvial Valley, 1950-69 -- An Analysis Based on Remote Sensing, U.S., Department of Agriculture, Economic Research Service, Agricultural Economics Report No. 215 (Washington, D.C.: Government Printing Office, 1970), p. 7.

13. Peter R. Crosson and Kenneth D. Frederick, The World Food Situation -- Resource and Environmental Issues in the Developing Countries and the United States, Research Paper R-6 (Washington, D.C.: Resources for the Future, Inc., 1977), pp. 162-163.

14. John Fraser Hart, "Loss and Abandonment of Cleared Farm Land in the Eastern United States," op. cit., pp. 515-516.

15. The comparison of land investment patterns with those of premium farmland on a national basis was facilitated by a map of the distribution, by county, of the percentage of area in the two highest classes of soil quality (Classes I and II), based on a classification by the Soil Conservation Service. The map was presented by Daniel R. Vining, Jr., Kenneth Bieri, and Anne Strauss in Urbanization of Prime Agricultural Land in the United States: A Statistical Analysis, RSRI Discussion Paper Series No. 99 (Philadelphia: Regional Science Research Institute, 1977), p. 9.

16. First applied to this region by Jean Gottmann in Megalopolis, The Urbanized Northeastern Seaboard of the United States (New York: Twentieth Century Fund, 1961).

17. David Berry, Ernest Leonardo, and Kenneth Bieri, The Farmer's Response to Urbanization: A Study of the Middle Atlantic States, RSRI Discussion Paper Series No. 92 (Philadelphia: Regional Science Research Institute, 1976), pp. 38-40.

18. Not to be overlooked is the historical advantage of the northern cities as suppliers of farm capital to the South and other parts of the nation, a situation at least hinted at by Brian J. L. Berry and Elaine Nells in their discussion, "Cumulative Heartland-Hinterland Relationships" in "Location, Size, and Shape of Cities as Influenced by Environmental Factors: The Urban Environment Writ Large," in The Quality of the Urban Environment, ed. H. S. Perloff (Baltimore: Johns Hopkins University Press, 1969), pp. 257-300.

19. Vining, Bieri, and Strauss, op. cit., p. 14.

20. Farms were multiplied by 1.5, the "man-equivalent" index applied by the Census of Agriculture to the annual labor contribution of a farmer and spouse. The number of full-time operator-equivalents contributed by part-time operators was obtained by multiplying them by the particular "man-equivalent" values assigned to them by the census: 1 man-equivalent = $1.28a + 0.75b + 0.23c$, where a = operators working off the farm <100 days, b = operators working off the farm 100-199 days, and c = operators working off the farm >199 days.

21. Wage rates for 1969 come from the U.S. Department of Agriculture, Statistical Reporting Service, Farm Labor, 13 January 1970, p. 10. The average weekly hour rate for labor is in Walter E. Sellers, Jr., Variations in Length of the Farm Workweek, U.S. Department of Agriculture, Economic Research Service, Statistical Bulletin No. 474 (Washington, D.C.: Government Printing Office, September 1971). The state regions and their average weekly hour rates, in descending order, are:
  Lake States (Minn., Wis., Mich.)--55 hrs.
  Mountain (Mont., Ida., Wyo., Nev., Colo., N.M., Ariz.) --55 hrs.

Northeast (Me., N.H., Mass., R.I., Conn., N.Y., Pa., N.J., Del., Md.)--54 hrs.
Northern Plains (N.D., S.D., Neb., Kan.)--52 hrs.
Corn Belt (Ia., Mo., Ill., Ind., O.)--47 hrs.
Pacific (Wash., Ore., Cal.)--38 hrs.
Southern Plains (Okla., Tex.)--37 hrs.
Southeast (S.C., Ga., Ala., Fla.)--35 hrs.
Appalachian (W. Va., Va., N.C., Ky., Tenn.)--34 hrs.
Delta States (Ark., La., Miss.)--32 hrs.

Although these estimates were for 1966, they were much more inclusive than the monthly reports issued by the Statistical Reporting Service for 1969 (Sellers, op. cit., pp. 1-2).

22. This was the latest date prior to the study year for which such information was available: U.S., Bureau of the Census, 1959 Census of Agriculture. Vol. I, Counties, Parts 48, 49, and 50. State Table 14.

23. Kenneth W. Korb, Dairy Farming: An Analysis of an Agricultural System in Eastern Lakeshore Wisconsin. Ph.D. dissertation, University of Wisconsin, 1968 (Ann Arbor, Mich.: University Microfilms, 1969), p. 379.

24. U.S., Bureau of the Census, 1954 Census of Agriculture. Vol. III, Farmers and Farm Production in the United States. Part 9. Special Reports: Chapter III, Tobacco and Peanut Producers and Production, p. 26, and Chapter IV, Poultry Producers and Poultry Production, p. 26. The figure for the large farms was for farms with gross sales of $25,000 or more.

25. Howard F. Gregor, "The Large Industrialized American Crop Farm--A Mid-Latitude Plantation Variant," Geographical Review, Vol. 60 (1970), P. 173.

26. Howard F. Gregor, An Agricultural Typology of California, Vol. 4 of Geography of World Agriculture, ed. György Enyedi (Budapest: Akademiai Kiado, 1974), pp. 88-91, 96-97.

27. Korb, op. cit., pp. 25, n. 10; 380.

28. C. Vogel, "Ökonomische Probleme der landwirtschaftlichen Mechanisierung," Berichte über Landwirtschaft, New Series, Vol. 36 (1958), p. 53.

29. John Lier, "Farm Mechanization in Saskatchewan," Tijdschrift voor Economische en Sociale Geografie, Vol. 62 (May/June 1971), p. 62.

30. Mark S. Monmonier and George A. Schnell, "The Tractor in New York and Pennsylvania, 1930-1974: A Study of Geographic Trends in Agricultural Mechanization," Proceedings of Association of American Geographers, ed. Richard E. Lonsdale, Vol. 4 (1972), pp. 70-75.

31. John Fraser Hart and Ennis L. Chestang, "Rural Revolution in East Carolina," Geographical Review, Vol. 68 (1978), pp. 456-457.

32. Ibid., pp. 456-457.

33. W. Herbert Brown, Peanut-Cotton Farms: Organization, Costs, and Returns, Southern Coastal

Plains, 1944-60, U.S., Department of Agriculture, Economic Research Service, Agricultural Economic Report No. 7 (Washington, D.C.: Government Printing Office, 1962), p. 14.

34. For a comparison of the larger and more mechanized farms of the "West Side" of the San Joaquin Valley with the smaller, more diversified, and more numerous farms of the "East Side," see Gregor, An Agricultural Typology of California, op. cit., pp. 60-67.

35. U.S., Department of Agriculture, Economic Research Service, Farm Real Estate Market Developments (Washington, D.C.: Government Printing Office, March, 1969), p. 14; (August, 1971), p. 36, cited in Michael D. Sublett, Farmers on the Road, Department of Geography Research Paper No. 168 (Chicago: Department of Geography, University of Chicago, 1975), p. 4.

36. Arthur J. Hawley and David W. Bunn, "Irrigation in the South," Southeastern Geographer, Vol. X, No. 2 (1970), p. 40.

37. Shown most clearly by the maps of the two items, and presented separately for the first time, in U.S., Bureau of the Census, 1974 Census of Agriculture. Vol. IV, Special Reports. Part 1. Graphic Summary, pp. 79 and 82.

38. C. Langdon White, Edwin J. Foscue, and Tom L. McKnight, Regional Geography of Anglo-America, 5th ed. (Englewood Cliffs, N.J.: Prentice-Hall, 1979), p. 340.

39. William E. Splinter, "Center-Pivot Irrigation," Scientific American, Vol. 234 (1976), p. 94.

40. Tom L. McKnight, "Great Circles on the Great Plains: The Changing Geometry of American Agriculture," Erdkunde, Vol. 33 (1979), p. 77.

41. U.S., Bureau of the Census, 1969 Census of Agriculture. Vol. I, Area Reports. Section 1. Summary Data.

42. Donald D. Durost and Warren R. Bailey, "What's Happened to Farming," in Contours of Change--The Yearbook of Agriculture 1970, ed. Jack Hayes, U.S., Department of Agriculture, 91st Congress, 2d Session, House Document No. 91-254 (Washington, D.C.: Government Printing Office [1970]), p. 3.

43. Ibid.

44. John C. Weaver, "Changing Patterns of Cropland Use in the Middle West," Economic Geography, Vol. 30 (1954), p. 47.

45. S. W. Warren, D. G. Sisler, and L. M. Plimpton, A Regional Summary of United States Farming, Department of Agricultural Economics, Cornell University Agricultural Experiment Station, A. E. Res. 292 (Ithaca, N.Y.: Cornell University, 1969), p. 43.

46. Korb, op. cit., p. 172

47. Warren, Sisler, and Plimpton, op. cit., pp. 39 and 42.

48. Hart and Chestang, op. cit., p. 453.

49. H. Thomas Frey and Henry W. Dill, Jr., <u>Land Use Change in the Southern Mississippi Alluvial Valley, 1950-69--An Analysis Based on Remote Sensing</u>, U.S., Department of Agriculture, Economic Research Service Agricultural Economic Report No. 215 (Washington, D.C.: Government Printing Office, 1971), p. iv.

50. Robert Estall, <u>A Modern Geography of the United States--Aspects of Life and Economy</u> (New York: Quadrangle/The New York Times Book Co., 1972), p. 159.

51. Howard F. Gregor, "Push to the Desert," <u>Science</u>, Vol. 129 (1959), pp. 1333-1334.

52. Howard F. Gregor, "Urbanization of Southern California Agriculture," <u>Tijdschrift voor Economische en Sociale Geografie</u>, Vol. 54 (1963), p. 275.

53. U.S., Bureau of the Census, <u>1969 Census of Agriculture. Vol. V, Special Reports. Part 10. Horticultural Specialties</u>, p. 7.

54. David L. Smith, "Superfarms vs. Sagebrush: New Irrigation Developments on the Snake River Plain," <u>Proceedings of the Association of American Geographers</u>, ed. Fritz L. Kramer, Vol. 2 (1970), pp. 127-131.

55. These and other comparisons of the distributions of individual yield-increasing inputs can be derived in more detail by consulting the maps in the Graphic Summary volumes of the Census Bureau's <u>1969 Census of Agriculture, Vol. V, Special Reports, Part 15</u>, pp. 91-97, and <u>1974 Census of Agriculture, Vol. IV, Special Reports, Part 1</u>, pp. 98-109.

56. U.S., Bureau of the Census, <u>1969 Census of Agriculture, Vol. II, General Report, Chapter 4, Equipment, Labor Expenditures, Chemicals</u>, p. 154.

57. Cited by Michael J. Perelman in "Farming with Petroleum," <u>Environment</u>, Vol. 14 (1972), pp. 8-13, and by Wilson Clark in "U.S. Agriculture is Growing Trouble as Well as Crops," <u>Smithsonian Magazine</u>, January 1975, both articles reproduced in Richard D. Rodefeld et al., <u>Rural America</u>, op. cit., pp. 48 and 96, respectively.

58. To glean the main arguments from the vast amount of literature, both pro and con, written on the problems of use of chemicals in agriculture, one could do no better than to compare the critical views collected by Rodefeld et al., ibid., with the optimistic outlooks offered by Marylin Chou et al., of the Hudson Institute, in <u>World Food Prospects and Agricultural Potential</u>, Praeger Special Studies in International Economics and Development (New York and London: Praeger Publishers, 1977).

59. Earl O. Heady et al., <u>Roots of the Farm Problem</u> (Ames, Ia.: Iowa State University Press, 1965, p. 107.

60. U.S., Bureau of the Census, <u>1969 Census of Agriculture, Vol. II, General Report, Chapter 4</u>,

Equipment, Labor, Expenditures, Chemicals, p. 157.

61. John M. Brewster, "Technological Advance and the Future of the Family Farm," Journal of Farm Economics, Vol. 40 (1958), p. 1607.

62. U.S., Department of Agriculture, Agricultural Statistics 1971, pp. 306, 322, 334, 372, 413, and 425. The price for sheep in Hawaii was unavailable and was computed on the basis of the U.S. ratio of sheep to hog prices. For the same reason, the average prices for broilers in Illinois, North and South Dakota, Montana, Idaho, Wyoming, Colorado, New Mexico, Arizona, Nevada, Alaska, and Hawaii were based on the national ratio of broiler to chicken prices; broiler values themselves were derived by multiplying the selling price per pound by two, two pounds being the estimated weight of average broilers on the farm at mid-growth. Turkey prices also were not provided for Nevada, Alaska, and Hawaii, and these were calculated on the basis of the U.S. ratio of turkey to chicken prices.

63. Ronald A. Gustafson and Roy N. Van Arsdall, Cattle Feeding in the United States, U.S., Department of Agriculture, Economic Research Service, Agricultural Economic Report No. 186 (Washington, D.C.: Government Printing Office, 1970), p. 48.

64. Walter M. Kollmorgen, "Farms and Farming in the American Midwest," Problems and Trends in American Geography, ed. Saul B. Cohen (New York and London: Basic Books, 1967), Ch. 7, p. 86.

65. U.S., Bureau of the Census, 1969 Census of Agriculture. Vol. II, General Report. Chapter V, Livestock, Poultry, Livestock and Poultry Products, p. 13.

66. William T. Ahlschwede, "Swine," Economic Atlas of Nebraska, ed. Richard E. Lonsdale (Lincoln, Neb., and London: University of Nebraska Press, 1977), p. 64.

67. Berry, Leonardo, and Bieri, op. cit., pp. 37-39.

68. Howard F. Gregor, "Industrialized Drylot Dairying: An Overview," Economic Geography, Vol. 39 (1963), pp. 315-316; Edward Higbee, "Metropolitan Agriculture," in Megalopolis, The Urbanized Northeastern Seaboard of the United States, ed. Jean Gottmann, op. cit., Ch. 6, pp. 289-291, 293.

69. Floyd A. Laskey and Charles N. Shaw, Economic Aspects of Dairying in the Northeast, U.S., Department of Agriculture, Economic Research Service, Agricultural Economic Report No. 188 (Washington, D.C.: Government Printing Office, 1970), pp. 39-46.

70. Jerry Dennis Lord, "The Growth and Localization of the United States Broiler Chicken Industry," Southeastern Geographer, Vol. 11, No. 1 (1971), p. 41.

71. Ibid., p. 40.

72. John Fraser Hart, The South, 2nd ed., rev. (New York: D. Van Nostrand Company, 1976), pp. 65-66.

73. Charles Bussing, "The Impact of Feedlots," The High Plains: Problems of Semiarid Environments, ed. Donald D. MacPhail, Contribution No. 15 of the Committee on Desert and Arid Zones Research, Southwestern and Rocky Mountain Division, A.A.A.S. (Fort Collins, Colo.: Colorado State University, 1972), pp. 84-86.

74. Howard F. Gregor, "A Sample Study of the California Ranch," Annals, Association of American Geographers, Vol. 41 (1951), pp. 296-299.

75. Gregor, "Urbanization of Southern California Agriculture," op. cit., pp. 273-278.

76. Gustafson and Van Arsdall, op. cit., p. 37.

77. Korb, op. cit., p. 362.

78. Ronald L. Mighell and Orlin J. Scoville, "Economic Effects of progress in Animal Feeding," Agricultural Economics Research, Vol. 8 (1956), p. 125.

79. David L. Wheeler, "The Cattle Feeding Industry in the Southern High Plains of the United States," Geography, Vol. 79 (1979), p. 50.

80. Howard F. Gregor, "Industrialized Drylot Dairying: An Overview," Economic Geography, Vol. 39 (1963), p. 303.

3
The Scale of Agricultural Industrialization

Although I have criticized the use of farm size as the principal indicator of agricultural industrialization, there is no question about its important implications for the capitalization process. Increased capital returns are best achieved on larger acreages, where greater production and larger economies of scale can be more easily realized. But larger farm size also tends to discourage the intensity of capitalization on a per-acre basis in favor of a more intensive application of capital to resources other than land. Therefore, the distribution of capitalization scale can be expected to depart, often drastically, from the pattern of capitalization intensity. For these reasons the amount of investment and expenditures applied to the principal forms of farm capital, but now on a per-farm basis, has to be considered.

The criterion used to determine the number of farms employed in the denominator, however, is more subjective than the farmland divisor used to compute capitalization intensity, and the implications of this difference for the scale values and patterns computed must be recognized. The greatest part of the basic data provided by the Census Bureau on farms, which are used in this study, is for farms selling at least $2,500 worth of products for the year. Yet the great proportion of farm production comes from a very small segment of even these farms, so many feel that a higher production threshold would be more realistic. Though it may be argued that the inclusion of the many less productive farms is not as much of a problem where the analysis of agricultural industrialization focuses on the amount of capitalization rather than production, the division of these additional farms into the capitalization totals does dilute the figures for capitalization scale. All major agricultural regions have many of these farms, but some distortion of the scale pattern can be expected in the western Dairy Belt, the Corn Belt, and the South, where the farms have their greatest distribution. Nevertheless, in most of these areas the concentrations are greatest in the poorer agricultural sections.

SCALE OF LAND AND BUILDING CAPITALIZATION

As one might expect, the scale pattern of farming capitalization is more or less the opposite of the intensity distribution, with the western part of the country now becoming the principal area of concentration because of its larger farms. But the exceptions to this reversed relationship are not trivial, and in those divergences is evidence of the true nature of the heavily capitalized farm as opposed to one that is large principally by virtue of its acreage. The point is well illustrated in the distribution of the scale of land and building investments per farm--the industrialization variable that most closely approximates farm acreage size--and its showing relative to the distributions of the other variables we have already considered.

The Western United States dominates in average amount of land and building investments per farm (Fig. 3.1). At least half of the territory of each of the nineteen western states ranks above the national median of $87,000 per farm, and nine of these states surpass this territorial minimum for the Class I rank as well, over $164,000 per farm. The highest scale class includes much of the western half of the Great Plains, much of the Rocky Mountain area, a majority of the Intermountain region, and practically all of the Pacific Southwest. But perhaps no less notable, in light of what we might normally expect because of the generally smaller farms, are the important concentrations of Class I counties in many of the important agricultural areas in the East as well. Most important is the South, with three extensive representations: the western Gulf Coast, most of the lower Mississippi Valley, and a majority of the Florida Peninsula. Smaller clusters are also scattered over the Piedmont and South Atlantic Coastal Plain. In the Middle West, it is the prime production center of east-central Illinois and its northeastern extension to Lake Michigan that clearly stand out, though a few outliers can be seen farther to the north and northeast in the Dairy Belt (Wisconsin, Michigan) and east in the Corn Belt (Indiana, Ohio). On the seaboard, Class I counties outline well over half of Megalopolis.

If all areas with above-median land values and building expenditures per farm are considered, the extent of large-scale capitalization becomes even more impressive. Most of the remainder of the West, from the Rocky Mountain states westward, now achieves parity with the Pacific Southwest in the overwhelming areal dominance by superior scale levels. In the six Plains states, the

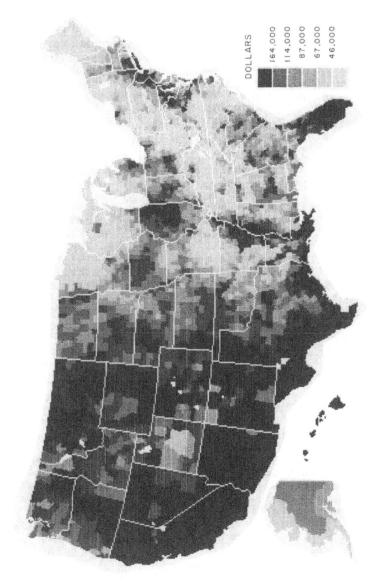

Figure 3.1. Land and building investments per farm

area of above-median scale now extends eastward to encompass the majority of the Plains, including all of the important Red River Valley section and most of the Winter Wheat Belt to the south. The expanded above-median area extends still further eastward in the Midwest, now bounding most of the Corn Belt and two small but important segments of the Dairy Belt: the extreme southeastern corner of Wisconsin and the southeastern segment of the Lower Peninsula of Michigan, running from Saginaw Bay to the Ohio border. The coastal belt of Megalopolis counties is also strengthened--an almost uninterrupted strip runs from Boston to Pamlico Sound in North Carolina. In the South, the western Gulf Coast and lower Mississippi Valley become one gigantic right-angled band of superior-scale territory, separated by only a few scattered counties from a Florida Peninsula that is now almost exclusively in the above-median group. The Coastal Plain outliers also expand to include county clusters of respectable size in South Carolina, southwestern Georgia, and the Alabama Black Belt.

The general distributional picture is quite different when farms with superior land and building capitalization scale are matched with those having above-median capitalization intensity (Fig. 2.1). At the Class I level (over $400 per farm acre and over $164,000 per farm), most of the West drops out; only the coastal valleys, most of the Central Valley of central California, and the strip comprising southern California and southwestern Arizona remain. In the East, the northeast quarter becomes more important relative to the South as east-central and northeastern Illinois and Megalopolis maintain their leading positions, whereas a somewhat lower land and building capitalization intensity reduces the rank of most counties on the western Gulf Coast and in the Lower Alluvial Valley of the Mississippi. The Mississippi Delta and a cluster of counties in central and southeastern Florida retain their positions.

When our view is broadened to include all areas having farms ranking in at least one of the above-median classes for both intensity and scale (over $210 per farm acre and over $87,000 per farm), we find the western pattern improved, though not extensively. The appearance of the Willamette Valley and the Puget Sound regions is the most obvious change, and practically all major agricultural counties in the Pacific Southwest are now indicated. Yet only the most important irrigated oases interrupt the otherwise unrepresented Intermountain area, and on the Great Plains, only the South Texas High Plains, the subhumid Winter Wheat Belt, and the middle Platte Valley in Nebraska relieve a still largely subpar national position. In the more humid eastern part of the nation, the greater intensity of land and building investment per farm definitely improves the areal extent of many important agricultural regions. Most of the Corn Belt, particularly the western part, now comes to the fore, as do the two northern extensions into the Dairy Belt, already perceived in the distribution of scale. Megalopolis is also somewhat reinforced in outline. All of the lower Mississippi Valley and much of the Florida Peninsula are the two principal above-median areas in the South, although the Acadian Prairies, the Gulf Coast of Mississippi and Alabama, and a few scattered counties on the Coastal Plain of Georgia and South Carolina should also be mentioned.

At this stage, it is appropriate to go one step further in our map comparisons, and that is to relate the scale and intensity patterns for land and building investment to the two patterns indicating more directly the physical extent of the farm: percentage of farms of 260 acres or more (Fig. 1.1) and percentage of farms with 100 acres or more of harvested cropland (Fig. 1.2). In this way, we come closer than in any other part of our study to uncovering the distribution of the large industrialized farm, as defined primarily by a heavy emphasis on the land resource: large acreages and both extensive and intensive capitalization of those acreages. It is a definition that is implicit in much of the debate over the advantages and disadvantages of the large farm. At the Class I level, it is apparent that such a discussion would have little value; no area of any sizable extent is represented in each of these four aspects of size. Only if pure farm size is excluded from consideration does a prominent area show up: east-central and northern Illinois. But if we widen our evaluation to include all areas with farms that simply surpass the U.S. median in all four farm size facets, then several concentrations can be recognized: the western Corn Belt; the lower Mississippi Valley; the subhumid Winter Wheat Belt; the south Texas High Plains; and a number of smaller foci dispersed over the Coastal Plain in Georgia and South Carolina, the southern Florida tip, the western Gulf Coast, the Texas Blackland Prairie, the northern and southern extremities of the California Central Valley, and the strip from extreme southeastern California to southwestern Arizona.

The lack of significant representation of Megalopolis and most of the prime agricultural areas of California, Hawaii, and the Florida Peninsula is evidence of the much smaller role of farm size relative to land capitalization. Emphasis here should be on the term <u>relative</u>, for despite the many and advanced ways technology has been used to enhance the modest land resources of the average farm, it has also been mobilized to create farms with some of the largest crop acreages and building complexes in the country. The contribution of these farms to the overall high intensity and large scale of land capitalization in these areas is considerable, despite the dilution of the values of the larger units by the greater number of smaller ones. This is especially true in Hawaii, where pineapple and sugarcane plantations, with their traditional array of residential, administrative, and maintenance and processing buildings, overwhelmingly dominate the croplands. There is probably no greater contrast anywhere in the country than between these truly industrial farms and the horticultural farms of only a few acres, also common in Hawaii. In California, the large cotton farms on the western side of the San Joaquin Valley have tens of thousands of acres and a complement of buildings that rival the Soviet collective farms in their number and variety of purpose. Many farms even have their own gins. These huge operating units furnish a dramatic contrast to the far greater number of smaller and more diversified farms on the eastern side of the valley. Large units offer strong competition to the smaller operator in Florida in all the principal crop groups, although their dominance is not quite as impressive as it is in many sections of California and Hawaii. Land capitalization on a per-farm basis plays the least role in Megalopolis because of the prevailing small farm size, with a greater share of the investment in buildings. The latter amount, though, is substantial on the larger farms and in the aggregate is still enough to influence heavily the average farm value of buildings in both county and state; that for New Jersey ($38,000), for example, is more than twice the figure for Wisconsin ($18,000), a third more than for Illinois ($23,000), and even more than for California ($34,000).[1]

Expansion of the farm plant (both buildings and land) has been going on for some time in all areas where the more landed industrialized farm is prominent. More buildings--and more specialized ones, particularly those housing machinery--are creating truly impressive farmsteads and are thus providing exceptions to the overall demise of farm structures as farms become fewer but bigger. The enlargement of the farm through annexation of noncontiguous lands has also become a widespread phenomenon as operators seek to increase their holdings within well-settled regions. Problems like increased fuel costs, heavier wear on machinery, impediments to movement of animals and equipment, greater risk of thievery and vandalism, and loss of timeliness in performance of farm functions have also accompanied this kind of growth in farm size.[2] Roads, however, have been improved, machinery has become more flexible, and communication technology has progressed to the stage of telephones, two-way radios, and closed-circuit television. These communication instruments have become common on farms where fragmentation has reached a level at which communication problems become the most serious matter confronting management. Nevertheless, farm expansion of the fragmented type has not been able to overcome completely the obstacles of other farms, and an increasing amount of leasing and renting has resulted. So widespread has this practice become in the South, for example, that a distinctive type of farm tenant is now well recognized: the multiple tenant.[3] This person is usually a small or medium-sized operator who is completely mechanized and, with the aid of several cash-wage employees, uses machinery at its economic optimum by working other farms that are no longer large enough to be viable operating units.

Farm expansion is also being accomplished through land reclamation, but in this case, because of much greater costs and concessionary tax policies, the larger farms have been particularly favored. Prominent examples found in several of the regions indicated by our maps are centers of larger landed farms with extensive land capitalization. Federal tax laws allow significant tax deductions for costs of reclamation activities such as land clearing or drainage, but for these provisions to be attractive it is necessary to have significant income. Thus, in the extensive land clearing operations carried out in the lower Mississippi Valley in the 1960s to make room for soybeans, the corporation farm was a favored organizational device for these activities.[4] In many cases, too, an already-established pattern of large properties--often itself the result of difficult environmental conditions with consequent sparse settlement--has further restricted the opportunities of the smaller operators. The accomplishment of drainage reclamation in the Everglades by large vegetable farms and the increasingly extensive irrigation of the west side of the San Joaquin Valley by even bigger units are examples of where this additional complication has been especially influential.

SCALE OF LABOR CAPITALIZATION

Labor, no less than land, has been a favorite criterion among investigators of the large industrialized farm. Yet, as noted earlier, the labor indicator runs afoul the problems of determining the minimum labor requirements of such a farm and obtaining sufficient data. By observing the areal distribution of the amount of labor expenditures per farm and comparing the pattern with that of intensity of labor expenditures, we may at least avoid these problems to the extent of determining where farms with heavy labor outlays are most concentrated. We shall also be advancing another step in our attempt to outline the distribution of what I have proposed as a more direct and comprehensive indicator of agricultural industrialization: the process itself.

The western part of the country is easily the most prominent area of labor capitalization by farm (Fig. 3.2). However, there is an an even more pronounced westward shift within the area itself, with a noticeable reduction of the Great Plains counties included in the highest category of labor expenditures per farm (over $7,300) and a broad extension into the Pacific Northwest and Alaska. All Pacific states now have massive majorities of their territories in the Class I group; Alaska, for the first and only time in our consideration of the sixteen intensity and scale variables posited for agricultural industrialization, shows all of its statistical-reporting units ranking above the national median ($5,000 per farm). Alaska also best illustrates the influence of isolation from major labor markets, a serious problem for much of the West. Here, in a location more removed from the national heartland than any other area except Hawaii, farm wage rates are high enough to place the majority of its farms in the top class of labor capitalization despite their predominantly modest size (Figs. 1.1 and 1.2) and very low labor capitalization intensity (Fig. 2.2). Farther south, in the other states of the Pacific area, high wage rates again greatly bolster the rankings of the predominantly small farms in scale of labor capitalization, though the much more intensive farming and the great scale of operations among the largest farms add their bit.

In the eastern part of the nation, the most obvious difference between the distributions of scale of land and building capitalization and labor capitalization is the reversal of the ranking of the Great Lakes region and particularly the Northeast relative to the Corn Belt. The high positions of the first two areas is especially noteworthy, considering the modest farm sizes. But unlike Alaska, the high wage rates here, in the densest labor concentration of the country, are more the result of the intense competition between the demands of intensive dairying and specialty cropping and those of the many and large industrial centers. The strong underlying role of the urban areas in this competition is quite evident in the Class I counties clustering in the major metropolitan areas of Chicago, Detroit, Pittsburgh, Milwaukee, Cleveland, and Minneapolis-St. Paul, culminating in the almost unbroken strip of extensive labor scale extending from Washington, D.C., to Boston. The heavy capitalization of labor on the farm at greater distances from urban centers, however, should not be underestimated. Class I counties mark much of the Western Michigan Fruit Belt; the fruit, truck, and dairy region of the Ontario Plain and Finger Lakes district in western New York state; the potato and cranberry section in

113

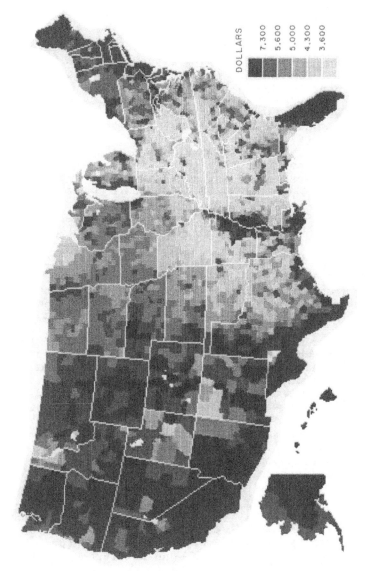

Figure 3.2. Labor expenditures per farm

northern Wisconsin; and the potato and pea area of northern Maine. On an even broader areal scale, most Wisconsin counties without Class I ranking still lie above the median in scale of labor capitalization, as do such counties in the Northeast.

The inferior position of the Corn Belt indicates in part the smaller role of urban competitiveness and stimulus, and hence the lower wage rates of the region, relative to those of the more urbanized lake states and the Northeast. Urban centers like Omaha, St. Louis, Columbus, Indianapolis, and Cincinnati do stand out, but none attains the highest scale-group rating. The scale of labor capitalization, in fact, decreases toward the east as urban populations increase, and in many counties in Indiana and Ohio it falls to the levels of the lowest scale class ($3,600 or less per farm). The much smaller farm size in this part of the Corn Belt is the most apparent explanation. The generally larger farms of Illinois, however, are not enough to raise the farm averages for labor capitalization above the national median either, and for this inability the greater emphasis on the more mechanized and less labor-intensive cash corn farming system, as well as less intensifying effect of urban centers, bears much responsibility. Only in northern and western Iowa and extreme southern Minnesota do labor capitalization values for farms rise above the median. Here the part played by the more labor-intensive cattle-hog and dairy farms is apparent.

In the South, the general distribution of heavy labor capitalization is similar to that for land and buildings. The principal areas, though, are more clearly outlined because of the very small scale of farm labor outlays elsewhere in the region. Rapid agricultural growth in the South has not improved average farm income status, and farm wages are nowhere near the national median. That wages are the lowest of any major U.S. agricultural region, however, is due to yet another reason: the general and historic lack of alternative job opportunities for the agricultural population. It is this "captive" labor force that has particularly retarded labor capitalization on the larger farms in the past. With the more recent heavy rural exodus, however, and increasing demands for a more specialized worker who often operates a particular type of machinery, wages on the larger farms have risen notably. Truck cropping and market gardening also have become quite important locally in several areas of the South, and although much of the labor used is still that of work gangs, the total amount of cash spent on a farm for labor is impressive. In addition, quite in contrast to what we have seen in the other principal farming regions, farms with extensive labor capitalization in the South are also usually the largest farms, and thus the sheer magnitude of operations swells the cash outlays for labor on a farm basis despite the generally lower wages compared with rates in the North and West. Peninsular Florida, the lower Mississippi Valley, and the Texas Gulf Coast easily stand out as the areas with the most extensive scale of labor expenditures. Scattered areas can also be distinguished on the Coastal Plain, especially in southwestern Georgia, the eastern Carolinas, and the Alabama Black Belt. Even smaller outliers, but with a scale of labor capitalization meriting the highest class, dot several sections in both interior and coastal areas. More prominent illustrations are the truck farming centers of the Sea Islands counties of South Carolina and Mobile County in Alabama.

Again, when scale and intensity patterns for the nation are combined, distributions of the high-ranking farms become much more selective. For the industrialized farm defined solely by an emphasis on labor, the distribution is widely dispersed, particularly when only the counties in the highest class of labor capitalization are taken into account (over $25 per farm acre and over $7,300 per farm). Counties above these minimums concentrate in the four extreme corners of the coterminous United States. Most extensive are the groupings of counties in Megalopolis, with its poultry and specialty crop extension into northern New England, and in the Pacific Southwest, including Hawaii. The Willamette Valley-Puget Sound strip in the Pacific Northwest and the central and southern portions of the Florida Peninsula take in the other two antipodes. Also scattered but somewhat more evenly distributed over the nation are the smaller Class I representations, in many instances consisting of only one county. Most conspicuous are the Ontario Plain-Finger Lakes region of western New York state and a narrow band across the Mississippi Delta in the New Orleans area. The metropolitan counties on the shores of the lower Great Lakes, the Lower Rio Grande Valley, and the Sea Islands shore of South Carolina also are unmistakable. Smaller places such as Ramsey County (Minneapolis-St. Paul), Minnesota; Wyandotte County (Kansas City), Kansas; Duval (Jacksonville) and Saint Johns counties in northeastern Florida and Gadsden County in the Florida Panhandle; Clark County (Las Vegas), Nevada; and Payette County in southwestern Idaho add to the dispersal of overall labor capitalization distribution.

When minimum expenditure levels are lowered to include all areas with above-median labor capitalization (more than $14 per farm acre and over $5,000 per farm), the northeast quarter definitely becomes supreme, with almost all of the counties in the Northeast represented and including most of the western Dairy Belt and a good part of the cattle-hog area in the western Corn Belt. Patterns of superior capitalization are expanded and reinforced in most other areas, too, the most extensive being the addition of large portions of the lower Mississippi Valley.

SCALE OF CAPITALIZATION IN MECHANIZATION

No other aspect of accelerating agricultural technology has rivaled mechanization in the intimacy of its association with large scale farming. The advantages that machinery offers to larger operators are many and have been well described. In more recent years, demands have been growing for the manufacture of smaller machines and other devices more suited to the smaller farmer, but the trend continues in the opposite direction, and in a way it suggests a reinforcing cycle. The growing dominance of a few giants in the farm machinery industry is leading to a smaller range and variety of available equipment, and because these concerns can produce most profitably for large and relatively homogeneous groups of farmers, they are not inclined to add new machinery lines of suitable capacity and cost for the small farm unit. This handicap, in turn, worsens the smaller farmer's already poor competitive situation and makes that operator even less attractive as a machinery customer. Meanwhile, the benefiting larger operators add their bit to the cycle by demanding still larger and more powerful equipment, a demand the manufacturers have shown themselves ready to satisfy.[5] Yet the progress of this interplay of profits and bigness has varied greatly over the country, as our maps of the scale of investments in and expenditures for machinery and equipment show (Figs. 3.3 and 3.4).

Machinery and Equipment Investments

For much of the cropland in the West, extensive capitalization in the form of machinery has been the story almost from the beginning of agriculture. And nowhere else have nature and events conspired to encourage this capitalization on so vast a territory as they have done on the Great Plains. A marginal precipitation condition that favors production volume rather than production intensity, a prior system of large landholdings that discouraged many would-be small farmers from even attempting settlement to begin with, and a vast amount of gentle terrain that has favored machine operation everywhere have been among the most forceful of the agents that have stimulated capitalization on a grand operational scale. In this region, then, the present technological events favoring large-scale and mechanized farming are only continuing an historical pattern, though at a faster rate.

117

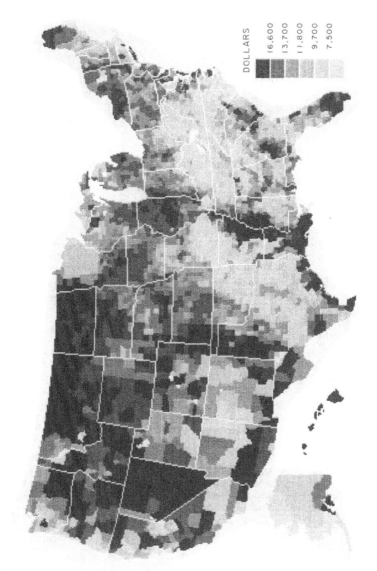

Figure 3.3. Machinery and equipment investments per farm

The showing of the Plains on the map is noteworthy in both areal extent and massiveness. Counties with above-median scale of capitalization in mechanization (over $11,800 per farm) embrace the great majority of Plains land. The similarity of the distribution to that of farm size as determined by amount of harvested cropland (Fig. 1.2) indicates how vital large acreages are to farmers who traditionally have had to depend on production scale to compensate for modest acre-yields. The scale of machinery and equipment investments made in this compensation, however, is much more voluminous than what is revealed by just the outline of the above-median area; the bulk of the counties represented rank in the highest two of the three above-median groups (more than $16,600 and $13,700 per farm). Both classes have their largest distributions on the northern Plains; the top class includes the vast part of Montana and North Dakota and describes a continuous band along the Canadian border, stretching from the Rockies on the west to the Laurentian Shield on the east. This is the heart of the Spring Wheat Belt in the United States, and here the full complement of machinery that has made wheat farming one of the most mechanized farming systems in the world becomes the farm standard. The combine has become the key machine, saving more labor than any other single piece of equipment; it is also the most expensive. The machine is not new, having been on the Great Plains farm scene in noticeable numbers as early as the 1920s. Now it is larger and self-propelled, and with adjustments, can be used for harvesting not only wheat and other small grains but also grain sorghum and beans. Corn picker headers can also be attached to some models. Combines and other agricultural machines in the Spring Wheat Belt are most prominent in the inventories of farms in Montana, where farms are the largest. In the Red River Valley, however, the better moisture conditions and the consequent greater production and crop variety reverse the general west-to-east decrease in machinery and equipment investment per farm, although the amount does not match the investment in the western end of the Belt.

Irrigated farms located along parts of the rivers flowing eastward across Montana, Wyoming, and the Dakotas have also been increasing their production as additional water is made available through federal water projects, and this has generated demands for a greater number and variety of machines, usually quite specialized. Potato and sugar beet harvesters are important examples. Hay production on both irrigated and unirrigated land has also sparked a large increase in hay balers and associated equipment. Where specialty crop joins with feed crop, the amount of machine use on a farm can increase substantially. All of these more intensive productions, though still concentrated in very small areas, have made sizable contributions to the scale of investment capitalization in mechanization in a number of counties in the western part of the Spring Wheat Belt, although the aggregation of the information by county makes it difficult to determine the importance of these contributions relative to the more areally-dominant wheat farm machinery inventory.

On the southern Plains, the distribution of the above-median groups describes a more contrasting pattern: the western area (High Plains) takes in most of the counties having a Class I rating, and the eastern part (subhumid Winter Wheat Belt) embraces the largest single group of the remainder. This is more evidence of the sharp east-west difference McCarty so graphically described in his 1940 account of the "old" and "new" Winter Wheat belts.[6] The contrast at that time was pictured as relating increasing drought in the West to a corresponding increase in farm size. Since then, the larger farms in the western part have benefited hugely from the rapidly accumulating economies of scale, and their expenditures, on mechanization at least, have strongly accentuated the east-west difference. This increased regional differentiation in scale of capitalization is also due, somewhat paradoxically, to the reduction of the sharp east-west differential in moisture availability through irrigation. The extensive tapping of the Ogallala Formation on the High Plains for sprinkler irrigation is a good illustration of how advancing irrigation technology on the Plains has favored operators with larger investments in machinery and equipment, even though irrigation is commonly assumed to be more a geographic correlate of smaller operations. Labor costs of irrigation have always been high, and it is these charges to which the larger farmers are particularly sensitive; yet the increased yields resulting from irrigation have enabled the bigger operators to use more mechanized plants to the fullest advantage, for with increased crop-acre production machine costs remain the same, whereas hand labor costs usually increase. Of course, increasing production also encourages further mechanization and thus more divergence between large and small farmers in scale of mechanization, for it is the larger farmer who can write off machinery costs most quickly. Phenomenal yields have been recorded in irrigated areas, the maximums for irrigated crops in Kansas, for example, being 160 bushels per acre for grain sorghum, 140 bushels for corn, 60 bushels for soybeans, and 33 tons to the acre for corn silage.[7]

The development of irrigation technology has conferred another advantage on the larger operator by making it possible to water much larger areas with considerably less labor for the same amount of land irrigated. The development of siphon tubes in the 1940s reduced some of the need for shoveling open and closing off furrows, and more recently the introduction of gated pipe (pipe with multiple, controllable outlets along its length) further reduced the labor needed for applying water to the individual furrows. The main advance, however, came with the advent of rotating sprinkler nozzles and the availability of comparatively cheap aluminum pipe. At first the entire system had to be dismantled and moved by hand from field to field, but now the pipes and attached sprinklers move automatically on wheels around a fixed pivot. Although center-pivot irrigation does not account for the majority of irrigated land on the southern Plains, it now makes up the largest part of the land being added to the irrigated area. This popularity and its high cost indicate a further winnowing of farmers by the pressures of technology. In Nebraska, the average cost of a complete center-pivot irrigation system for 133 acres was $25,256 in 1969, and rose to an estimated $60,000 in 1975.[8]

Irrigation plays an even greater part in the rapidly growing machinery and equipment inventories of farms elsewhere in the West, although the dryfarmed wheatlands of the Palouse in eastern Washington and of adjoining northeastern Oregon offer an important exception. The dependence on the more limited water supplies of the West produces a much spottier distribution pattern of areas to the west and south of the Great Plains, one that would be even more fragmented were it not for the areal exaggerations of the large counties, especially in the Intermountain area and egregiously so in Nevada. Nonetheless, where the concentrations of extensive mechanization scale do occur, they are often of a higher value than what farm size alone would suggest, whereas on the Plains there are many above-median counties that do not match their high rankings in size (cf. Figs. 3.3 and 1.1 and 1.2). This greater ratio of mechanization investment scale to farm size is most evident in the Pacific Southwest, where a milder climate allows more intensive cropping in the irrigated areas, thus increasing the need of growers for a larger and more varied machinery and equipment plant.

Nevertheless, as is the case for the patterns of land and building capitalization scale (investment), many of the larger farms have such immense investments in machinery and equipment that they definitely influence the average farm figures. Again, Hawaii is probably the most spectacular example, where the pineapple and sugarcane plantations, especially the latter with their large and specialized complements of field machines, trucks, repair shops, and even refineries, stand in sharp contrast to the far more numerous small farms specializing in everything from sugarcane to orchids and coffee. In California, the large rice farms in the Sacramento Valley often have more money tied up in machinery than in the expensive land. Self-propelled combines, land planes, contour plows, ditchers, disk harrows, tractors, bank-outs, trucks, and pumping and well apparatus make up the standard equipment, not to mention the aircraft that are rented to fertilize and sow the fields and spray them with herbicides and pesticides. Even this typical array is exceeded by that employed on the large cotton farms on the west side of the San Joaquin Valley, where plows, tractors, bulldozers, harrows, land planes, planters, earth movers, ditchers, trucks, grain combines, cotton pickers, and aircraft are all standard equipment. Also vital to operations are deep wells and powerful pumping equipment, with pumping costs alone amounting to $50,000 to $100,000 for the average west side cotton farm.[9]

High costs of water extraction and distribution are increasingly conferring upon larger capital sources an advantage in reclaiming western land, particularly where land is of more marginal quality and thus less capable of providing the large and dependable returns vital to the farmer with fewer capital resources. The beginning of irrigation on the west side of the San Joaquin valley is one of the best examples of this capitalization favoritism, but there are many others. Smith notes, for instance, how large corporate organizations and groups of entrepreneurs have begun to irrigate large acreages on the benchlands of the Snake River Plains with the aid of powerful pumps and extensive sprinkler systems.[10]

Although the eastern part of the country definitely does not match the overall prominence of the West in the scale of machinery and equipment investments, it does not lack for prominent agricultural areas that rank above the national median or in the very highest class. Both North and South have these areal distinctions, but they also differ in their distributions of them. The South leads in areas with farms in the highest group for mechanization investment, those averaging over $16,600 per farm, but the North definitely leads in area with farms topping the investment median of $11,800. The North also has a majority of its territory in areas of above-median scale, whereas the South has practically the opposite ratio.

The stronger concentration of Class I farms in the South is closely related to a long period of large landholdings. The legacy of the plantation is clear in the single most prominent distribution, that of the lower Mississippi Valley, and in the smaller, more fragmented areas of the southeastern Coastal Plain. Machinery and equipment inventories in the valley are sizable because of the heavy demands of a wide variety of field crops, particularly sugarcane, cotton, corn, soybeans, and rice. On many a plantation the "tractor station" has become the focus of activity, for it also shelters harvesting, cultivating, and accessory machinery, spare parts, repair tools, and fuel.[11] In size and function, it compares favorably with similar facilities in the Pacific Southwest. The relatively recent mechanization of peanut harvesting is one of the more important reasons why southwestern Georgia has become the largest Class I areal representative of mechanization scale on the southeastern Coastal Plain, although cotton and corn add materially to machinery requirements. An inheritance of large landholdings also has facilitated a quite extensive scale of mechanization along the Texas-Louisiana Gulf Coast and on the southern tip of Florida, though there was little plantation history in many parts of these areas. Vegetables, sugarcane, and rice have become the principal machine crops.

These leading areas of machinery and equipment investment scale in the South are also deriving more and more of that leadership from irrigation, with its need for pumps and pipes and its indirect stimulus of machinery needs through its ensuring more consistent and higher acre-yields. Flood irrigation of rice in the Mississippi lowlands and on the Gulf Coast is a well-established practice and is continuing to expand, but it is sprinkler irrigation that has been most impressive in the extent and recency of diffusion. Though used only supplementally and practiced by a minority of farms, irrigation of this kind is now important enough to allow us to discern concentrations in the specialty crop areas of peninsular Florida, southern Louisiana, and the portion of the Delta lowlands shared by Arkansas and Mississippi.[12] Other important centers are in the tobacco areas of Kentucky, North Carolina-Virginia, and Georgia-Florida, but here the farms are too small to allow the effects of irrigation to have any significant impact on mechanization investment scale, at least by national standards. With persisting pressures such as the cost-price squeeze and the growth of contract farming for specialized products in specified quantities and of uniform quality, the rapid increase in sprinkler irrigation in the South seems bound to continue.

The superiority of the North over the South in overall regional representation of significant machinery and equipment investment scale can be attributed to more extensive good farmland and larger markets. But farm size is no less important a variegator of the regional pattern in the North than it is in the South. Thus the two most important areas of investment scale--the western Corn Belt with extensions into the Dairy Belt, and the middle or New York State portion of the Northeast with overlaps into Vermont and Pennsylvania--correlate fairly well with the two largest areas of above-median farm size. But even the largest farms in the North average smaller than the largest ones in the South, so the counties in the highest scale category do not dominate the above-median distribution as they do in the South. Only two sections with material county representation in Class I are outlined--east-central Illinois and the Ontario-Mohawk Plain--with smaller scatterings of similar values in such places as the Minnesota River and Hudson valleys.

There is, however, less correlation between mechanization investment scale and farm size in the North than in the South, with the largest discrepancy occurring in the Dairy Belt. Most counties around the lower Great Lakes and in Megalopolis fall in the lowest class for percentage of farms of 260 acres or more (less than 21 percent--Fig. 1.1); yet most of these counties rank above the national median in mechanization investment scale. The intensiveness of dairying, as well as that of the many fruit, vegetable, and truck enterprises in these areas, comes readily to mind when looking for an explanation of this divergence. Only in the Pacific Southwest can one find a similar situation on such an extensive areal scale, and here the distorting effects of very large farms on the mechanization investment scale averages must be remembered. A reversal of the ratio of large investment scale to farm size can also be detected in the western Corn Belt when cropland acreage rather than farm acreage is considered; many counties in this area, though well above the median in both investment scale and percentage of farms with one hundred acres or more of harvested cropland, do not maintain a level of investment scale commensurate with their cropland acreages. Rather than interpreting this variance as a diseconomy, it is better to see it as evidence of the continuing trend toward use of fewer but larger machines and the resort to more auxiliary power sources, whereas the higher ratio of mechanization investment scale to cropland acreage in other important farming areas of the Midwest might well be viewed, at least in part, as a symptom of over-mechanization.

Farm size is least useful as a clue to the regional ordering of mechanization investment when evaluating its extent on the basis of the combined ranks for scale and intensity (Figs. 2.3 and 3.3). The East now replaces the West as the focus of an agricultural industrialization that emphasizes investment in machinery, and even some of the most important eastern concentrations correspond with areas having some of the smallest farm sizes. Areas with the highest industrialization rank, i.e. those falling in Class I for both intensity (over $55 per farm acre) and scale (over $16,600 per farm) of mechanization investment, are extremely limited though widely distributed. Only three regions stand out, a part of the Illinois Grand Prairie, the Ontario-Mohawk Plain in New York State, and parts of the prairies and adjoining delta land in southern Louisiana. More island-like patterns, sometimes made up of only one or two counties, complete the eastern pattern: parts of the Minnesota River Valley; Aroostook County in Maine; the Hudson and upper Connecticut valleys; and scattered counties in New Jersey, in eastern Pennsylvania, on the Delmarva Peninsula, on the Virginia mainland shore, and on the southeastern tip of Florida. The West stands out as practically a blank; only four Hawaiian counties and two California counties (neither in the important San Joaquin Valley) show up. Here the prevalence of small fruit farms, with their small machinery inventories, suggests itself as one of the important reasons for this insignificant representation. The similarly poor showing of most of the Florida Peninsula also supports such a deduction.

Eastern superiority becomes even greater when intensity and scale thresholds are lowered to the median, $33 per farm acre and $11,800 per farm. The Middle West and Northeast also become the dominant regions, with the best showing in the smaller-farm areas of the eastern Corn Belt, the Lower Lakes region, and Megalopolis. In the South, all of the Lower Alluvial Valley now appears, as well as portions of the inner Coastal Plain in South Carolina and Georgia and a few counties along the eastern and western Gulf coasts. Thus, in contrast to the North, more of this improvement results from the large scale than the high intensity of mechanization investment. The West is also now restored to its more traditional patterns: southern California and southwestern Arizona; Central Valley; Willamette Valley; oases of the Snake River Plains. And as in the South, it is a distribution of industrialization based more on scale than intensity.

Operational Expenditures

The West again becomes the principal part of the national pattern when the scale of mechanization capitalization is computed for machine hire, customwork, and fuel expenditures (Fig. 3.4). Indeed, farm size and capitalization scale are more closely correlated here than they are for machinery and equipment investments, with the West standing out even more and the South gaining an unqualified second position, superior to the Northeast quadrant in both Class I and above-median areal coverage (over $2,000 and $1,250 per farm, respectively). On the Great Plains, the area with values well above the median (i.e., Classes I and II, or over $1,500 per farm) now extends without a break from Canada to Mexico. The relative locations of these two higher classes of operational expenditures also indicate the even greater role of farm size: on the northern Plains the Class I counties are concentrated more in the western and drier sections, where farms are larger; on the southern Plains Class I counties greatly enlarge the areal extent of the High Plains, which has larger farms and was already

125

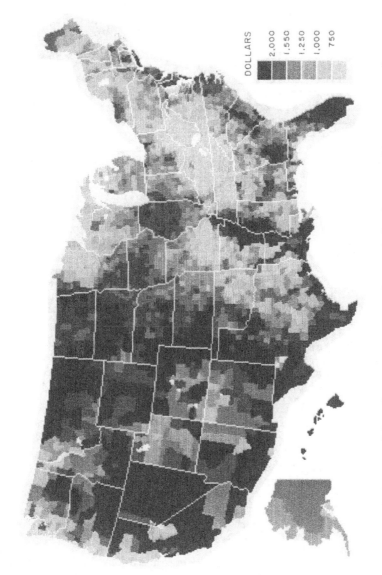

Figure 3.4. Machine hire, customwork, and fuel expenditures per farm

dominant in mechanization investment. Custom combining, the hiring of workers and machines to cut the grain, has proven particularly attractive to the larger operator, who has the greater supply of capital but who also is relatively more sensitive to labor peaks because of particularly heavy specialization on one crop. More machinery can be hired and usually the custom operator furnishes operators for the machines. With this greater investment and expenditure mobility, the larger operator also has been able to increase the production base by acquiring still more land, not infrequently distributed over several states and offering perhaps the grandest example of the type of fragmented farm that is resulting from agricultural industrialization. Even the smaller operators are beginning to find custom combining economical as machines become larger and more costly. This motivation, plus the federal wheat acreage controls instituted since the mid-1950s, has reversed an earlier trend toward addition of combines to farm inventories, when, after World War II, farmers acquired enough land and money to make such purchases feasible. More than 16,000 custom cutters and 8,000 combines and grain trucks work their way north every summer, beginning on the Texas plains in May, moving to Oklahoma and Kansas in June, Nebraska in July, the Dakotas in August, and Montana and the Canadian Prairie Provinces in September. Crews work fourteen hours a day between rainstorms.[13] Average size of these harvesting units is difficult to determine, although Mather, in his description of "megalophilia" on the Great Plains, mentions the "agricultural service man, with ten custom combines in his fleet and the necessary complement of trucks,...with about a third of a million dollars of capital investment."[14]

Custom combining on the Great Plains originated on a large scale in the Winter Wheat Belt, and it is there that the greatest number of custom operators still locate. They have nonetheless continued to extend their operations to other parts of the Plains, particularly to the north, and the increasing substitution of winter wheat for spring wheat in that direction is closely related; greater familiarity with the winter type of grain and the larger yields that especially increase the profitability of large-scale machine harvesting are two of the more salient reasons for the similarity between these two poleward movements. Over a third of the Great Plains wheat crop is combined by migratory crews, and the proportion is twice as great in much of the Winter Wheat Belt.

Fuel expenditures on a per-farm basis pretty much duplicate the scale of mechanization investment on the Plains. Although machinery operations make the biggest demands on fuel supplies, center pivot irrigation is becoming an increasingly important customer; by 1978

almost a quarter of all irrigated land on the Great
Plains was watered by this system. Although center-pivot
irrigation is not a monopoly of the larger farms, the
current fuel shortage in the country often poses an even
more critical problem for the larger farm users, especially where greater depths must be pumped and thus more
energy must be consumed, as in many sections of the
western Plains.

The showing of the rest of the West in scale of
operational expenditures is also noticeably improved over
its already respectable representation in scale of
mechanization investments. Machine hire and customwork
are resorted to by both irrigation and grain farmers, and
by both large and small operators. Although the larger
operators heavily influence farm averages by controlling
much of the cropland, in many sections the smaller ones
also depend a great deal on larger growers and specialized machinery operators for spraying and harvesting
their crops. Expenditures for fueling machinery are also
heavy. Where frost is a threat to subtropical crops, as
in California, Arizona, and the Rio Grande Valley, much
oil is used for heaters, although wind machines
("blowers") are taking their place because they require
much less labor, do not pollute the air, and--increasing-
ly pertinent in the present energy crisis--use
hydroelectric power instead of fossil fuel.

The improved national position of the South in areas
of high operational expenditures is due to an increase in
the scale of capitalization in areas beyond the lower
Mississippi Valley and the western Gulf Coast. Those two
areas maintain their Class I rankings, whereas central
Florida now joins the southern tip to make another significant segment of this top-class pattern. Here we can
explain the improvement in much the same way that we did
in accounting for the improved showing of the specialty
crop areas of the Pacific Southwest. There is also some
slight strengthening of the Class I distribution on the
Inner Coastal Plain of South Carolina and Georgia,
although the increase in coverage by the combined classes
I and II is much more obvious in both this area and the
Black Belt of Alabama and Mississippi. A large part of
the Texas Blackland Prairie is also now above the median.
The heavy fuel expenditures on farms raising cotton and
other cash field crops undoubtedly exaggerate the ranking
of many counties on the southeast Coastal Plain, but not
enough to make those counties the principal centers of
the above-median areas.

Of the three broad regional divisions of the
country, West, South and North, only the North has a less
important areal representation in scale of expenditures
for machinery operation than it does in the scale of
mechanization investment. Only a minority of its territory now ranks above the median, and of the area that

does, a very small fraction is in the top scale class.
By far the largest above-median representation is in the
western Corn Belt. With Class II counties congregating
in northern Iowa, southern Minnesota, and Illinois, and
with practically all of the few Class I counties also in
Illinois, it is apparent that the farms with a greater
emphasis on cash corn place the greatest demands on
machine hire, customwork, and fuel expenditures.

Next largest in size is a more or less continuous
band of counties in Megalopolis; despite its much smaller
area, it rivals the western Corn Belt in number of counties in the Class I group. Here the pressures and
attractions of mechanization of specialty-crop operations, the immense profitability of the markets, and the
constraints of small farm size join to encourage a dependence by operators on others for machine work. Completing the above-median pattern is a sprinkling of
counties, most of which, as in western New York State and
northern Maine, still do not equal their national importance in mechanization investment scale. The small
grouping of Class I counties in the vicinity of
Cleveland, especially when compared with its below-median
ranking in mechanization investment scale, reflects
particularly well the large expenditures for fuel in
greenhouse agriculture, expenditures that are also important in several Megalopolitan counties but are not as
large relative to costs for fueling machinery as they are
in the Cleveland area. Why the Cleveland area stands out
so markedly has never been satisfactorily explained.[15]

Higher-Order Mechanization Patterns

With the distribution of the scale of capitalization
of mechanization expenditures now in hand, it is possible
to make further generalizations about pertinent distributions of a higher order. Three of these distributions
can be distinguished on the basis of a two-way comparison, the kind made almost exclusively up to now; two
can be described with a four-way comparison.

The first distribution, that of the combined
intensity and scale of operational expenditures associated with mechanization, reveals a definite southern
orientation (Figs. 2.4 and 3.4). This locational bias is
particularly evident among areas with Class I ratings in
both intensity and scale (more than $6 per acre and more
than $2,000 per farm); it is also a configuration that
sharply contrasts with the one outlining the overlappings
of intensity and scale patterns for mechanization investments, where, as we have seen, the distribution heavily
favors the northeast quarter and is much sparser. The
Pacific Southwest and the lower Mississippi Valley are
the largest parts of this southern pattern, followed by
the concentrations in central and southern Florida, the

South Texas High Plains, and the more restricted cases of the San Luis and lower Rio Grande valleys. The northern section of the country is not without important counties, though, with most in Illinois and Megalopolis. Some counties on the Snake River Plains also add to the more northerly pattern.

Including in our comparison all areas with above-median ranking (over $3.50 per acre and over $1,250 per farm) adds three significant regions to the overall distribution, though it does not seriously lessen the southern edge: western Corn Belt, South Texas High Plains, and South Atlantic Coastal Plain.

Total mechanization scale, as delineated by Class I minimums in investments and expenditures (over $16,600 and over $2,000 per farm, respectively), duplicates the broad regional ranking for expenditures, with a few intraregional modifications. The West is the leader, but now the High Plains definitely dominates the Plains, with the smaller representations on the northern Plains confined to the drier portions (Montana and central South Dakota). West and south of the Rockies, the wheat area of interior Washington and Oregon again is prominent, but the conspicuousness of the irrigated sections is reduced somewhat in much of the San Joaquin Valley and considerably so in many of the counties of the Colorado Plateau and in the Rio Grande Valley south of El Paso. For the South, the overall-scale distribution of Class I investment areas is essentially the same as that for expenditures, with the lower Mississippi Valley forming the premier center. Also extremely high in both scale categories are several counties strung out along the western Gulf Coast. Distribution is halved, however, on the Florida Peninsula, as the central part of the state has mostly submedian investments. The fragmented strip of very high overall scale on the Inner Coastal Plain of Georgia and South Carolina offers a sharp contrast to the showing of southern Appalachia, the largest single area in the United States ranking in the lowest class of total mechanization scale, with no more than $7,500 of investments and $750 of expenditures per farm. Scatterings of counties with rankings in the top class characterize the pattern in the northeast quarter, and these are principally in northern and central Illinois and in Megalopolis.

Lowering the two combined mechanization scale minimums to include all values above the median (more than $11,800 investment and $1,250 expenditures per farm) produces no areal overlaps large enough to change the broad regional ranking, but it does give more prominence to the northern part of the country; the northern Plains now joins with the western Corn Belt to form the largest representation anywhere. Sections of the eastern Corn Belt, more counties on the mid-Atlantic Seabord, practically all of the Ontario-Mohawk Plain, much of the

Willamette Valley, and even the Matanuska Valley in Alaska further strengthen the northern display. In the southern band of the nation, almost all the major agricultural counties of California are now represented, the counties on the western Gulf Coast are combined into a single strip joining with the Delta, and the majority of the counties in the Black Belt and the Georgia-Carolina Inner Coastal Plain become almost a continuous strip as well.

The next two of our pattern comparisons involving the scale of mechanization expenditures disclose the distribution of still further aspects of labor capitalization. The first and simplest of the two is the distribution of the scale of mechanization expenditures compared with the distribution of the scale of labor expenditures (Figs. 3.4 and 3.2, respectively), providing a fuller view of the scale of labor capitalization. I have already noted the labor dimension of mechanization expenditures that is represented by the workers who operate the hired machines and perform the contracted customwork, and how these cash outlays consequently inform us almost as much about mechanized labor as labor expenditures do about hand labor. Counties with farm expenditures for both kinds of labor at the Class I level definitely concentrate in the West: the oases and particularly the Pacific Southwest; the High Plains; and the more intensive ranching areas where irrigated feed crops support livestock operations. Irrigation, and often large farm size as well, are obviously the principal catalysts in the creation of this heavy labor demand. Most of the lower Mississippi Valley and the peninsula of Florida are the major areas in the East.

Another group of regions can be added to the area of superior scale of labor capitalization if minimums are relaxed to include Classes II and III. The northern Plains is the most prominent and advanced member of this new collection, followed in area but not necessarily in scale level by the extreme western end of the Corn Belt, western Gulf Coast, Megalopolis, and smaller areas in such places as the Alabama Black Belt, sections of the South Atlantic Coastal Plain, the Ontario-Mohawk Plain, and northern Maine. A comparison of the rankings of these regions also shows that except in the Megalopolitan area, the scale of mechanized labor rather than hand labor is most important. The part of the Corn Belt west of Illinois is the least advanced of this regional group in the scale of combined expenditures for hand and mechanized labor, although this area of intensive cattle and hog feeding nonetheless keeps the Middle West from being almost a complete blank on the map.

The second of the pattern comparisons bearing on labor capitalization gives us an even more comprehensive view from an industrialization standpoint. It is a view that can be obtained by comparing the congruent parts of four distributions, two of the scale of expenditures for hand and mechanized labor and two of the intensity of expenditures for the two labor types (Figs. 3.2 and 3.4 and Figs. 2.2 and 2.4, respectively). Here, admittedly, we are approaching the limits to which visual comparisons can be carried, and any spatial analysis that goes beyond broad regional delineations is better served by the application of statistical techniques. At the Class I level, the most extensive regional representation in all four labor categories is provided by the Pacific Southwest, particularly the Central Valley, the oases of southeastern California and southwestern Arizona, and the islands of Oahu and Kauai in Hawaii. Smaller areas, but with equally high class ranks in all labor categories, are centers in central and southern Florida and the Mississippi Delta. Still smaller overlaps in high labor input values can be noted in several counties scattered along the North Atlantic Seaboard, the shores of Lakes Erie and Ontario, and the middle and lower courses of the Snake River in Idaho.

When representation thresholds include areas with Class II and III rankings, the lower Mississippi Valley, with its lesser intensity of hand labor expenditures, and much more of Megalopolis, with its generally lower scale of mechanized labor expenditures, join the comprehensive labor capitalization pattern. Much of the Willamette Valley and most of the Ontario-Mohawk Plain, both areas with a smaller scale of mechanized labor expenditures, also come in. In the Middle West, only the extreme western end of the Corn Belt is added to the distribution, so minimal is the scale of manual labor expenditures in most of the belt. Much of the Dairy Belt also remains unrepresented because of the smaller scale of mechanized labor expenditures; the same situation applies to the lower Willamette Valley and most of the Puget Sound area. On the southern Texas High Plains, however, it is the lower intensity of these outlays for mechanized labor that prevents representation. On the other hand, expenditures for mechanized labor in the metropolitan counties of coastal northern and southern California, though not of Class I stature, are still of sufficient intensity and scale to add the areas to the national distribution of above-median labor capitalization.

As with labor capitalization, using a four-way comparison also enables us to perceive in coarse outline the distribution of a more inclusive type of capitalization in mechanization, this time by combining the scale of investments and expenditures with the intensity of those outlays (Figs. 3.3 and 3.4 and 2.3 and 2.4, respectively). At the Class I level, few areas display a highly advanced stage of mechanization in all four categories, despite the popular assumption of a one-to-one relationship of mechanization to agricultural industrialization. Also, what counties do show up indicate that it is not, as is often believed, western areas like California or the Great Plains that display the most extensive mechanization, but areas in the East that do. Only two counties in the Sacramento Valley and two in Hawaii prevent the West from being completely excluded from representation. In the East, counties are numerous enough to allow us to recognize four areas: the prairies and Mississippi Delta of southern Louisiana, forming the largest single concentration in the country; a sprinkling of counties in Megalopolis; several counties in central Illinois; and the Gold Coast counties of extreme southeastern Florida.

Widening the areal perspective to include all counties ranking above the median expends the distribution considerably, although there are noticeable contrasts between the regions represented in their levels of capitalization in mechanization. The Corn Belt, especially from Illinois westward, is now the largest areal representative, yet it is the lower Mississippi Valley that is most impressive in ranking, falling below the Class I minimum only in the intensity of machinery and equipment investments. Western New York State and Aroostook County in Maine, though smaller areas, also show up well in overall ranking, dropping below the top class level only in the scale of machinery and equipment investments. In contrast, California, which is now also represented in all four categories of mechanization capitalization, achieves only a Class III rating in the intensity of mechanization and equipment investments in many of its most important agricultural counties. Most surprising, perhaps, is that even with the relaxation of minimums for capitalization in mechanization to include all above-median counties, the region long held to be the land of agricultural mechanization par excellence, the Great Plains, fails to attain any significant representation. Counties along the middle Platte in Nebraska and on the southern Texas High Plains are the only areas that stand out.

SCALE OF CAPITALIZATION IN CROPPING

Crop Investments

Extensive capitalization scale is more widely distributed for crop investments than for any other of the agricultural industrialization inputs considered so far (Fig. 3.5). But the pattern is also well dispersed, reflecting the highly variegated productive capabilities of the land and the pronounced selectivity of the agricultural industrialization process. The western half of the country still is the most prominent, though its

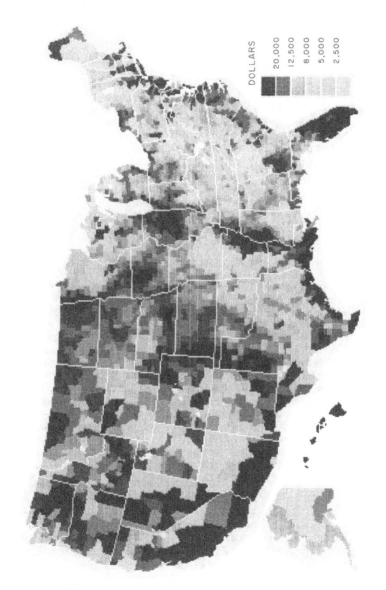

Figure 3.5. Crop investments per farm

leadership is now much more dependent on the inclusion of all counties with above-median investment scale (more than $8,000 per farm); for Class I counties (those with crop investments of more than $20,000 per farm) western regional primacy is thinner, especially when the areal exaggeration of the data by the many large counties is taken into account. This reduced eminence of the West is obviously closely tied to the more extensive, rather than intensive, nature of operations on its many large farms. Yet many farms are also objects of heavy crop investment, and farms that are smaller but nevertheless heavily capitalized are likewise numerous in many areas. The result is a widely varying ratio of crop investment capitalization to farm size from place to place, one whose range surpasses that of any in the East on a similar areal scale.

Farms that rank high, i.e., in Class I, for both crop investments and size have their greatest representation on the High Plains (cf. Fig. 3.5 and Figs. 1.1 and 1.2). A good part of the Red River Valley is noticeable farther north, as is the eastern part of the Columbia Basin in Washington. Still smaller and more widely scattered examples can be noted in such places as the Humboldt Valley in Nevada and the San Luis Valley in Colorado. A greater diversity of crops and often a large amount of irrigation are the two most obvious explanations for these distributions. For farms in any of the three above-median classifications in both crop investments and acreage, almost all of the northern Plains and the subhumid eastern part of the southern Plains become the principal domiciles; the ratio of large investment scale to farm size, however, now becomes a negative one. There is also a respectable sprinkling of counties in the basins and on the plateaus of Oregon, Idaho, Colorado, Utah, and Nevada with the same kind of ratio; some of this relationship may be a statistical artifact because of the aggregation of the data for counties having a number of both larger and more extensively operated farms and smaller and more intensively irrigated units. Farms with crop investments that surpass their acreage rankings definitely outline the intensively irrigated crop-specialty areas of the Pacific Southwest, with extensions northward to the Willamette Valley and eastward to the middle and lower Rio Grande Valley. Nowhere else in the West is the divergence between scale of crop investment and farm size as great as it is here, particularly in California and Hawaii. An important part of this wide differential can also be traced to the more massive and often equally intensive operations of the very large farms, although their contributions are obscured by the averaging of the many more smaller farms into the crop investment totals for the counties.

Eastern farms with Class I rankings in both crop investments and size are not numerous enough to show up in the county distributions, although they are significant in a few counties along the western Gulf Coast and the southern tip of Florida. The picture changes completely when all farms simply ranking above the median in both crop investments and acreage are viewed, with all of the better agricultural areas except the Dairy Belt now standing out. As in the West, there are still few places in this broader distribution where farms have equally high levels of crop investments and acreage. But unlike the West, there are also very few places in this pattern where crop investment scale is exceeded by farm size. Areas prominently outlined in this distribution are the Corn Belt--especially east-central Illinois and western Iowa, most of the Texas-Louisiana Gulf Coast Prairies and the lower Mississippi Valley, and large parts of the Coastal Plain in South Carolina and Georgia. Another set of areas can be detected where farms with above-median crop investment scale are paired with those of submedian acreage. Peninsular Florida is the largest of the representative areas, but counties scattered through Megalopolis and along the shores of the lower Great Lakes are also easily identifiable. Intensive farming of truck and specialty crops characterize these areas, thus providing an eastern parallel to the Pacific Southwest, where a high ratio of crop investment scale to farm size also obtains. Indeed, the ratio in most of the eastern distribution is even greater, for large farms control much less of the total acreage and thus do not skew the averages to the extent they do in the West. Many small farms close to or on the edges of the populous urban centers of the Midwest and Northeast find it profitable to invest heavily in cropping; how attractive these locations are is clearly evident in the island-like patterns of Class I counties pinpointing all major metropolitan areas and several smaller cities as well.

In spite of its varying influence on the scale of crop investment, farm size continues to increase almost everywhere, and crop investment increases with it. At least a coarse correlation between scale and acreage can be noted for most of the major agricultural areas, and even in parts of Megalopolis and the Pacific Southwest, where scale outranks size to the maximum, some similarities between the patterns of crop investment scale and average farm cropland acreage are visible (Figs. 3.5 and 1.2). The ability of operators on larger farms to invest more in crops than those on smaller units is obvious; what is often overlooked is the growing ability of the larger operators to produce both higher acre-yields and a greater variety of money crops. To assume that it is easier for smaller farmers to increase their acre-yields overlooks the fact that intensification is turning increasingly to the use of capital rather than labor, and capital can usually be amassed easier on larger farms. Machinery, the most important part of this working capital, ensures a larger crop area and reduced labor costs, and thus increases revenue that can be used to buy more fertilizers, better seeds, and other tools for increasing acre-yields. Furthermore, this advantage in acre-yields continues to increase because of the mutually reinforcing effects of increased yields and mechanization. Increasing yields encourage mechanization because machine costs stay the same, whereas hand labor costs customarily increase with yield. In turn, mechanization encourages greater yields because writeoff costs can be paid so much more quickly. Machinery costs are usually long-term costs because they can be used only at certain times.[16]

More machinery and equipment also have allowed many larger operators to produce a greater number of cash crops. Although it is one of the most potent forces favoring single-crop cultivation, mechanization also makes available more area and cultivation time, not all of which necessarily has to be given to one and the same crop. Given enough machinery and acreage, then, it becomes possible for the large farm to diversify and intensify production to a sizable degree. The typical large-scale farm in the Imperial Valley raises and sells cotton, sugar beets, alfalfa, flax, barley, and a wide variety of vegetables. Southern plantations now concentrate on groups of specialties, with one 38,000-acre operation drawing income from sales of cotton, corn, rice, soybeans, spinach, wheat, cattle, and pulpwood.[17] Heavier emphasis by the larger farms on the money crops, in production intensification and often in variety, has now become a nationwide phenomenon. The resulting divergences in land use between larger and smaller operations had already become important enough by 1968 to prompt Heady to observe that land use changes among individual farms had been greater than those for the nation.[18] Among crop farms with enough cash to support at least five resident workers with families, specializations are different enough from those of crop farms in general to make for a national pattern quite unlike that usually perceived. Thus, what is usually outlined as the Corn Belt is better designated a "horticultural belt," as far as large crop farms are concerned. Emphasis on production of horticultural specialties for the large urban markets of the Northeast extends this belt to the Atlantic Seaboard. In the Dairy Belt, larger crop farms of this kind capitalize on particularly favorable environmental and market situations to form what could be called a "fruit-and-potato belt." Even in the Spring and Winter Wheat belts, where large farms are widespread, the average farm fails to convey the true specialty-crop character of many of the largest and most productive farms. Potato farms are the most numerous of the heavily capitalized farms in North Dakota, horticultural farms dominate South Dakota, and cotton farms are the most common of the large units in Oklahoma.[19]

This marked concentration by the larger farms on specialty crops, especially vegetables, is not surprising. They offer more attractive profit margins than field crops but at the same time require more capital because of the higher risks involved and the greater expense of harvesting and marketing. Larger operators also use to advantage their large machinery inventories by cultivating fewer types of vegetables and stressing those that are easiest to cultivate and harvest mechanically. Vegetable production also lends itself to vertical integration and is possibly the most effective way for large-scale operators to make their operations pay. Middleman costs are eliminated and additional sources of profit are opened up. An excellent illustration is that of many large-scale sprinkler-irrigated potato farms in Idaho. The operators control upstream links by sharing heavily in the profits of machinery, pipe, fuel, and seed companies, and, often, of financial institutions. They control downstream items by having their own storage cellars and warehouses for shipment to market, and sometimes even process the product as well.[20]

Large farm size understandably plays much less of a role in crop investment when both scale and intensity distribution patterns are taken into account (Figs. 3.5 and 2.5, respectively). The largest area with significant investment at both farm and per-acre levels is in the East, where crop investment customarily outranks farm size on a national basis. For the Class I grade ($60 per farm acre and $20,000 per farm), the East-West disparity is especially sharp. The only extensive representation of major crop investment in the West is the Pacific Southwest, and there farm size for most counties averages among the lowest in the nation. Only the Imperial, Salt River, and Sacramento valleys have farm acreages that average above the median and come close to the Class I rankings of those areas for both scale and intensity of crop investment. Four conspicuous regions of overall heavy crop investment are in the East: the prairie cores of the Corn Belt in Iowa and Illinois; most of the lower Mississippi Valley; the middle band and southern tip of Florida; and several large clusters of counties roughly outlining Megalopolis. Less agglomerated but also marked in their delimitation of areas with heavy crop investments at both farm and per-acre levels are counties along the shores of the Lower Great Lakes and around many more inland metropolitan centers such as Minneapolis-St. Paul, St. Louis, Pittsburgh, and Cincinnati. In these areas and in Megalopolis, farm size is the least reliable indicator of the massiveness of farm investment. The lower Mississippi Valley north of the Delta most closely approaches its high investment classification with its extensive farm acreages.

The poor showing of the West is definitely improved when distributions are expanded to include all areas represented in any of the three leading classes (I, II, III) for both scale and intensity categories. The principal region of large farms, the Great Plains, now appears with farms in several major areas that closely approach that size distinction in overall crop investment: the Red River Valley, the middle Platte Valley, the subhumid Winter Wheat Belt, and especially the High Plains, with the South Texas High Plains as the leading center. The Pacific Northwest and the more important oases of the southern Intermountain region also now come into view, although their ratio of farm size to crop investment is the reverse of that of the Plains areas. Except for some additions to the margins of the Sacramento Valley and the inclusions of the Gila Basin and the island of Hawaii, little change affects the already prominent rating of the Pacific Southwest. Eastern representations of above-median scale and intensity of crop investment also are much more extensive than those based on scale alone. However, the additions, unlike many of those in the West, reinforce rather than contradict the dominant national pattern of a high ratio of overall crop investment to farm size, which is so evident for just crop investment. Most of this distributional expansion is accounted for by the rest of the Corn Belt; some larger fragments of the Dairy Belt, including now an almost continuous coastal strip along both the lower Great Lakes and the mid-Atlantic Seaboard; and the majority of the Southeast Coastal Plain, extending from Virginia to southern Alabama. The Louisiana-Texas Gulf Coast prairies add to this enlarged pattern and link up with the lower Mississippi alluvial lands, a region with which it also shares the distinction of having farm sizes nearly matching the high national ranking of its crop investments.

Cropping Expenditures and Higher-Order Cropping Patterns

Cropping expenditures, the other dimension of the scale of capitalization in cropping, also display a widely dispersed spatial pattern, although the West now cedes leadership to the East (Fig. 3.6). For the West, the change is most obvious in the widespread disappearance of above-median counties (those with crop expenditures over $1,500 per farm) from the Great Plains and Intermountain area. The largest farms in the nation, in both total and cropland acreage, are concentrated in these two regions. Here the scale of capitalization in

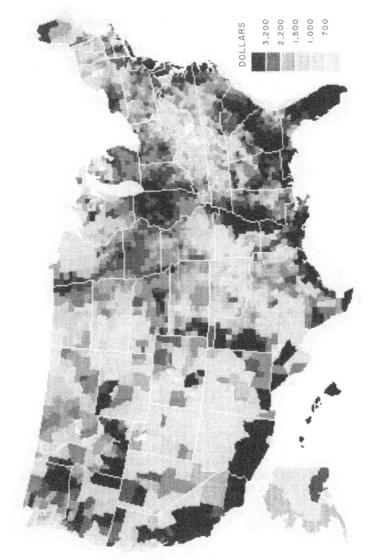

Figure 3.6. Crop expenditures per farm

cropping comes closest to being a direct function of area, because land is the cheapest of the production factors. Only where land costs increase relative to the rest of the factor mix do cropping expenditures become nationally significant, and in the West these are places where more humid conditions or irrigation water are found. They are also customarily the places where farms are smaller, as is evident by the close correlation of very large cropping expenditure scale with extremely small farm size in most of the principal agricultural counties west of the Rockies. On the Great Plains, this relationship is less intimate, and despite the poor representation of much of the region in scale of cropping expenditures, it is also there that one finds the kind of large farm that is at least large enough to achieve Class I status in not only acreage and cropping expenditures (over $3,000 per farm), but in crop investments as well. This regional exception is essentially the High Plains, though some counties in the part of the Red River Valley nearest the Canadian border and in the Palouse area of eastern Washington also may be included. If the majority of the farms in the major agricultural areas elsewhere in the West were as large, they too could be classified as large in all three scale categories.

For eastern farms, the improvement of the distribution of cropping expenditures over that of crop investments can be accepted as commonplace, although some noticeable differences between the Middle West, the Megalopolitan strip, and the South are observable in the relative shares of the three above-median class patterns (I, II, and III). All important cropping areas of the Middle West now rise above the national median, but with most of the distributional expansion being accounted for with the accession of counties to classes II and III rather than I. These additions are mostly those of the Dairy Belt and the eastern Corn Belt; the western Corn Belt maintains its above-median status, but with Class I counties now concentrated almost exclusively in east-central and northern Illinois and a bordering fringe in Indiana. Larger farms and greater emphasis on cash grain production thus make this latter area the most important part of the American agricultural heartland in the scale of both crop investments and cropping expenditures. Much the same type of pattern improvement occurs in Megalopolis, with some contraction of the Class I areas in the expenditure distribution but with a somewhat greater expansion of the overall area ranking above the median.

Easily the most impressive areal gain of the cropping expenditure pattern over the crop investment distribution is recorded by the South. Peninsular Florida, the lower Mississippi Valley, and the Louisiana-Texas Gulf Coast prairies are now joined by a vast Coastal Plain section and important adjoining segments of the Piedmont. Additionally, an extremely large proportion of this addition is expansion of the Class I distribution. With the three other regions, this new block of territory makes the South probably the most extensive regional representative of large cropping expenditure scale. In the Lower Alluvial Valley of the Mississippi, farm values for crop investments, cropping expenditures, and farmland acreage come closest of any place in the East to the good showing of the large crop farms of the High Plains.

The extensive representation of Class I counties in the South combines with similarly impressive distributions on the High Plains and in the Pacific Southwest to give a southern cast to the overall pattern of cropping expenditure scale. A longer and warmer growing season, with its heavy crop production and resulting major demands for fertilizers and crop-protection agents, quickly comes to mind as an important locational determinant. Heavy emphasis on specialized crops and the inherently poor conditions of many southern soils also contribute to this southerly orientation. The influence of large-scale farming also cannot be overlooked, particularly in the South. Large farm units prevail along the western Gulf Coast, in the Mississippi Valley between Illinois and southern Louisiana, and on sizable parts of the Southeast Coastal Plain in Georgia and South Carolina (Figs. 1.1 and 1.2), and it is in these areas where the expenditure scale patterns make the South stand out more prominently than the North, just the reverse of the regional relationship for expenditure intensity (Fig. 2.6). Large farms use more fertilizers and chemicals than smaller units not only because of their greater needs, but also because they can obtain those inputs more cheaply by securing volume discounts through purchasing agent techniques. They negotiate directly with the manufacturers, jobbers, or distributors of these and many other items. Bids by suppliers in these kinds of transactions can often substantially reduce or eliminate distributor and dealer costs.

A sharper division between East and West vies with the southerly emphasis in the national distribution of overall cropping expenditures, i.e., inputs in terms of combined intensity and scale. The very low intensity of cropping expenditures in much of the West eliminates the vast majority of counties between the Pacific mountain system and the Middle West and South from significant ranking. Even the clusters of counties that maintain their above-median classifications in both categories of cropping expenditures (more than $4.70 per farm acre and $1,500 per farm) are diminished in their national, if not regional, standings. The oases of the Snake River Plains and the South Texas High Plains have only a few counties in Class I for both kinds of cropping expenditures (over $10.50 per farm acre and $3,200 per farm), and the Palouse country of eastern Washington and the middle Platte and Red River valleys have no representative units. In the East, the South is again the most important region, with Class I patterns outlining much of the coastal plain, extending from South Carolina to extreme southern Alabama and the Florida Panhandle, and the lower Mississippi Valley. Central and southern Florida and the lower Rio Grande Valley are also delineated. Again, too, the Middle West and Megalopolis come next in significant areal representation, with the most impressive clustering of Class I counties taking place in east-central and northern Illinois. In the Far West, the areal distribution pattern also remains essentially the same as that of the scale of cropping expenditures, with the Pacific Southwest dominating, followed by a good part of the Willamette Valley.

This double areal orientation, east-west and north-south, also generally repeats itself when all four distribution patterns associated with cropping activity are considered: investment intensity and scale, and expenditure intensity and scale. Only the Southeast Coastal Plain suffers a significant reduction in importance at the Class I level, with only southwestern Georgia standing out in the scale of crop investment. At simply the level above the median, similar deficiencies in investment scale exclude notable segments of the eastern Corn Belt and the Dairy Belt.

SCALE OF CAPITALIZATION IN LIVESTOCK AND POULTRY RAISING

Livestock and Poultry Investments

If large-scale capitalization is more extensively distributed for crop investments than for any other of the agricultural industrialization inputs, then it is also most regionally pronounced in the distribution of animal investments. Here the West stands out more than it does for any of the other scale variables (Fig. 3.7). About a third of the nation is involved, and the overwhelming portion has a capitalization level that surpasses the Class I threshold, $19,500 of investment per farm. Only the grazing of large herds and flocks on extensive acreages can ensure a profit in a region handicapped by drought, poor soil conditions, and rugged terrain in so much of its territory.

It would be a mistake, however, to infer from this kind of economic adjustment to the environment that the livestock enterprise is carried on only at the minimum permissible level of agricultural technology. This traditional view of the livestock ranch is rapidly being outmoded by extensive modifications of orientations and

143

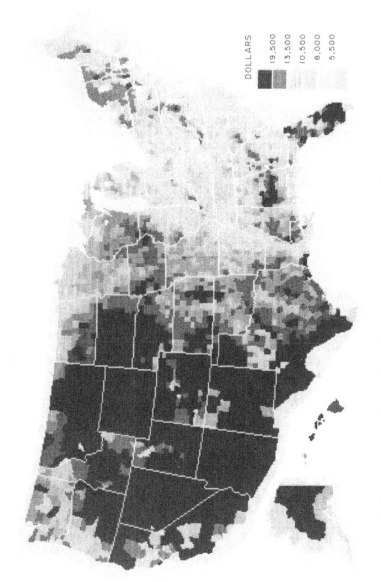

Figure 3.7. Livestock and poultry investments per farm

operations. Ranchers have been steadily increasing their irrigated lands for both pasture and feed crops, and in some areas the volume of feed production and the inventory of feed-handling equipment have become so great that it is no longer possible to differentiate clearly between livestock and cropping enterprises. Ranchers also have been attuning their operations more and more to the demands of the highly capitalized and accelerated functions of feedlot fattening, either contractually or by developing or expanding their own feedlot facilities. Even the traditional modes of moving livestock from pasture to pasture have been changed in many areas. Trailing of cattle has been losing ground to trucking, especially where roads are good. Movement is rapid with this method of transportation, and the possibility of animals being struck by vehicles is virtually eliminated. Weight loss is also considerably reduced, and the need for providing rest and feed on the trail is also eliminated. In mountainous terrain, trucked cattle are generally unloaded at the lowest elevations of the range and guided to higher altitudes, although even at these levels varying pasture conditions or property barriers can make truck transportation intermittently useful. Increasing concerns over the worsening fuel situation, however, are causing a growing number of operators to reconsider the feasibility of trailing. Sheepherding has also become increasingly receptive to the truck as labor costs associated with seasonal migrations continue to grow faster than total operating costs and problems of trespass become more serious with multiplying land purchases. But trucking has not been able to relieve sheepmen of a serious profits squeeze that has been operating since the late 1950s, so there has been a growing shift from seasonal migrations to untended, fenced grazing. This kind of operation has become so successful that some believe fenced grazing may replace transhumance even in the arid Great Basin.[21]

The incentive to intensify and to rationalize livestock raising operations has naturally been greatest in areas where physical and marketing conditions are the best, and even in the West the consequent variations are great enough to make for broad intraregional differences. Livestock investment scale reaches its peak on many of the ranches in the drier Intermountain area, but it is on the Great Plains and the Pacific margins that it becomes most prominent in number of farms and, in some places, in dominance of operating units as well. Both of these areas have more moisture, either in the form of precipitation or irrigation or both, and both have greater access to markets. Of these two more favored areas, the Great Plains is the most impressive, and particularly so for the northern Plains, where the distribution of farm size in the Class I category is practically as extensive as the Class I pattern for livestock investment per farm (cf. Figs. 1.1 and 3.7). Much of the High Plains also fits into this superior group of livestock investment scale. A small but important outlier lies to the east in the form of the Flint Hills of eastern Kansas and the connecting Osage Hills of northeastern Oklahoma, although farm size does not quite match the scale of livestock investment.

Extensive grasslands and a growing bounty of fodder crops provide firm support for the extensive herds and flocks of the Plains. North of the Platte River both short and mid-grasses abound, tall grasses cover much of the landscape in the Nebraska Sand Hills and the Flint-Osage Hills of Kansas and Oklahoma, and short grasses predominate farther south. The variety of feed crops raised, both through rainfed and irrigation cropping, is also impressive. Corn, corn silage, and legume hay are the leading feeds on the northern Plains. On the High Plains, grain sorghum, barley, wheat, corn and sorghum silage, cottonseed hulls, and alfalfa hay are the primary feeds. Where irrigation is especially important, the volume and varieties of crops increase further. Thus, on the Colorado Piedmont and in the South Platte Valley in northeastern Colorado, major feeds are corn, grain sorghum, barley, corn silage, legume hay and silage, and beet pulp, as well as some sorghum silage and vegetable residues. But the rapid expansion of irrigation should not obscure the rapid spread of still another method of extending and stabilizing the livestock industry over much of the Plains: the construction of small stock dams. Well over 300,000 of them have been built in the region in the last thirty years.

Good cropping conditions do not promote large-scale livestock investments everywhere on the Plains. On the eastern margins, more moisture, smaller farms, and better market accessibility encourage farming that is more intensive than extensive and oriented more toward crops than livestock. On the southern margins, good irrigation supplies and a longer growing season help to do the same thing. In certain areas the falloff in livestock investment scale is especially sharp, as along the edges of the Spring Wheat Belt in North Dakota, the Palouse wheat area of eastern Washington and northern Idaho, and the cotton-sorghum-vegetable center of the South Texas High Plains just south of Lubbock. In all these areas scale values drop to the lowest of the six value classes, i.e., less than $5,500 of livestock investment per farm. Parts of the subhumid Winter Wheat Belt in Kansas and Oklahoma also clearly show up as submedian areas, and even in the lower Platte Valley, which can be considered an integral part of the Corn Belt with its corn-cattle-hog economy, several counties have similarly low ranks; this undoubtedly is attributable largely to the diluting effect of smaller farms. Beef cows, however, are also being raised in increasing numbers in these more favored cropping areas--in some of those places to such an extent that livestock investment is still maintained at scales above the national median. This is especially obvious where the Class I values of the ranching "peninsula" in South Dakota and Nebraska grade into the lesser but still respectable scale values of the Corn Belt to the east. Increasing herd size is also proving extensive enough to preserve sizable livestock investment scale in several spots on the High Plains in the face of intensive cash cropping.

The ability to achieve large-scale livestock investment in areas of intensive cash cropping and small farms is even better demonstrated in the lowlands of the Pacific Southwest and western Washington and Oregon. No match for the Great Plains in the number of high-value counties, these two regions nevertheless exhibit a sharp contrast between levels of livestock investment scale and farm size. Practically all major agricultural counties in Arizona, California, and Hawaii rank below the U.S. median in farm size; farms in California and Hawaii rank in the bottom class (less than a fifth of all farms are 260 acres or larger); yet almost as many of these counties post above-median values in the scale of livestock investment. Probably nowhere else in the country is the force of the market for livestock products displayed on so extensive an areal scale as here, for despite the tremendous competition of a host of highly profitable specialty crops, livestock production for the rapidly growing populations in this region continues to gain on other sectors of the agricultural economy in many sections. Not all operators who emphasize cropping exclude every activity related to livestock raising. They sell feed crops, field stubble, byproducts like sugar beet tops and cottonseed cake, and even animals, to operators of primarily livestock systems. Increasing specialization, nonetheless, is forcing an ever sharper spatial separation of livestock raising and cropping activities, and as land costs continue their rise the pressures for such a separation grow even more. For animal farming, this has meant a concentration of the growing herd and flock sizes on as small a farm as possible. Feedlot fattening, drylot dairying, and mass-poultry farming are all important ways the agriculturist in this region has modified traditional livestock enterprises to capitalize on markets and still compete for land.

Although the West is the undisputed leader in scale of livestock investment, the East is not without important representation. Above-median investment scale is especially well distributed in the South, where several prominent areas match those on the Plains having Class I

status in both investment scale and farm size. One such
area is in Texas, where parallel prongs of slightly less
investment scale extend northeastward from the Rio Grande
Valley through the Edwards Plateau and Cross Timbers, the
Post Oak Strip, and the Coastal Prairies. Within this
region, the immense size of the livestock ranches in the
more western parts, commonly averaging in the tens and
sometimes in the hundreds of thousands of acres, accu-
rately reflects the leading position of Texas among the
states in beef cattle raised. The densest concentrations
of cattle, however, are to be found on the smaller units
to the east, but where feeding conditions are better.
These conditions are best on the Coastal Prairies, where
rice is rotated with pasture, which benefits from the
residual effects of fertilizer applied to the rice in
addition to an ample supply of moisture.[22]

Another prominent southern area is the Alabama Black
Belt, the leading dairy and beef cattle region of the
state, and the middle portion of a more extensive pattern
extending as a shallow arc from the Loess Bluffs and Pine
Hills in southwestern Mississippi to the lower piedmont
of Georgia and South Carolina. Here the "livestock
revolution" has had its greatest effect, with some of the
most remarkable transformations of agricultural systems
in the United States since World War II. The conversion
of plantations to ranches is the most striking example of
these changes, but the addition of livestock raising to
cropping enterprises also has been widespread. An
impressive example of the latter development is the
Deltapine plantation complex in northwestern Mississippi,
where several thousand beef cattle are fed in feedlots,
slaughtered in Deltapine's own meat packing plant, and
transported to market by company-owned refrigerated
trucks; yet even this prodigious operation is overshad-
owed by the greater investments and proceeds associated
with the cropping of cotton and a large variety of other
crops.[23] Large farms have led the way in the introduction of cattle raising, for the required initial investments and incidence of risk in beef cattle raising are
high. Both medium and large farms, though, are profiting
from the steadily expanding practice of "stocker-grazing," in which lightweight calves are purchased in the
fall, raised on pasture and fodder crops through the
following spring, and then sold to midwestern or Texas
feedlot operators for fattening and slaughter. Prunty
has observed pastures of 200 to 600 acres on these farms,
supporting 400 to 1,500 stocker calves.[24]

A third notable concentration of significant scale
in livestock investment in the South is on the Florida
Peninsula, where the relatively close juxtaposition of
beef cattle raising, dairying, and poultry farming somewhat parallels the situation in the Pacific Southwest.
Extensive scale is particularly well distributed in the

southern part of the peninsula, where the cattle ranches in the Lake Okeechobee area are the largest and most stocked and where dairy and poultry operations reach a maximum of investment scale on the fringes of the heavily urbanized Gold Coast. As this urban area has expanded, these more extensive farms have had to be abandoned, although many have benefited from the growing market by relocating farther west and expanding their properties and operations over cheaper land. What may be the ultimate in massiveness of single-unit dairying in eastern United States has been described by Higbee in his account of a firm that moved to north of Lake Okeechobee and cleared thousands of acres out of the wilderness for pasture: 8,000 cows, refrigerated trucks for hauling milk, bottling plants, and villages for the families of herdsmen and milkers, complete with buses and schools.[25] Dairy and poultry activities also attain markedly high scale levels in the Tampa-St. Petersburg and Jacksonville areas, despite the very small farm sizes in those places.

In the North, livestock investment scale above the national median describes much of the western Corn Belt, especially Iowa; much of the western Dairy Belt, mostly in Wisconsin; and in the Northeast, principally in the Appalachian Highlands. Investments in beef cattle are especially responsible for the Iowa concentration, and they are large enough to form two clusters of counties with Class I status, in the northwestern corner of the state and in the extreme east, where Iowa, Illinois, and Wisconsin meet. Investments in dairy cattle stamp the Wisconsin area, although the highest scale levels are in southwestern Wisconsin, where cattle feeding adds to the dairy income. The advanced scale of livestock investment is also impressive in that it is achieved on generally small farms, the ratio of investment to farm size equaling that in many counties of California and Hawaii. The large livestock investment scale in the Corn Belt is also noteworthy in view of the smaller farm sizes, but it cannot match that produced by the heavy stocking of dairy farms in Wisconsin. The preeminence of "America's Dairyland" on this score is by no means evidence of a generally uniform distribution of advanced investment scale; even in eastern Lakeshore Wisconsin, where smaller farms easily predominate, herd sizes are twice as large on the larger units.[26]

The attraction of the large urban markets of Megalopolis and the commonly larger farm sizes account for the extensive scale of livestock investment in the Northeast. Farm livestock inventories on the Allegheny Plateau and Lake Champlain-St. Lawrence Plain and in the Mohawk-Black River valleys are particularly sizable and in most counties exceed the herd size averages for the majority of Wisconsin counties. This region also compares with Wisconsin in its large sales of dairy heifers to farmers in areas where it is uneconomic to raise their own replacements, here principally on the urban fringe along the Atlantic Seaboard. Poultry notably add to the investment input in a few counties in Maine and southeastern New York, and beef cattle investment contributes some major islands of above-median scale to the distribution in the Ridge-and-Valley and Piedmont areas of Virginia.

The paradoxical low ranking of most seaboard counties in the Northeast in livestock investment scale refers not only to the small farm sizes of the area but to the impact of urbanization in its less favorable influence on dairying. Greater competition from market gardening, increasing attractiveness of part-time farming to the detriment of more time-demanding farm schedules, and insufficient capital flexibility in the face of rapidly changing political and social situations all continue to put greater pressure on livestock enterprises closest to urban centers. Similar blanks in the distribution of high livestock investment scale can easily be noted in metropolitan counties elsewhere in the nation, the pattern being even more emphatic than the one already observed for livestock investment intensity. That pattern also lends weight to the conclusion by Cummins, in his detailed statistical study of dairying in the Great Lakes states, that dairy farms form a declining proportion of commercial farms within a radius of fifty miles from urban-industrial complexes and that this decline had already started at least as early as 1950.[27]

Higher-Order Patterns of Crop and Livestock-Poultry Investments

Western leadership in livestock investment is considerably qualified when the scale of capitalization is collated with its intensity (Fig. 2.7), though probably not quite as severely as often assumed. The distribution of areas in the West having above-median ratings in both intensity and scale of livestock investment (more than $27 per farm acre and more than $10,500 per farm) is extremely limited, but the ratio of counties with highest intensities and scales (more than $46 per farm acre and more than $19,500 per farm) to all above-median counties is still higher than in the East. These higher-value counties embrace the irrigated areas, where the feed base and market conditions reach their optimum. Almost all western counties with any significant irrigation are included in the distribution when any above-median value becomes the criterion, thus essentially duplicating the list of areas already noted for heavy livestock capitalization per acre. Beyond irrigation, population becomes the most important areal delineator, as shown especially by the county concentrations on the

Pacific rim. Heavy capitalization intensity and extensive capitalization scale clearly focus on the metropolitan and bordering counties of southern California and southern Arizona, the San Francisco Bay Area, and the Puget Sound region. The island of Oahu, with Honolulu, stands out in Hawaii. In several of these more heavily populated areas, too, both poultry and dairy cows begin to compete with beef cattle for local and sometimes even national importance. Central and southern California are particularly conspicuous in this respect.

However, easily the most extensive area of significant intensity and scale of livestock investment begins on the moist edges of the Plains and extends eastward, encircling much of the western Corn and Dairy belts and the western Gulf Coastal Plain in Texas and Louisiana. Much of the Northeast, the Pine Hills of southern Mississippi, the Coastal Plain of Alabama, the lower Piedmont of Georgia and South Carolina, and sections of northern, central, and southern Florida also exceed the national median in both livestock investment categories. As we might expect in the East, the intensity of investment in these areas is generally more important than the scale of capitalization--particularly in the northern half, where the investment intensity patterns of the very highest class (more than $46 per farm acre) are almost identical to those of above-median investment scale (over $10,500 per farm). Nevertheless, a few areas with both scale and intensity values in the Class I group can be seen: the extreme northwest corner of Iowa and adjoining northeast corner of Nebraska; the extreme northwest corner of Illinois and adjoining counties of eastern Iowa; and a few isolated counties in the Northeast. The well-distributed patterns of Class I livestock investment intensity in the South do little to enhance the importance of the region in combined intensity and scale because so many of the counties with the highest intensity are precisely those with some of the smallest farms in the nation. This contradiction is especially obvious in the major poultry areas of northern Alabama and Georgia and in the beef cattle and dairy cow areas of middle Kentucky and Tennessee. Contrarily, the extensive distribution of Class I livestock investment scale on the Florida Peninsula cannot make up for the below-median showing of investment intensity in the majority of counties, although it is equaled in or near the metropolitan areas of Jacksonville, Tampa Bay-St. Petersburg, and Miami. Class I investment scale also is matched by above-median, though not Class I, investment intensity in the Alabama Black Belt.

With the national pattern of livestock investment scale now before us, it also becomes possible to view in more detail the spatial nature of a higher order of industrialized farming activity, that of the combined importance of crop and livestock investment scale (Figs. 3.5 and 3.7). This pattern qualifies a common assumption that because of better environmental and market conditions it is the eastern part of the country that has most of the area with major investments in both crops and livestock. For the intensity of investment, on a per-acre basis, that is undoubtedly so; for the scale of investment, on a per-farm basis, the regional weight is in the West. The Great Plains is particularly responsible with two extensive representations, a broad strip running between the heart of the Spring Wheat Belt to the northeast and the ranching country to the southwest, and most of the High Plains to the south, excluding the irrigated cotton section at the southern end. The Pacific Southwest is also prominent, as are all major oases between it and the Plains. Only the western end of the Corn Belt (essentially Iowa), the Coastal Prairies of the western Gulf Coast, and southern Florida stand out in the East. Also, fewer of these areas have equally high ratings in both crop and livestock investment scale than the important distributions in the West; only southern Florida has Class I ranking in both scale categories, whereas most of the High Plains and the Pacific Southwest similarly qualify. An even more negative showing in the East, however, is the widespread mutual exclusiveness of the two investment scale patterns. Areas with very small livestock investment scale but with extremely large scale of crop investment are exemplified by the Red River and upper Minnesota valleys, the Illinois Grand Prairie, most of the lower Great Lakes littoral, all of the Mississippi alluvial lands south of Illinois, and almost the entire Atlantic Coastal Plain, not to mention smaller but still important agricultural areas like the extreme southern end of the Great Plains and the northern section of Maine. Areas with the converse of this highly contrasting relationship (i.e., dominance of livestock investment) are also evident, although much more restricted. The Driftless Area, where Wisconsin, Illinois, and Iowa come together, is the largest illustration, but widely dispersed places like Sullivan County in southeastern New York, Androscoggin County in southwestern Maine, Nassau County in northeastern Florida, Marin County in central California, and the Tanana Valley in central Alaska (obscured on the map by the large reporting area) also show up.

Livestock and Poultry Expenditures and Higher-Order Patterns

A more positive areal showing by the East is evident in the distribution of the scale of livestock and poultry expenditures (Fig. 3.8). The western Corn Belt increases its ranking and expands its Iowa center of

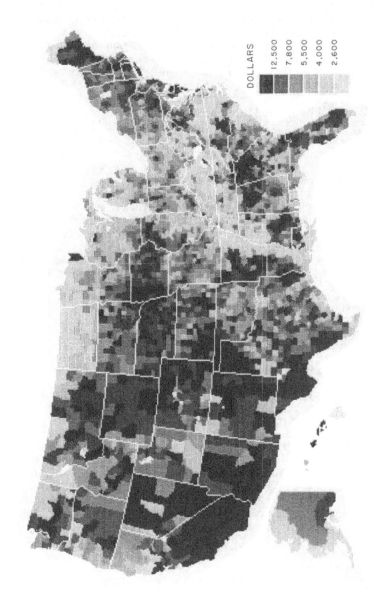

Figure 3.8. Livestock and Poultry expenditures per farm

above-median values (over $5,500 per farm) well into western and northern Illinois and southwestern Minnesota. The Northeast improves even more, particularly in Megalopolis and its margins. Areal coverage increases the most in the South, and much of the above-median area fits in the Class I group (over $12,500 per farm). Although better feed conditions and greater market stimulus come immediately to mind in explaining the enhanced display of the eastern regions, the part of small farm size and a resulting greater need for purchasing animals and supplies must not be overlooked. Most of the counties with a large scale of animal and feed expenditures are in the areas with the smallest farms (Fig. 1.1). This is especially obvious in the South and Northeast, where the negative correlation between large expenditure scale and small farm size clearly designates the principal poultry areas. Only in the Pacific Southwest and western Washington is substantial expenditure scale so impressively independent of farm size, and there too the distribution of above-median scale is more widespread than it is for investment intensity.

Large farm size contributes much more to the premier position of the rest of the West in scale of feed and animal purchases, although even there size has an inferior role in large sections of territory. This qualification is particularly noticeable in the much lesser importance of the northern Plains, in both grain and ranching areas, relative to the leading national position of the region in dominance by large farms. Only where irrigation and better cropping temperatures obtain do size and expenditures keep the same high rank, and this ratio is most extensively represented by counties in the southern Plains. High rankings in the scale of both livestock investment and livestock expenditures are also typical of these more physically favored areas. Feedlot operations increasingly contribute to the massive scale of some of these units, and when combined with their growing number they may be influential enough to outweigh the diluting effect on scale averages by the more numerous smaller livestock farms. Mather stated in 1972 that one hundred feedlots were supplying 16 percent of all the fed cattle in the nation and that most of these were on the Great Plains or in the Southwest.[28] How far-flung and extensive the influence of such gargantuan operations can be is illustrated by the requirements of the Montfort feedlots, a pioneer prototype of this enterprise form in northeastern Colorado. On that farm, 200,000 head are fed simultaneously, or 600,000 annually, drawing upon a total land area of approximately 25 million acres for the support of 700,000 brood cows and bulls, for the raising of 600,000 yearlings to feedlot stage, and for the production of 250,000 tons of silage, 365,000 tons of green chopped alfalfa, 25 million bushels of corn, and minor feed ingredients.[29]

The strong intensiveness of livestock expenditures that was indicated indirectly by the high ratio of inputs to farm size can be appreciated even more by noting the combined scale and intensity distributions for expenditures (Figs. 3.8 and 2.8). The East stands supreme, with the poultry areas of the South, the western Corn Belt, and the dairy-poultry area of the Northeast being the principal above-median concentrations. The West is certainly represented, as the southern Plains, Pacific Southwest, and western Washington still match the overall expenditure levels of the eastern sections; but for the great majority of the region, the inability to approach anywhere near the national median of expenditures on a per-acre basis is patent. Even many of the oases are unable to meet median standards of expenditure intensity, although data aggregation by counties undoubtedly degrades the high values of many of the smaller centers.

A further alteration of the national pattern becomes apparent when all of the individual distributions that we have analyzed so far for livestock capitalization are studied as a group: the intensity and scale of livestock and poultry investments and expenditures (Figs. 2.7, 2.8, 3.7, and 3.8). From the four maps, one can quickly conclude that livestock capitalization of some significance is associated with the majority of U.S. agricultural land. The second impression, though, when noting the places where livestock capitalization reaches significant levels in all four capitalization categories, is of a distribution that is much more impressive for its dispersal than for any large compact areas. Most prominent of the areas with values at or near Class I levels are the western Corn Belt, the Pacific Southwest, the vicinity of the three main population centers on the Florida Peninsula, the Colorado Piedmont and South Platte Valley, the South Texas High Plains near Amarillo, the lower and middle Snake River oases, and a few scattered counties in southern New York, Vermont, and Maine. The conspicuous absence from this list of the southern poultry areas and the northeastern dairy and poultry areas, as well as the western Washington area, are remedied if their submedian investment scale is disregarded. And if, instead, a deficiency in the intensity of investment is excepted, much of the High Plains and the Flint Hills can be added to the distribution.

A Summary Pattern of Total Crop and Livestock-Poultry Capitalization

A consideration of the distribution pattern of overall livestock capitalization also invites comparison with the spatial ordering of total cropping capitalization (Figs. 2.7 + 2.8 + 3.7 + 3.8 with Figs. 2.5 + 2.6 + 3.5 + 3.6). Again, examining such a large number of distributions allows us to obtain only the broadest of pictures, but it is enough to inform us of the principal areas. The western Corn Belt and the Pacific Southwest are the only centers of any significant areal extent that meet above-median minimums in all eight aspects of crop-livestock capitalization, and of these two regions, the Pacific area appears to be superior because of its larger scale of cropping expenditures. Central and southern Florida, a smaller portion of the livestock center southwest of Amarillo on the Texas High Plains, and the Snake River oases in Idaho form smaller centers of uniformly high crop-livestock capitalization.

NOTES

1. Computed from data published by the U.S. Department of Agriculture, Major Statistical Series of the U.S. Department of Agriculture. Vol. 6. Land Values and Farm Finance, U.S. Department of Agriculture Handbook No. 365, April 1971, pp. 11-12.
2. Michael D. Sublett, Farmers on the Road--Interfarm Migration and the Farming of Noncontiguous Lands in Three Midwestern Townships, 1939-1969. Department of Geography Research Paper No. 168 (Chicago: Department of Geography, University of Chicago, 1968), pp. 125-148.
3. Merle C. Prunty, "Some Contemporary Myths and Challenges in Southern Rural Land Utilization," and James S. Fisher, "Federal Crop Allotment Programs and Responses by Individual Farm Operators," both in Southeastern Geographer, Vol. 10, No. 2 (1970), pp. 4-5 and 50-51, respectively.
4. Philip M. Raup, "Corporate Farming in the United States," Journal of Economic History, Vol. 33 (1973), p. 281.
5. G. F. Donaldson and J. P. McInerney, "Changing Machinery Technology and Agricultural Adjustment," American Journal of Agricultural Economics, Vol. 55 (1973), p. 832.
6. Harold Hull McCarty, The Geographic Basis of American Economic Life (New York and London: Harper & Brothers Publishers, 1940), pp. 228-229.
7. Huber Self, Environment and Man in Kansas--A Geographical Analysis (Lawrence, Kan.: The Regents Press of Kansas, 1978), pp. 105 and 107.
8. Leslie F. Sheffield, "Irrigation," Agricultural Atlas of Nebraska, ed. Merlin P. Lawson, James H. Williams, and Doug Murfield (Lincoln, Neb., and London: University of Nebraska Press, 1977), p. 16.
9. Howard F. Gregor, An Agricultural Typology of California, Vol. 4 of Geography of World Agriculture,

ed. György Enyedi (Budapest: Akademiai Kiado, 1974), pp. 55 and 62.

10. David Lawrence Smith, "Superfarms vs. Sagebrush: New Irrigation Developments on the Snake River Plain," *Proceedings of the Association of American Geographers*, ed. Fritz L. Kramer, Vol. 2 (1970), pp. 127-131.

11. Merle Prunty, Jr., "The Renaissance of the Southern Plantation," *Geographical Review*, Vol. 45 (1955), p. 486, and idem, "Deltapine: Field Laboratory for the Neoplantation Occupance Type," in *Festschrift: Clarence F. Jones*, ed. Merle Prunty, Jr., Northwestern University Studies in Geography No. 6 (Evanston, Ill.: Northwestern University Department of Geography, 1962), p. 167.

12. Arthur J. Hawley and David W. Bunn, "Irrigation in the South," *Southeastern Geographer*, Vol. 10, No. 2 (1970), pp. 42-44. Especially informative are the maps on pages 42 ("Southeastern United States Farms Irrigated") and 44 ("Counties Containing Specified Proportions of Farms Irrigated").

13. Stephen H. Sosnick, *Hired Hands--Seasonal Farm Workers in the United States* (Santa Barbara, Calif.: McNally & Loftin, 1978), p. 5.

14. E. Cotton Mather, "The American Great Plains," *Annals*, Association of American Geographers, Vol. 62 (1972), p. 254.

15. Dana G. Dalrymple, *Controlled Environment Agriculture: A Global Review of Greenhouse Food Production*, U.S., Department of Agriculture, Economic Research Service, Foreign Agricultural Economic Report No. 89 (Washington, D.C.: Government Printing Office, 1973), p. 128, fn. 1.

16. Howard F. Gregor, "Farm Structure in Regional Comparison: California and New Jersey Vegetable Farms," *Economic Geography*, Vol. 45 (1969), p. 219.

17. Prunty, "Deltapine: Field Laboratory for the Neoplantation Occupance Type," op. cit., p. 165.

18. Earl O. Heady, *Capacity and Trends in Use of Land Resources*, Center for Agricultural and Economic Development (Ames, Ia.: Iowa State University of Science and Technology, 1968), p. 6.

19. Howard F. Gregor, "The Large Industrialized American Crop Farm--A Mid-Latitude Plantation Variant," *Geographical Review*, Vol. 60 (1970), p. 158. Distributions are based on computations from published and unpublished census data, which were aggregated by states.

20. Ronald R. Boyce, *The Bases of Economic Geography*, 2d ed. (New York: Holt, Rinehart and Winston, 1978), p. 213.

21. Daniel Alexander Gómez-Ibáñez, "The Rise and Decline of Transhumance in the United States," unpublished Master's thesis, Department of Geography, University of Wisconsin, Madison, 1967, p. 72.

22. John Fraser Hart, *The South*, 2d ed., New Searchlight Series (New York: D. Van Nostrand Company, 1976), pp. 118-119.

23. Prunty, "Deltapine: Field Laboratory for the Neoplantation Occupance Type," op. cit., pp. 165-167.

24. Prunty, "Some Contemporary Myths and Challenges in Southern Rural Land Utilization," op cit., p. 9.

25. Edward Higbee, *Farms and Farmers in an Urban Age* (New York: The Twentieth Century Fund, 1963), pp. 41-42.

26. Kenneth W. Korb, *Dairy Farming: An Analysis of an Agricultural System in Eastern Lakeshore Wisconsin*. Ph.D. dissertation, University of Wisconsin, 1968 (Ann Arbor, Mich.: University Microfilms, 1969), p. 379.

27. David E. Cummins, *Effect of Urban Expansion on Dairying in the Lake States, 1949-69*, U.S., Department of Agriculture, Economic Research Service, Agricultural Economic Report No. 196 (Washington, D.C.: Government Printing Office, 1970), p. 7.

28. E. Cotton Mather, "The American Great Plains," Annals, Association of American Geographers, Vol. 62 (1972), p. 257.

29. Ibid.

4
The Structure of Agricultural Industrialization

By now it is thoroughly evident that the importance of the capitalization variables relative to each other varies greatly from place to place. It is also quite clear that these variations describe patterns of varying consistency, thus providing spatial insights into the structure of the agricultural industrialization process. I have already attempted to provide such insights, but only for the input variables that appear to be most functionally related and without the benefit of maps representing specifically those relationships. With all the distribution patterns of the individual variables now in hand, we can inquire about the still broader aspects of agricultural industrialization structure and the way they are distributed.

THE GENERAL INTENSITY STRUCTURE

An important first step in discerning the more general lineaments is to determine the extent of association of each capital-input variable with each of the others. The most common approach to such a problem is to compute a matrix of Pearson product moment correlation coefficients, with 1.0 indicating a perfect correlation and 0.0 indicating absolutely none. The average coefficients of the variables I have chosen to represent the intensity of agricultural industrialization show labor and mechanization to be most important, followed by cropping and land and finally livestock and poultry (Table 4.1).[1]

These figures, however, only hint at the areal distribution of the intensity structure, and they do not reveal the substructures that may exist. For these and other characteristics of this more comprehensive industrialization complex, we can turn to the techniques of factor analysis, and more specifically, of components analysis.[2] In this procedure, no particular assumption about the underlying structure of the variables is

Table 4.1. Correlations between capital-input criteria for the intensity of agricultural industrialization

Criteria	1	2	3	4	5	6	7	8	Ave.
1. Labor expenditures/ farm acre (LREXPA)	1.00	.89	.90	.84	.83	.78	.64	.59	.78
2. Machine hire, customwork, and fuel expenditures/ farm acre (MFEXPA)		1.00	.91	.85	.90	.85	.59	.47	.78
3. Machinery and equipment investments/farm acre (MEINVA)			1.00	.82	.85	.79	.56	.53	.77
4. Land and building investments/farm acre (LBINVA)				1.00	.83	.78	.57	.47	.74
5. Crop expenditures/ farm acre (CREXPA)					1.00	.87	.48	.36	.73
6. Crop investments/ farm acre (CRINVA)						1.00	.34	.21	.66
7. Livestock-poultry expenditures/farm acre (LVEXPA)							1.00	.80	.57
8. Livestock-poultry investments/farm acre (LVINVA)								1.00	.49

required, and one only asks what would be the linear combination of variables accounting for more of the variance in the data as a whole than for any other linear combination of variables. When the correlation coefficient matrix of the intensity variables is factor-analyzed, the resultant "principal component" yields essentially the same structure given by the correlation matrix averages for the variables, although the variable representing mechanization and mechanized labor now takes the leadership from the manual labor variable (Table 4.2).[3] This latter shift in analysis appears to bear out the general observation that mechanization in American agriculture has now proceeded from a stage of reducing need for year-round labor and sharpening labor peaks to one of reducing labor peaks and putting greater stress on a year-round labor supply more geared to the needs of mechanization.[4]

More than 74 percent of the variance is statistically explained by the principal component, so we may safely assume that it represents the intensity structure of general agricultural industrialization from this standpoint. Only the livestock variables owe less than 50 percent of their variance to the influence of this component, a statistic arrived at by squaring the Pearson correlation coefficient ("loading") of the variable. The joint product, computed by multiplying the loading by the factor score regression weight (not shown in Table 4.2), refines the outlines of the intensity structure even more; almost half of the variance explained by the component structure is derived directly and indirectly from the labor and mechanization variables, whereas no more than 14 percent comes from the two livestock variables.

No less beneficial geographically is that once the component (intensity) structure is developed by factoring, it becomes possible to use it to compute weights for each variable and to apply them to the standardized variable values of each case (county). It thus becomes as easy to map in detail the distribution of the component of general agricultural industrialization as it has been to map the distributions of the individual industrialization intensity variables, but now areal comparisons are derived from the factor scores on the component rather than the ratio data on the individual variables (Fig. 4.1). The scores are standardized values and are grouped into six classes, with class limits made small enough to ensure a detailed distribution pattern. General intensity of agricultural industrialization is above the mean (i.e., any positive factor score) for all major agricultural regions of the United States except the Great Plains; both the High Plains and subhumid Winter Wheat Belt are clearly profiled, but only the middle Platte Valley in southern Nebraska, the Colorado

Table 4.2. The intensity structure of general agricultural industrialization

Capital Inputs	Loading	% Variance Explained	Joint Product
Machine hire, customwork, and fuel expenditures/farm acre	.9572	.9162	.1545
Labor expenditures/farm acre	.9492	.9010	.1502
Machinery and equipment investments/farm acre	.9408	.8851	.1492
Crop expenditures/farm acre	.9113	.8305	.1401
Land and building investments/farm acre	.9110	.8299	.1399
Crop investments/farm acre	.8455	.7149	.1206
Livestock-poultry expenditures/farm acre	.6946	.4825	.0813
Livestock-poultry investments/farm acre	.6084	.3702	.0624

163

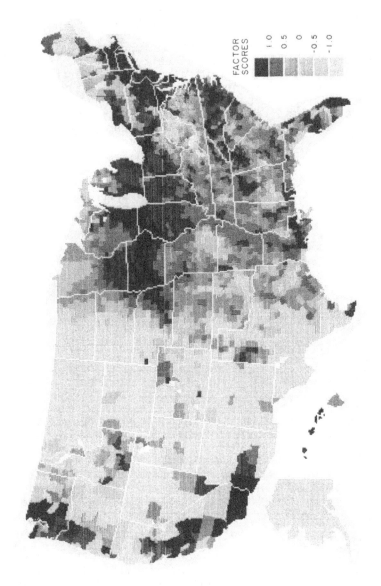

Figure 4.1. Intensity of general agricultural industrialization

Piedmont and South Platte Valley in northeastern Colorado, and the southern end of the Texas High Plains in the vicinity of Lubbock form notable patches of significant intensity. The Snake River oases in Idaho stand out in the Intermountain area, although the irrigated valleys of southeastern California, southwestern Arizona, and west-central Washington make up important eastern extensions of the major high-intensity areas of the Pacific Southwest and Trans-Cascade Pacific Northwest.

In the more prominent East, the Middle West and Northeast form the most extensive block, although even here there are important variations. The western Corn Belt joins northern Illinois and southeastern Wisconsin to outline the largest single concentration of very high intensity (over one standard deviation) in the Middle West. Equally high values stamp much of the lower Great Lakes littoral. But the largest area of such high intensity embraces southern New England and the Middle Atlantic section to the south. It is the best evidence of all of what can be observed in many parts of the distribution of the leading intensity class: the powerful influence of metropolitanization on the agricultural industrialization process; fourteen of the top twenty counties in the scoring on the intensity component are in this easternmost region (Table 4.3). Urban influence also shows clearly in the clustering of the highest-scoring areas in the vicinity of the three leading population clusters on the Florida Peninsula, but it is the intensive poultry-tobacco-mixed farming operations that are most responsible for the largest area of Class I intensity in the South, a belt extending through northern Alabama and Georgia and across the entire length of North Carolina. Few of the major Class I intensity areas in the nation, in fact, score at that class level for all the individual capitalization intensity variables, a reminder that the intensity structure produced by the factoring is for the country as a whole and not precisely for any one region. Iowa drops back in field labor expenditures, while the Pacific Southwest and most of the Florida Peninsula fall below the Class I threshold in mechanized labor inputs. Somewhat surprisingly, practically all of Wisconsin and the lower Great Lakes margins do not match Class I values for livestock expenditures, whereas the Willamette Valley, parts of the Central Valley in California, most of Hawaii, and eastern North Carolina are deficient in livestock investments. Definitely lower intensities in both livestock expenditures and investments characterize the overall highly intensive Mississippi Delta and lower Rio Grande Valley. Only the Megalopolis region scores in the highest intensity class for all the variables in the general industrialization component.

Table 4.3. The twenty leading counties in intensity of general agricultural industrialization[a]

1.	Suffolk, Mass.	5.42	11.	Middlesex, Mass.	3.08
2.	Union, N.J.	5.08	12.	Hartford, Conn.	2.98
3.	Nassau, N.Y.	4.97	13.	Dade, Fla.	2.95
4.	Hudson, N.J.	4.93	14.	Middlesex, Conn.	2.94
5.	Passaic, N.J.	4.79	15.	Newport, R.I.	2.87
6.	Queens, N.Y.	4.29	16.	Hood River, Ore.	2.86
7.	Bergen, N.J.	4.16	17.	Lake, O.	2.77
8.	Cuyahoga, O.	3.88	18.	Santa Cruz, Cal.	2.76
9.	Suffolk, N.Y.	3.65	19.	Westchester, N.Y.	2.65
10.	Ramsey, Minn.	3.26	20.	Gloucester, N.J.	2.60

[a]Ranks are based on the county scores on the agricultural industrialization component for general agricultural intensity. Scores have been standardized so that their mean is equal to zero.

THE INTENSITY SUBSTRUCTURES

Another value of factor analysis for our study of industrialization structure is the ability of the procedure to isolate substructures. Whereas our first concern was simply to uncover the intensity structure responsible for the greatest amount of variation among the variables, we can now look for structures characterizing the principal clusters of variables. These clusters are not so much subsets of the agricultural intensity structure just described as they are more detailed indicators of the total complex from a different point of view. This different and more elaborated view was achieved through varimax rotation, a nondeterministic algebraic method of sorting out the factors or components around the particular groupings of variables.[5] Two major component structures were extracted from the correlation matrix via the rotation process, one oriented around cropping (Table 4.4) and the other even more tightly around livestock and poultry raising (Table 4.6). The cropping component, though, is twice as important as the other component in the amount of explained variation of the intensity variables: 60 percent versus 29 percent. Within the cropping structure, fully 50 percent of its statistical explanation comes directly and indirectly from the two cropping variables. Each of the variables, crop investments and crop expenditures, contributes more to the intensity structure than any other variable, with investments being the most important. Labor, mechanization, and land make up the next most important variable grouping, although mechanization now surpasses labor as the variable for hand labor drops to a much lower rank in the intensity structure than it has in the structure of general agricultural industrialization (from 2 to 6).

The factor score pattern is as well distributed over the country as general agricultural industrialization intensity, and actually even more so if the distribution of the highest intensity class is noted (Fig. 4.2). On this last basis, the South even exceeds the Middle West, with the lower Mississippi Valley and the Coastal Plain in the Carolinas forming the two most prominent areas, followed by sections in southwest Georgia, central and southern Florida, and scatterings along much of the Gulf Coast from the Florida Panhandle to the mouth of the Rio Grande. The only important difference between cropping and general intensity distributions in the Middle West is a closer focusing on the best agricultural lands, with the Grand Prairie of Illinois now easily the most impressive single area, followed by other favored sections like the Iowa Prairie, upper Minnesota Valley, Maumee Valley, and the less irregular terrain connecting the Saginaw Plain with the Lake Michigan littoral. Metropolitan centers, however, also exert strong influence, as can be

Table 4.4. The intensity structure of industrialization in cropping

Capital Inputs	Loading	% Variance Explained	Joint Product
Crop investments/farm acre	.9504	.9033	.2799
Crop expenditures/ farm acre	.9292	.8637	.2237
Machine hire, customwork, and fuel expenditures/farm acre	.9016	.8129	.1738
Machinery and equipment investments/ farm acre	.8611	.7415	.1459
Land and building investments/ farm acre	.8439	.7122	.1452
Labor expenditures/farm acre	.8221	.6758	.1096
Livestock-poultry investments/farm acre	.1743	.0304	-.0347
Livestock-poultry expenditures/farm acre	.3027	.0916	-.0434

168

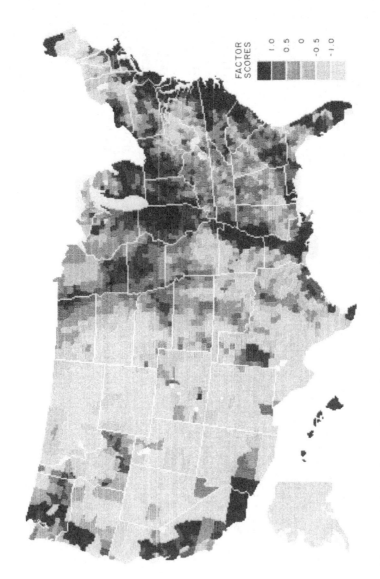

Figure 4.2. Intensity of industrialization in cropping

seen in the many Class I counties along the shores of the lower Great Lakes. Megalopolis also demonstrates greater centering on both the more favored lowlands and around the big population centers; thirteen of the twenty leading counties in the intensity of cropping industrialization are in this region (Table 4.5). The same reshuffling of the above-mean factor score areas can be seen in the Pacific area, although the Willamette and Sacramento valleys are added to the Class I distribution. Little is changed in the meager Great Plains pattern, although the Red River Valley now joins the middle Platte Valley and South Texas High Plains with ranking in the top two intensity classes. The even sparser cropping intensity distributions of the Intermountain area are punctuated principally by the above-average values of the Columbia Basin and Snake River Plain. The majority of the irrigated areas, however, are definitely inferior to their standings in general agricultural intensity.

A key to the much lesser ability of the livestock intensity component to explain the variation in the intensity distribution is provided by the low contributions of most of the variables to the livestock intensity component (Table 4.6). Six of the eight loadings show a moderately good correlation of all but the cropping variables with the component, but the number of significant variables is cut to three on the basis of percentage of variance of each variable explained by the component; even this figure is reduced to simply the two livestock variables when the most important criterion of the importance of the variable in the component structure is considered, i.e., the combined direct and indirect contribution of the variable to the explanatory power of the component. Conversely, however, the uncommonly great weight of the livestock intensity variables makes them quite representative in the factor score pattern, even more widespread than cropping industrialization intensity (Fig. 4.3). Also, the fact that livestock industrialization intensity does have much more of a locational correlation with crop and other intensity variables than is shown by the overall national factor structure further ensures a wide distribution. Thus, although locational patterns for the major center of livestock intensity in the western parts of the Dairy and Corn belts depart from those of cropping intensity in finer detail, they nevertheless form a large overlap. The same situation can be observed for the leading livestock intensity areas of Megalopolis, the southern Plains, the Intermountain oases, central and southern California, and western Washington. The South, on the other hand, counters this balance with the location of most of its leading and predominantly poultry intensity centers well outside the chief cropping intensity areas. Also contributing to this negative relationship is the extremely high level of

Table 4.5. The twenty leading counties in intensity of industrialization in cropping[a]

1. Queens, N.Y.	7.08		11. Dade, Fla.	3.78
2. Hudson, N.J.	6.27		12. Camden, N.J.	3.56
3. Union, N.J.	5.87		13. Ramsey, Minn.	3.51
4. Nassau, N.Y.	5.69		14. Milwaukee, Wis.	3.39
5. Suffolk, Mass.	5.31		15. Santa Cruz, Cal.	3.12
6. Cuyahoga, O.	4.77		16. Middlesex, N.J.	3.11
7. Passaic, N.J.	4.41		17. Atlantic, N.J.	3.05
8. Suffolk, N.Y.	4.39		18. Barnstable, Mass.	2.97
9. Bergen, N.J.	4.06		19. Hartford, Conn.	2.95
10. Hood River, Ore.	3.86		20. Chelan, Wash.	2.90

[a] Ranks are based on the county scores on the agricultural industrialization component for cropping intensity. Scores have been standardized so that their mean is equal to zero.

Table 4.6. The intensity structure of industrialization in livestock and poultry raising.

Capital Inputs	Loading	% Variance Explained	Joint Product
Livestock-poultry investments/farm acre	.9417	.8868	.5380
Livestock-poultry expenditures/farm acre	.8876	.7878	.4448
Labor expenditures/farm acre	.4747	.6758	.0426
Machinery and equipment investments/farm acre	.3868	.1496	.0083
Land and building investments/farm acre	.3564	.1270	.0022
Machine hire, customwork, and fuel expenditures/farm acre	.3477	.1209	-.0053
Crop investments/farm acre	.0287	.0008	-.0068
Crop expenditures/farm acre	.2029	.0412	-.0239

172

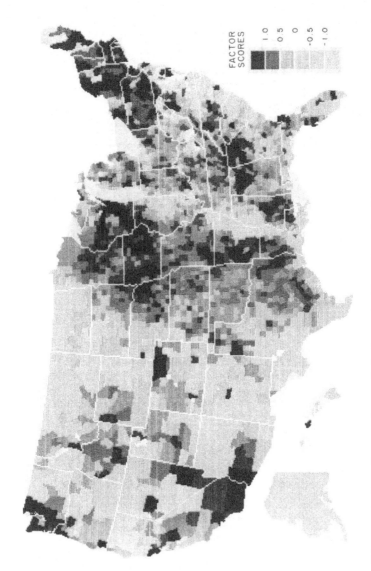

Figure 4.3. Intensity of industrialization in livestock and poultry raising

poultry raising intensity in the South, with sixteen of the leading twenty counties in the U.S. in intensity of industrialization of livestock and poultry raising located in the region (Table 4.7). In turn, northern Georgia dominates the southern pattern with eleven of those sixteen counties. Less regionally prominent examples of a strong negative correlation between livestock and cropping industrialization intensities are seen in the Appalachian Highlands of the Northeast, the Maumee Valley, and the Grand Prairie of Illinois.

THE GENERAL SCALE STRUCTURE

The structural aspects of the scale of agricultural industrialization can be studied in the same way as intensity. The correlation matrix for the capitalization variables representing industrialization scale shows the average coefficients for mechanization and labor to be the most important, although those for field labor expenditures are now secondary in importance compared with their leading rank in the intensity correlation matrix (Table 4.8). Land, cropping, and livestock variables follow, pretty much duplicating the sequence for intensity correlation averages. Mechanization and mechanized labor also stand out more sharply from the variable group, as do the livestock variables at the low end of the scale. The generally lower correlations of all the variables compared with the intensity coefficients are also quite obvious, a natural consequence when one remembers that large capitalization scale can often be achieved as easily with heavy applications of capital on smaller farms as it can be with less applications on larger farms; the spatial result is a softening of the sharp East-West contrasts exhibited in industrialization intensity.

Mechanization and the associated labor also come out clearly in the scale structure of general agricultural industrialization, as represented by the principal component (Table 4.9). These two variables also are more important in industrialization scale than they are in industrialization intensity, contributing directly and indirectly almost 39 percent of the variance explained by the component (scale) structure, versus a figure of 30 percent for the intensity structure. However, less of the total scale variation is accounted for by the scale structure than for the intensity component (52 percent vs 74 percent), reflecting the lower correlation matrix coefficients, which, as in the factoring of the intensity variables, furnished the data base. The ranking sequence of scale variables presented by the correlation matrix is repeated in the scale structure, although hand labor loses some of its importance relative to land and cropping.

Table 4.7. The twenty leading counties in intensity of industrialization in livestock and poultry raising[a]

1.	Lumpkin, Ga.	3.16	11.	Washington, Ark.	2.85
2.	Douglas, Ga.	3.12	12.	Habersham, Ga.	2.75
3.	Dawson, Ga.	3.11	13.	Pickens, Ga.	2.75
4.	Hall, Ga.	3.07	14.	Stephens, Ga.	2.70
5.	Forsyth, Ga.	3.04	15.	Simpson, Miss.	2.66
6.	Cherokee, Ga.	3.00	16.	Nassau, Fla.	2.65
7.	White, Ga.	2.94	17.	Windham, Conn.	2.63
8.	Towns, Ga.	2.92	18.	Androscoggin, Me.	2.61
9.	Livingston, La.	2.86	19.	Cullman, Ala.	2.61
10.	Wahkiakum, Wash.	2.85	20.	Island, Wash.	2.60

[a] Ranks are based on the county scores on the agricultural industrialization component for livestock and poultry raising intensity. Scores have been standardized so that their mean is zero.

Table 4.8. Correlations between capital-input criteria for the scale of agricultural industrialization

Criteria	1	2	3	4	5	6	7	8	Ave.
1. Machine hire, customwork, and fuel expenditures/ farm (MFEXPF)	1.00	.81	.66	.73	.66	.59	.24	.28	.57
2. Machinery and equipment investments/farm (MEINVF)		1.00	.59	.59	.68	.59	.09	.20	.51
3. Labor expenditures/ farm (LREXPF)			1.00	.65	.55	.46	.22	.20	.48
4. Land and building investments/farm (LBINVF)				1.00	.44	.37	.27	.39	.45
5. Crop investments/ farm (CRINVF)					1.00	.76	-.11	-.18	.40
6. Crop expenditures/ farm (CREXPF)						1.00	-.01	-.20	.37
7. Livestock-poultry expenditures/farm (LVEXPF)							1.00	.66	.19
8. Livestock-poultry investments/farm (LVINVF)								1.00	.19

Table 4.9. The scale structure of general agricultural industrialization

Capital Inputs	Loading	% Variance Explained	Joint Product
Machine hire, customwork, and fuel expenditures/farm	.9219	.8499	.2059
Machinery and equipment investments/farm	.8685	.7543	.1827
Labor expenditures/farm	.7993	.6389	.1547
Land and building investments/farm	.7923	.6277	.1520
Crop investments/farm	.7849	.6161	.1493
Crop expenditures/farm	.7210	.5198	.1260
Livestock-poultry investments/farm	.2475	.0613	.0149
Livestock-poultry expenditures/farm	.2444	.0597	.0145

All important agricultural areas of the nation are outlined by above-mean values in the factor score pattern (Fig. 4.4). With the heavy emphasis on western areas, the Great Plains, which were largely absent in the general intensity distribution, now become the most impressive area in territorial extent. But it is the Pacific Southwest that attains the highest levels of general agricultural industrialization scale, with twelve of the leading twenty counties in the country (Table 4.10). In contrast to the good showing of the West, above-mean representation is heavily eroded in the Dairy Belt, leaving the western Corn Belt (principally Illinois and Iowa) and Megalopolis as the principal areas in the Middle West and Northeast. Except for the tobacco sections in Kentucky, Tennessee, the Carolinas, and Virginia, all notable agricultural areas in the South are outlined by high to very high factor scores (0.5 to over 1.0 standard deviation). The Mississippi alluvial lands, all of the Gulf Coast from the Rio Grande to Louisiana, and most of the Florida Peninsula are the largest distributions, although many counties on the Inner Coastal Plain are also highly visible. The good showing of the Alabama Black Belt, and the thoroughly insignificant performance of most of the counties in northern Georgia and Alabama and in western North Carolina, indicate that cattle easily outclass poultry as an important ingredient in general farming scale despite the unusually intensive industrialization of poultry raising. With a better representation in Class I scale values than the North, the South in effect reinforces the southern emphasis already noted in the higher scale values in the Pacific Southwest. Florida, in fact, is the only eastern state with representation in the list of the top twenty counties in industrialization scale, with five representatives in its southern tip. A southern tier becomes even clearer when the almost solid band of Class I counties on the High Plains is noted. Yet even this strong southern orientation is not without its qualifications. California and Florida clearly do not equal their impressive showing in general industrialization scale with their scale of machinery and equipment investment, and the Inner Coastal Plain is obviously less prominent in the scale of labor expenditures and land and building investments. In the northern half of the country, Illinois and much of Iowa actually fall below the mean in labor expenditure scale, and Megalopolis is certainly spotty in the distribution of above-mean mechanization investment scale.

THE SCALE SUBSTRUCTURES

As with the intensity of agricultural industrialization, rotation of components reveals a substructure based

178

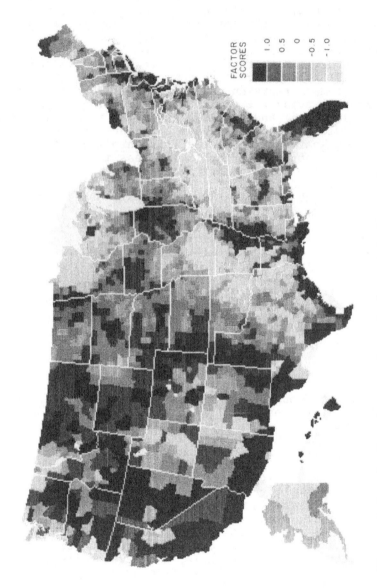

Figure 4.4. Scale of general agricultural industrialization

Table 4.10. The twenty leading counties in scale of general agricultural industrialization[a]

1. Imperial, Cal.	3.44		11. Maricopa, Ariz.	3.25
2. Pinal, Ariz.	3.44		12. Mauai, Haw.	3.22
3. Kern, Cal.	3.42		13. Kauai, Haw.	3.12
4. Hendry, Fla.	3.39		14. Yolo, Cal.	3.10
5. Palm Beach, Fla.	3.36		15. Kings, Cal.	3.09
6. Monterey, Cal.	3.32		16. Glades, Fla.	3.04
7. Collier, Fla.	3.30		17. Colusa, Cal.	2.98
8. Yuma, Ariz.	3.30		18. Elmore, Ida.	2.89
9. Reeves, Tex.	3.29		19. Honolulu, Haw.	2.87
10. Martin, Fla.	3.26		20. Pershing, Nev.	2.84

[a] Ranks are based on the county scores on the agricultural industrialization component for general agricultural scale. Scores have been standardized so that their mean is zero.

on a crop-livestock dichotomy, but with some modifications (Table 4.11). The most important scale component is cropping, but with a stronger role for mechanization-- so much so, in fact, that the two mechanization variables separate the leading crop variable (investments) from the other crop variable (expenditures) in the joint product rankings. The two cropping variables nevertheless contribute more in total to the component than do the mechanization variables (39 percent vs 36 percent). A little surprising is the greater importance of hand labor and the lesser showing of land in comparison with their ranking in the intensity of agricultural industrialization. Total variance explained by the cropping component is less than that explained by cropping for the intensity component (50 percent vs 60 percent), although the figure is still almost twice that of the livestock component (26 percent).

The national distribution of major scale in cropping industrialization is quite close to that of scale in general industrialization, though with some reinforcement of all major agricultural regions in the East. In the Middle West, the strengthening is enough to make central Illinois the largest single area of Class I cropping scale (Fig. 4.5). In the South, values are increased enough to put the region on a par with the Pacific Southwest in representation among the leading twenty counties in scale of cropping industrialization, thus further enhancing the showing of the southern tier (Table 4.12).

Livestock and poultry raising monopolize their factor structure for scale almost as much as they do for intensity (Table 4.13). The domination of the factor score pattern by the West is no less strong (Fig. 4.6). Only a scattering of counties interrupt the above-mean distribution in the conterminous western United States, and a majority of the area with positive values qualifies for Class I ranking. On the eastern margins, a salient from the northern Plains carries positive scale values into Iowa and the bordering fringes of Illinois and Wisconsin, while still farther east an important outlier is formed by the extreme Northeast. More impressive, though, is the eastern extension of above-average scale through a large part of the South, for which both poultry and cattle raising are substantially responsible. Highest scale values nevertheless remain in the western core, particularly in western Texas and New Mexico, where large farm size and milder climates favor bigger herds (Table 4.14).

NOTES

1. Prior to computation of the correlation matrix, the ratio data were standardized and all case (county)

Table 4.11. The scale structure of industrialization in cropping

Capital Inputs	Loading	% Variance Explained	Joint Product
Crop investments/farm	.8715	.7595	.2100
Machinery and equipment investments/farm	.8634	.7454	.1849
Crop expenditures/farm	.8025	.6440	.1783
Machine hire, customwork, and fuel expenditures/farm	.8818	.7776	.1713
Labor expenditures/farm	.7601	.5778	.1363
Land and building investments/farm	.7090	.5027	.1097
Livestock-poultry investments/farm	.0360	.0013	-.0017
Livestock-poultry expenditures/farm	.0531	.0028	-.0020

182

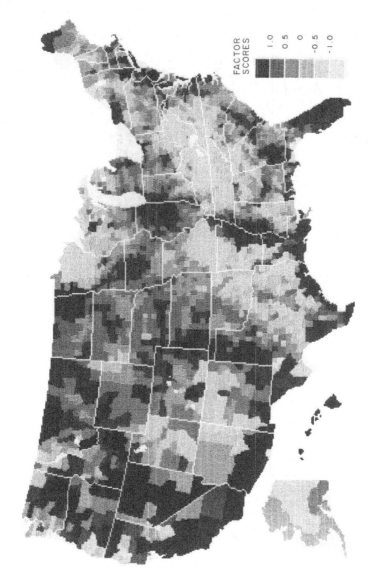

Figure 4.5. Scale of industrialization in cropping

Table 4.12. The twenty leading counties in scale of industrialization in cropping[a]

1. Yolo, Cal.	3.26	11. Coahoma, Miss.	3.05
2. Sharkey, Miss.	3.18	12. Hendry, Fla.	3.04
3. Kauai, Haw.	3.17	13. Kern, Cal.	3.03
4. Tunica, Miss.	3.14	14. Leflore, Miss.	3.03
5. Crittenden, Ark.	3.11	15. Imperial, Cal.	3.01
6. Collier, Fla.	3.10	16. Martin, Fla.	3.01
7. Colusa, Cal.	3.10	17. Pinal, Ariz.	3.01
8. St. Mary, La.	3.09	18. Washington, Miss.	3.00
9. Maui, Haw.	3.07	19. Bolivar, Miss.	2.97
10. Palm Beach, Fla.	3.07	20. Monterey, Cal.	2.96

[a] Ranks are based on the county scores on the agricultural industrialization component for cropping scale. Scores have been standardized so that their mean is zero.

Table 4.13. The scale structure of industrialization in livestock and poultry raising

Capital Inputs	Loading	% Variance Explained	Joint Product
Livestock-poultry investments/farm	.9215	.8492	.4255
Livestock-poultry expenditures/farm	.8361	.6991	.3492
Land and building investments/farm	.4442	.1973	.0799
Crop investments/farm	-.2738	.0750	.0525
Crop expenditures/farm	-.2595	.0673	.0468
Machine hire, customwork, and fuel expenditures/farm	.2770	.0767	.0235
Labor expenditures/farm	.2588	.0670	.0216
Machinery and equipment investments/farm	.1234	.0152	.0011

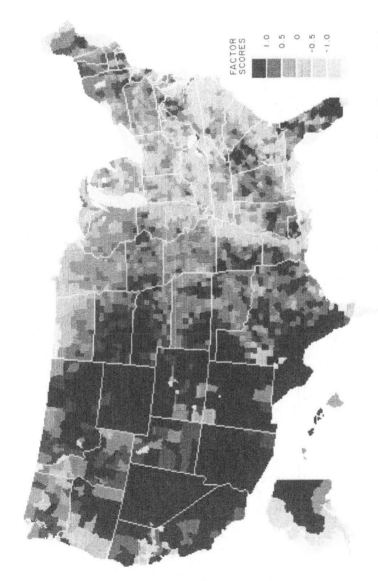

Figure 4.6. Scale of industrialization in livestock and poultry raising

Table 4.14. The twenty leading counties in scale of industrialization in livestock and poultry raising[a]

1.	Brewster, Tex.	4.18	11.	Irion, Tex.	2.70
2.	Coconino, Ariz.	3.46	12.	Inyo, Cal.	2.69
3.	Guadalupe, N.M.	3.35	13.	Hinsdale, Colo.	2.68
4.	Fairbanks, Alas.	3.31	14.	Marin, Cal.	2.68
5.	Grant, Neb.	3.02	15.	Jeff Davis, Tex.	2.64
6.	Val Verde, Tex.	2.98	16.	Santa Fe, N.M.	2.64
7.	Carbon, Wyo.	2.92	17.	Mariposa, Cal.	2.63
8.	Elko, Nev.	2.88	18.	Sublette, Wyo.	2.63
9.	Terrell, Tex.	2.77	19.	Catron, N.M.	2.61
10.	Jackson, Colo.	2.72	20.	Potter, Tex.	2.55

[a]Ranks are based on the county scores on the agricultural industrialization component for scale of livestock and poultry raising. Scores have been standardized so that their mean is zero.

outliers in the data distributions were eliminated if their values exceed three standard deviations. The distributions were then normalized, using the most appropriate of the three transformations found most effective in treating all the distributions for the data group: log X, $X^{1/2}$, X^2. The effects of the various forms of truncation and transformation on distribution curves are well illustrated by R. J. Rummel, Applied Factor Analysis (Evanston, Ill.: Northwestern University Press, 1970), pp. 280-286.

2. Although components analysis is different in several ways from all other types of "classical" factor analysis, I follow common practice by considering the components method as a type of factor analysis because of its general similarities and, where not ambiguous, by using the terms "component" and "factor" interchangeably.

The most widely circulated book on the nature of factor analysis is probably Harry H. Harman's Modern Factor Analysis, 2d ed., rev. (Chicago and London: University of Chicago Press, 1967). A most succinct description for newcomers to the technique is provided by Jae-on Kim, "Factor Analysis," in SPSS: Statistical Package for the Social Sciences, ed. Norman H. Nie et al., 2d ed., rev. (New York: McGraw-Hill Book Company, 1975), Ch. 24, pp. 468-514. R. J. Rummel, op. cit., provides a fuller account of the procedure in the same introductory vein.

3. The computer program used for factor analysis was Subprogram Factor, Statistical Package for the Social Sciences (SPSS).

4. G. Vogel, "Ökonomische Probleme der landwirtschaftlichen Mechanisierung," Berichte Über Landwirtschaft, New Series, Vol. 36 (1958), pp. 17-68.

5. Rummel (op. cit., pp. 368-422) provides a good explanation of the various rotation types, including varimax. Although components are commonly rotated, many researchers object to the practice because the principal purpose of rotation, to clarify the details of factor structure, runs counter to the primary aim of components analysis, to account for as much variation as possible. Components analysis, however, is not only nondeterministic; it also provides an exact spatial representation of the factor structures, so if the structures produced by the components approach are similar to those yielded by other factor analytic types, rotation of the components would appear to be more beneficial geographically. I have found this especially to be the case when the number of variables to be factored is small, and even more so when the factors are less important but still statistically significant [H. F. Gregor, "Factorial Reality and Spatial Exactness--An Empirical View," AAG Program Abstracts, New Orleans, 1978, ed. Robert C. West and

Clarissa Kimber (Washington, D.C.: Association of
American Geographers, 1978) p. 112].

5
The Types of Agricultural Industrialization

The availability of factor scores for both intensity and scale structures in agricultural capitalization logically suggest another, and final, step in our spatial summation of agricultural industrialization: the determination of types of industrialization based on the comparative levels of intensity and scale. Because intensity has proven itself more influential than scale in industrialization, we can also formulate a gauge of overall industrialization as we proceed with establishing typologies. What constitutes high, moderate, or low intensity and large, moderate, or small scale can be defined only relatively, using the standardized values of the factor scores. I have selected standard deviation values of 0.5 and -0.5 as sufficiently discriminating delimiters for the three intensity and scale levels, yet they are generous enough to ensure an adequate view of regional variation. In a normal (Gaussian) statistical distribution, this grouping framework makes one-third of the 3,036 U.S. counties studied eligible for each of the three classes. Of the various combinations of intensity and scale possible within this group format, five can be constructed in which some significant intensity or scale is demonstrated, i.e., over 0.5 standard deviation.

TYPES OF GENERAL AGRICULTURAL INDUSTRIALIZATION

When the comparative rankings of counties in the intensity and scale of general agricultural industrialization are evaluated, it becomes apparent that the national distribution pattern is quite different in several respects from the one of popular perception (Fig. 5.1). "Factory farms," as characterized by capitalization, may be considered most numerous in the southern part of the nation, but the industrialization process is actually much more extensive in the north, particularly in the Middle West and Northeast, where barriers to farm expansion are most formidable. The South, in contrast, a

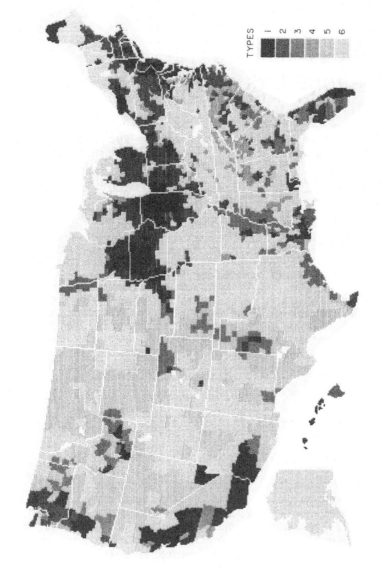

Figure 5.1. Types and levels of general agricultural industrialization

region with a long tradition of large scale farming operations, is less well represented even in some of its most favorable farming areas; on the Plains, the locale of the earlier "bonanza" wheat farms, only a minority of counties exhibit any important industrialization. The quintessence of industrialization types (Type 1: high intensity and large scale) also emphasizes the general pattern. This type is represented by 332 counties, the biggest share of which are in Illinois and Iowa, especially in the cash grain sections. Megalopolis and the Pacific Southwest also are prominent regions, as are smaller outliers like the specialty crop centers in central and southeastern Florida and along the Gulf Coast, the Ontario-Mohawk Plain, the Willamette Valley, and the interior oases of Washington and Idaho, and northern Maine. Type 1 counties comprise 11 percent of the U.S. total and 21 percent of the 1,564 counties having some significant agricultural industrialization.

The most extensive areal coverage, however, is reserved for the next most important type--Type 2: high intensity but moderate scale. A third (480) of all the counties with some important industrialization fit into this class, and they account for the majority of the advanced industrialization area in both the Middle West and Northeast, although there is also a quite noticeable distribution in western Washington and North Carolina. Livestock raising and dairying obviously play more of a part in this type of industrialization than they do in Type 1, but the intensive fruit and specialty crop production in many sections of some of the most important dairy areas must not be underestimated.

Type 3 agricultural industrialization, moderate intensity but large scale, claims the smallest number of counties (252) having some significant capitalization in both industrialization categories. But this group also has the most widespread distribution of areas of respectable size. The largest representation is in the South and includes most of the leading agricultural areas of the region: lower Mississippi Valley, South Atlantic Coastal Plain, and the western Gulf Coast. On the Great Plains it is the Red River Valley and the High Plains. In the Pacific Northwest it is the wheat-specialty portion of the Columbia Plateau and the Snake River Plains.

An important break occurs after the first three industrialization types, for now capitalization no longer attains high levels in both intensity and scale. Two types are represented, and both contrast sharply with each other as well. Type 4, representing general agricultural industrialization of high intensity but small scale, has 141 counties and the smallest representation of the industrialization types; it is also the most concentrated in distribution. A few widely scattered sections are found in northeastern United States, most notably in eastern Wisconsin and western Pennsylvania, but the major part is outlined by the poultry and livestock specializations in northern Alabama and Georgia, eastern Tennessee, and western North Carolina, and by tobacco-mixed crop farming in both Carolinas. Contrarily, Type 5, which denotes industrialization of large scale but low intensity, is one of the most extensively distributed of all five industrialization types; its 267 counties include the rangelands of much of the Great Plains and the Intermountain West. The remaining areas on the map, designated by Type 6, include all counties in which no significant industrialization (less than 0.5 standard deviation) was achieved in intensity or scale, and here the East is more prominent than the West.

The concentration of the highest levels of general agricultural industrialization in the populous Great Lakes and Megalopolis areas, as well as in the fertile Corn Belt and on the milder margins of the nation, raises the interesting question as to which has had the most immediate locational influence: markets or physical environment. A more detailed breakdown of the Type 1 distribution, using standard deviation values that ensure an approximately equal apportionment of counties among the classes, suggests the superiority of the environment, but not without strong urban leavening (Fig. 5.2). Both California and Florida, especially their southern parts, stand out, while in the Corn Belt, the very hearts of the prairie cores in Illinois and Iowa figure prominently, though not at the comparable California and Florida levels. On the other hand, Megalopolis is a supreme example of urban sway; Imperial County in California is surpassed by three counties in the New York metropolitan area for national leadership in industrialization (Table 5.1). Northeastern Illinois actually exceeds the industrialization levels of the more extensive sections downstate and in Iowa, and the market pull of Los Angeles and Miami certainly is not negligible.

TYPES OF INDUSTRIALIZATION IN CROPPING AND IN LIVESTOCK-POULTRY RAISING

Of the three typologies erected for agricultural industrialization--general, cropping, and livestock and poultry raising, cropping has the most extensive spread, with 1,781 (60 percent) of all U.S. counties having some significant scale or intensity (Fig. 5.3). The most important type, with both high intensity and large scale, is also more widespread than the same type in general agricultural industrialization. Its 502 counties not only essentially duplicate the main Type 1 areas of general capitalization, they also include the main southern agricultural areas beyond Florida: Mississippi alluvial lands, Texas Gulf Coast, Inner Coastal Plain.

193

Figure 5.2. Type 1 levels of general agricultural industrialization

Table 5.1. The twenty leading counties in both intensity and scale of general agricultural industrialization (over 1.64 standard deviations)[a]

	Intensity	Scale	Total			Intensity	Scale	Total
1. Nassau, N.Y.	4.97	1.98	6.95	11. Middlesex, Conn.	2.94	1.93	4.87
2. Union, N.J.	5.08	1.71	6.79	12. Broward, Fla.	2.26	2.58	4.84
3. Suffolk, N.Y.	3.65	2.30	5.95	13. Santa Cruz, Cal.	2.76	1.84	4.60
4. Imperial, Cal.	2.27	3.44	5.71	14. Orange, Cal.	2.23	2.30	4.53
5. Honolulu, Haw.	2.78	2.87	5.65	15. Ventura, Cal.	2.03	2.50	4.53
6. Dade, Fla.	2.95	2.44	5.39	16. Riverside, Cal.	2.11	2.39	4.50
7. Middlesex, N.J.	2.86	2.49	5.35	17. Orange, Fla.	2.02	2.46	4.48
8. Yuma, Ariz.	1.99	3.30	5.29	18. Delaware, Pa.	2.68	1.61	4.29
9. Hartford, Conn.	2.98	2.19	5.17	19. Westchester, N.Y.	2.65	1.62	4.27
10. Palm Beach, Fla.	1.69	3.36	5.05	20. Washington, R.I.	2.16	1.73	3.89

[a] Ranks are based on the totals of the county scores on the agricultural industrialization components for general agricultural intensity and scale.

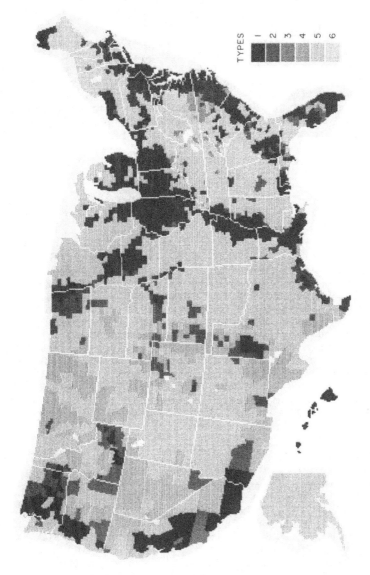

Figure 5.3. Types and levels of industrialization in cropping

Type 1 coverage also extends now to the Red River Valley and notably expands in the Columbia Basin and on the South Texas High Plains.

Type 2, highly intensive industrialized cropping but of only moderate scale, claims 355 counties that are like the Type 2 counties in general agricultural industrialization in their heavy focus on the Middle West and Northeast. Type 2 cropping industrialization, however, fails to include the principal cattle-feeder counties of the western Corn Belt. In contrast, the Type 2 area in the Carolinas is almost twice as large as it is for general industrialization.

The third type, constituting 182 counties with moderately intensive but large scale cropping industrialization, is now more a western phenomenon, dominating the Red River and Platte valleys, Colorado Piedmont, High Plains, Columbia Basin, and the Gila and Salt River basins in southern Arizona. Eastern representations are mostly in the South, where they include the majority of counties on the Texas Gulf Coast and in the Alabama Black Belt and furnish important fringes for the Type 1 areas in Georgia and Florida.

Counties with notable capitalization in only one of the two industrialization dimensions are much fewer than those in similar groups for general industrialization, although the distributions are still roughly the same. Only forth-nine counties represent Type 4, high intensity but small scale, but they are enough to outline clearly the oldest growing area for flue cured tobacco in the United States, the Piedmont of North Carolina and Virginia. Also quite area-specific is Type 5, low intensity but large scale, its 167 counties providing representation in all of the nineteen western states except Alaska and Hawaii. But with the emphasis on cropping, distribution is more restricted in the drier parts of the Great Plains and Colorado Plateaus than it is for the Type 5 representation in general agricultural industrialization. However, areas with no significant industrialization in intensity or scale, those of Type 6, are still more extensive in the eastern half of the country.

A more discriminating regionalization of Type 1 cropping industrialization, as was done for general industrialization, reveals a more southerly emphasis than is evident in the overall Type 1 pattern (Fig. 5.4). From this we can at least infer a greater locational role for growing conditions and a lesser one for urban influence than was evident in the detailed Type 1 distribution for general industrialization. This shift also shows up at a smaller scale, as in the improved position of the Central Valley in California compared with the southern part of the state and in the reduced gap between the Illinois Grand Prairie and northeastern Illinois; the Grand Prairie now surpasses the Iowa Prairie, though it

Figure 5.4. Type 1 levels of industrialization in cropping

falls behind the lower Mississippi Valley. On a leadcounty basis, however, the evidence is much less clear, with seven of the first nine counties in cropping industrialization appearing in Megalopolis (Table 5.2).

The proportion of counties with some significant industrialization in livestock or poultry raising is almost as great as that for general industrialization (54 percent vs 59 percent). But the 1,625 counties form a distribution pattern that is much more at odds with the patterns of both general and cropping industrialization (Fig. 5.5). The West is certainly better represented, although it does not overwhelm the national distribution as it does in just the scale of operations; in fact, it is still secondary to the East in areal coverage if only the two highest types of industrialization in livestock and poultry raising are considered. Distribution in much of the South is almost the converse of the cropping industrialization pattern, whereas in the North both divergence and overlap characterize the relationship between the two spatial orderings. The tendency of livestock and poultry industrialization to locate in important cropping areas in some places and less cropped areas in others is best illustrated by the locations of the two leading industrialization types. Type 1, with 299 counties, involves the greatest number of farmers in the feeder center of eastern Nebraska and western Iowa, and Type 2, with 566 counties, greatly expands that center to include much of the western Corn Belt and the western Dairy Belt in Wisconsin and Minnesota. Both types, however, fail to appear in much of the eastern Middle West, partly because of more emphasis on cash cropping, and partly because of the smaller farms and greater incidence of part-time farming. Both types also have important representations in the Northeast, but more specialized cropping and pressures of urbanization make for blank spots along the lower Great Lakes and the Atlantic Seaboard. In the South, Types 1 and 2 account for and share almost all important industrialization centers, very few of which are in the better croplands; in the West, where intensity falls off rapidly with distance from irrigated lands and population centers, Type 2 has little showing and Type 1 closely correlates with cultivated areas. Southern California and southern Arizona, central California, and western Washington are most favored, but Type 1 counties are also scattered across the Intermountain area and the southern Plains.

The best showing in the West, however, is provided by Type 3, moderately intensive but large scale industrialization. The type is almost exclusively a western one, though counties in the more important livestock areas of Florida are also represented. Type 3 adds a transitional zone on the western edge of the Corn Belt, in South Dakota and Nebraska; it outlines much of the High Plains

Table 5.2. The twenty leading counties in both intensity and scale of industrialization in cropping (over 2.05 standard deviations)[a]

	Intensity	Scale	Total		Intensity	Scale	Total
1. Queens, N.Y.	7.08	2.52	9.60	11. Sutter, Cal.	2.46	2.72	5.18
2. Union, N.J.	5.87	2.35	8.22	12. Palm Beach, Fla.	2.09	3.07	5.16
3. Nassau, N.Y.	5.69	2.48	8.17	13. Orange, Fla.	2.32	2.45	4.77
4. Suffolk, N.Y.	4.39	2.62	7.01	14. St. John the Baptist, La.	2.11	2.60	4.71
5. Dade, Fla.	3.78	2.70	6.48	15. Lake, Fla.	2.32	2.29	4.61
6. Middlesex, N.J.	3.11	2.61	5.72	16. St. Johns, Fla.	2.08	2.52	4.60
7. Northampton, Va.	2.85	2.65	5.50	17. Assumption, La.	2.07	2.52	4.59
8. Kauai, Haw.	2.07	3.17	5.24	18. Ventura, Cal.	2.15	2.41	4.56
9. Hartford, Conn.	2.95	2.28	5.23	19. Orange, Cal.	2.20	2.30	4.50
10. Santa Cruz, Cal.	3.12	2.06	5.18	20. St. James, La.	2.15	2.06	4.21

[a] Ranks are based on the totals of the county scores on the agricultural industrialization components for cropping intensity and scale.

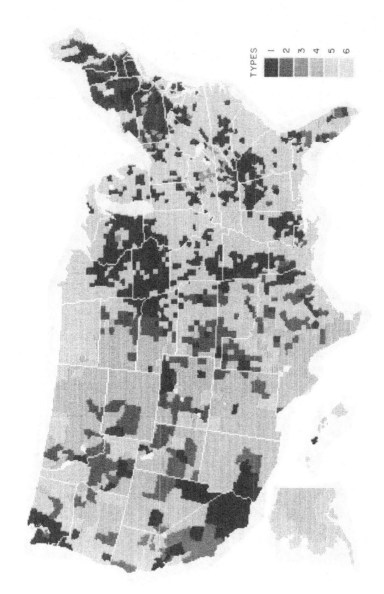

Figure 5.5. Types and levels of industrialization in livestock and poultry raising

and lesser areas in the Flint Hills and in central and eastern Texas; it takes in a good part of the San Joaquin Valley and surrounding rangeland; and it claims large areas in the Intermountain region, including respectable portions of the Snake Basin, Wyoming Basin, Gila and Salt basins in Arizona, Western Slope of Colorado, and basin lands of Utah.

The remaining two industrialization types, those lacking even moderate capitalization in either intensity or volume, resemble the same types for general and cropping industrialization. Type 4, with high intensity but small scale, has the least county representation (42) of any agricultural industrialization type. The counties nevertheless are consolidated enough to outline areas of smaller dairy and cattle farms in central Kentucky, eastern Tennessee, and southwestern Virginia, although an important secondary area of smaller dairy farms around the major manufacturing complex of western Pennsylvania and northeastern Ohio can also be recognized. Industrialization of low intensity but large scale is again a western monopoly, and it takes up the vast proportion of the territory not included by the other industrialization types; even Alaska figures in this expansive distribution, the only time it is represented by an industrialization type. And again, Type 6 counties, those with no significant agricultural industrialization in intensity or scale, are more prominent in the East.

Yet another view of the often wide differences between the distribution of industrialization in livestock and poultry raising and the patterns of general and cropping industrialization is offered by the more detailed resolution of the distribution of the most important livestock-poultry type (Fig. 5.6). Unlike the other two maps using this approach (Figs. 5.2 and 5.4), this one shows considerably less correlation of its overall pattern with either major cropping or market centers. The difference is not so great, however, that one would fail to recognize the influence of nearby markets on the prominence of southeastern California and southwestern Arizona, as well as some counties on the fringe of Megalopolis; nor is it so large that one would overlook the pertinence of readily accessible rich feed supplies to the conspicuousness of the eastern Nebraska-western Iowa center. Some resemblance to the southern orientation in cropping industrialization can also be detected, with sixteen of the leading twenty counties in livestock and poultry industrialization located in the southern half of the country (Table 5.3). However, most of these important counties outline a quite different pattern from that of cropping industrialization.

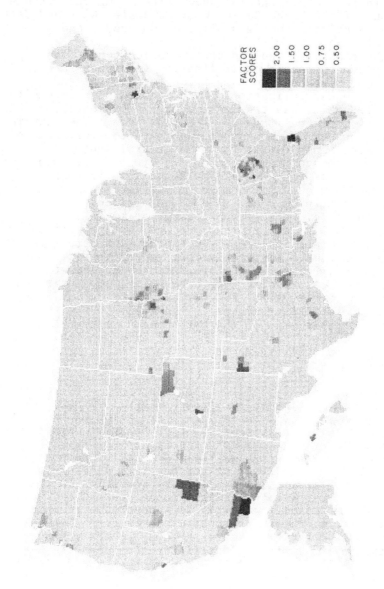

Figure 5.6. Type 1 levels of industrialization in livestock and poultry raising

Table 5.3. The twenty leading countries in both intensity and scale of industrialization in livestock and poultry raising (over 1.47 standard deviations)[a]

	Intensity	Scale	Total			Intensity	Scale	Total
1. Douglas, Ga.	3.12	1.89	5.01	11. Imperial, Cal.	2.02	2.20	4.22
2. Stanton, Neb.	2.38	1.48	4.86	12. Cuming, Neb.	2.54	1.63	4.17
3. Sullivan, N.Y.	2.88	1.89	4.77	13. Riverside, Cal.	2.22	1.91	4.13
4. Nassau, Fla.	2.65	2.10	4.75	14. Sarpy, Neb.	2.37	1.53	3.90
5. Lumpkin, Ga.	3.16	1.57	4.73	15. Deaf Smith, Tex.	1.71	2.12	3.83
6. Hinsdale, Colo.	1.94	2.68	4.62	16. Honolulu, Haw.	2.18	1.49	3.67
7. Duval, Fla.	2.47	2.07	4.54	17. Randall, Tex.	1.49	2.17	3.66
8. Marin, Cal.	1.78	2.68	4.46	18. Putnam, Ga.	1.92	1.73	3.65
9. Sabine, Tex.	2.96	1.48	4.44	19. Lincoln, Nev.	1.83	1.78	3.61
10. Washington, Ark.	2.85	1.54	4.39	20. Parmer, Tex.	1.53	1.76	3.29

[a] Ranks are based on the totals of the county scores on the agricultural industrialization components for the intensity and scale of livestock and poultry raising.

TYPES OF LIMITED INDUSTRIALIZED AGRICULTURE

So far we have not devoted much attention to geographical patterns of limited agricultural industrialization. Yet if we accept overall farming prosperity as synonomous with a high level of capitalization, then it is exactly these "negative" distributions that become the objects of most immediate social concern. For these patterns we can turn to the counties that failed to qualify for any of the five types of significant industrialization. Four types of intensity-scale combinations can be defined at this lower level, and they complete the number of discrete pairs that can be extracted from the scores using 0.5 and -0.5 as class breaks; their combined distribution thus complements that of significant industrialization and corresponds to the area represented in Figs. 5.1, 5.3, and 5.5 by the undifferentiated Type 6. The ordering of these four additional types, however, is reversed from that used on the other maps so as to correspond with the emphasis on least industrialization (Fig. 5.7). The fifth type shown on the maps of limited industrialized agriculture refers to areas with at least some significant industrialization in either intensity or scale.

The distribution of areas with at best only moderate intensity and scale of general agricultural industrialization clearly demonstrates that capitalization, no matter how advanced overall, is still discouraged in wide sections of the country, and that much of the problem is the poorer promise of returns in the more difficult physical environments and the partial concomitant of those conditions, isolation from major markets. Moreover, as agricultural industrialization increasingly favors the better farming areas, it deepens and widens the economic slough in which the inhabitants of the less favored areas find themselves. The correlation of environmental handicaps with low levels of agricultural industrialization is also evidenced by the predominance in the western patterns of the two most under-capitalized types (Type 1: low intensity and small scale, and Type 2: low intensity but moderate scale), whereas in the East, with its generally better physical and market conditions, the less-capitalized types are comparatively less inferior. Evidence is no less clear at a lower regional level. Alaska is the most extensive regional example, with the Fairbanks area topping all counties in negative intensity and scale values for general agricultural industrialization (Table 5.4). In the coterminous United States, the Ozark-Quachita Highlands join with the eroded plateau surfaces of central Texas and the hilly Cross Timbers of eastern Texas to form the most extensive section of limited industrialized land, with ten of the twenty lowest-ranking counties in general industriali-

205

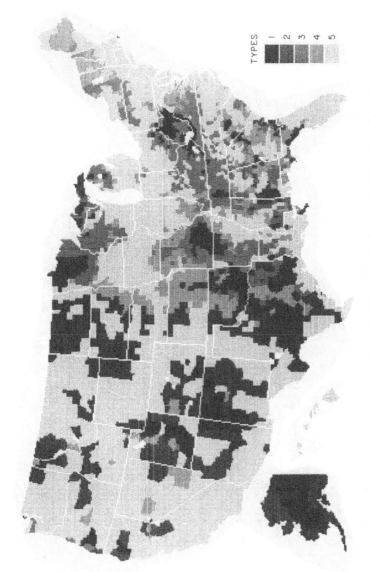

Figure 5.7. Types and levels of limited industrialized agriculture

Table 5.4. Twenty lowest ranking counties in both intensity and scale of general agricultural industrialization (over -1.15 standard deviations)[a]

	Intensity	Scale	Total		Intensity	Scale	Total
1. Fairbanks, Alas.	-3.25	-1.80	-5.05	11. Kimble, Tex.	-2.07	-1.24	-3.31
2. Brewster, Tex.	-2.82	-1.16	-3.98	12. Reynolds, Mo.	-1.32	-1.94	-3.26
3. Boone, W. Va.	-1.43	-2.44	-3.87	13. Glynn, Ga.	-1.81	-1.43	-3.24
4. Calhoun, W. Va.	-1.53	-2.28	-3.81	14. Latimer, Okla.	-1.69	-1.55	-3.24
5. Doddridge, W. Va.	-1.44	-2.19	-3.63	15. Burnet, Tex.	-1.60	-1.41	-3.01
6. Carson City, Nev.	-2.01	-1.38	-3.39	16. Pocahontas, W. Va.	-1.28	-1.70	-2.98
7. Ritchie, W. Va.	-1.28	-2.10	-3.38	17. Harlan, Ky.	-1.21	-1.73	-2.94
8. Shoshone, Ida.	-1.55	-1.79	-3.34	18. Gilmer, W. Va.	-1.16	-1.75	-2.91
9. Taos, N. M.	-2.03	-1.30	-3.33	19. Pushamtaha, Okla.	-1.50	-1.37	-2.87
10. Jack, Tex.	-1.74	-1.58	-3.32	20. Creek, Okla.	-1.23	-1.59	-2.82

[a] Ranks are based on the totals of the county scores on the agricultural industrialization components for general agricultural intensity and scale.

zation intensity and scale within its boundaries. Extensive sections of deficit industrialization are also located on the Colorado Plateaus, the Great Plains, in the Great Lakes Cutover, and in Appalachia.

On the margins of these deficit industrialization centers, however, where environmental conditions are less severe and isolation is less, delimitation is less clear cut and subject even more to the arbitrary class breaks used for the typology. Scale of capitalization is still great enough to exclude large blocks of the West from the areas defined as having no significant industrialization, while in the East intensity is high enough to exclude poultry farming areas from the less industrialized areas of the Piedmont and dairying areas from the deficiently industrialized Cutover and Appalachia. In contrast, areas with more favorable physical resources, like much of the subhumid Winter Wheat Belt and the Texas Grand and Blackland prairies, are included within the pattern of no significant industrialization.

The peripheries of the limited industrialized areas also have particular pertinence because a larger number of farmers suffering from the competition of the more industrialized regions generally locate here. More farmers also hinder industrialization by making it difficult to expand the land resource. The handicap of small farm size is vividly illustrated by the inferior industrialization ranking (Type 3: moderate intensity but small scale) of the Nashville and Blue Grass basins, both above-average agricultural regions but also the most populated parts of the areas without significant agricultural industrialization.

The unfavorable implications of a larger farm population are of course not restricted to the much less industrialized agricultural economies. Even more farmers and farm laborers feel the pressures of industrialization within the regions of significant agricultural capitalization, although competitiveness often takes place on a finer, intraregional scale, and rural unemployment is commonly exported to less fortunate farming regions with the homeward flows of migrant workers.

What has been said about the distribution of the limited industrialized types of general agricultural industrialization can be repeated even more for the patterns of limited industrialized cropping. With emphasis on cultivation, environmental conditions become even more crucial in the calculations of farm operators, and this is reflected in the expanded coverage for all four types of industrialization falling below the significant level (Fig. 5.8). The West is still more conspicuous, but more because of the expansion of Type 2 than Type 1. The single most extensive distribution of Type 1 in the coterminous United States, running through Missouri, Arkansas, Oklahoma, and Texas, also becomes larger; its

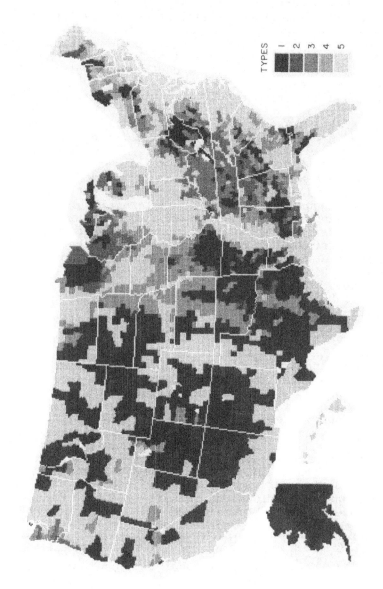

Figure 5.8. Types and levels of limited industrialized cropping

enlargement is the principal reason for the almost 50 percent increase in the number of Type 1 counties over those of little general agricultural industrialization (467 vs 265). Domination by this region of the Type 1 counties also shows up in the list of the twenty counties ranking lowest in both cropping intensity and scale, with fourteen in this one area, nine just in Texas (Table 5.5). Southern Appalachia owes most of its wider distribution to the increase in counties of Type 3. The biggest addition comes from inclusion of the poultry areas in Alabama, Georgia, and North Carolina. Type 4 patterns, representing moderate intensity and scale in cropping industrialization, reach out from eastern Kansas and northern Missouri to include most of the cattle and hog feeding areas of the Corn Belt west of Illinois as well. Only the cash grain section of north-central Iowa and southern Minnesota remain within the limits of significant industrialization in this part of the belt.

The less favored position of livestock raising in agricultural industrialization is well shown by the distribution of the limited industrialized types, for in the majority of the areas where land has proven eventually very good for cropping (and therefore a good base for a combined livestock-crop economy), the opportunity has been rejected for a cash crop. This rejection has been so complete that these areas include most of the principal centers of the lowest level of livestock industrialization: Spring Wheat Belt, Grand Prairie of Illinois, South Atlantic Coastal Plain, lower Mississippi Valley, and large strips of the Gulf Coast (Fig. 5.9). The leadership of the South in number of major regions of minimum livestock industrialization is also borne out by individualized county rankings; seventeen of the twenty counties that are lowest in both intensity and scale are in the South, and all but one of those are situated in the Lower Alluvial Valley (Table 5.6). Less spectacular illustrations are the Type 3 patterns in the eastern Middle West and the Type 4 patterns in the subhumid Winter Wheat Belt. Still more examples can be detected at a lower regional level: Maumee Valley, Aroostook County, centers in central and extreme southeastern Florida, Texas High Plains south of Lubbock, Palouse, and Willamette and Sacramento valleys, to name the most obvious. A material exception to this mutual exclusiveness of cropping and livestock industrialization can be noted in most of the highly productive irrigated lands of California and southern Arizona, although the combination in many sections may be more a function of aggregate data than farming enterprise.

Though livestock industrialization is least important in premium cropping areas, it also is discouraged by poorer physical environments. Extremely low capitalization marks the coastal lands of Alaska and scattered

Table 5.5. The twenty-one lowest ranking counties in both intensity and scale of industrialization in cropping (over -1.32 standard deviations)[a]

	Intensity	Scale	Total		Intensity	Scale	Total
1. Fairbanks, Alas.	-2.55	-2.63	-5.18	12. Burnet, Tex.	-1.58	-1.66	-3.24
2. Brewster, Tex.	-2.18	-2.19	-4.37	13. Lewis, W. Va.	-1.33	-1.91	-3.24
3. Catron, N.M.	-2.24	-1.69	-3.93	14. Real, Tex.	-1.74	-1.38	-3.12
4. Calhoun, W. Va.	-1.48	-2.23	-3.71	15. Creek, Okla.	-1.34	-1.71	-3.05
5. Edwards, Tex.	-1.93	-1.69	-3.62	16. Highland, Va.	-1.33	-1.69	-3.02
6. Jack, Tex.	-1.71	-1.82	-3.53	17. Lampasas, Tex.	-1.62	-1.39	-3.01
7. Carson City, Nev.	-1.76	-1.73	-3.49	18. Taos, N.M.	-1.57	-1.36	-2.93
8. Kimble, Tex.	-1.77	-1.62	-3.39	19. Haskell, Okla.	-1.35	-1.55	-2.90
9. Taney, Mo.	-1.36	-1.97	-3.33	20. Glynn, Ga.	-1.41	-1.45	-2.86
10. Llano, Tex.	-1.76	-1.52	-3.28	21. Gonzales, Tex.	-1.43	-1.34	-2.77
11. Ozark, Mo.	-1.35	-1.91	-3.26				

[a] Ranks are based on the totals of the county scores on the agricultural industrialization components for cropping intensity and scale.

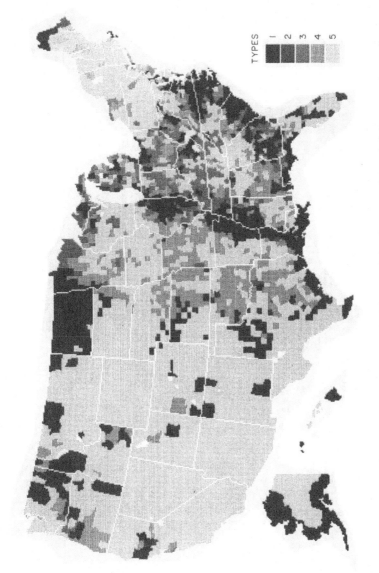

Figure 5.9. Types and levels of limited industrialized livestock and poultry raising

Table 5.6. The twenty lowest ranking counties in both intensity and scale of industrialization in livestock and poultry raising (over -2.15 standard deviations)[a]

	Intensity	Scale	Total			Intensity	Scale	Total
1. Queens, N.Y.	-3.92	-9.93	-13.85	11. Mississippi, Ark.	-2.70	-2.67	-5.37
2. St. John the Baptist, La.	-2.86	-4.24	-7.10	12. Quitman, Miss.	-2.64	-2.55	-5.19
3. Assumption, La.	-2.90	-3.47	-6.37	13. Arkansas, Ark.	-2.65	-2.44	-5.09
4. Monroe, Ark.	-2.84	-3.43	-6.27	14. Humphreys, Miss.	-2.61	-2.40	-5.01
5. Chelan, Wash.	-2.41	-3.68	-6.09	15. Aroostook, Me.	-2.17	-2.80	-4.97
6. Poinsett, Ark.	-2.68	-2.88	-5.56	16. St. Mary, La.	-2.64	-2.16	-4.80
7. Pemiscot, Mo.	-2.64	-2.89	-5.53	17. St. Francis, Ark.	-2.55	-2.18	-4.73
8. St. Bernard, La.	-2.34	-3.17	-5.51	18. Craighead, Ark.	-2.16	-2.53	-4.69
9. Crittenden, Ark.	-2.85	-2.53	-5.38	19. Cross, Ark.	-2.48	-2.20	-4.68
10. Lake, Tenn.	-2.73	-2.64	-5.37	20. Gulf, Fla.	-2.31	-2.37	-4.68

[a]Ranks are based on the totals of the county scores on the agricultural industrialization components for the intensity and scale of livestock and poultry raising.

counties in the mountains and plateaus of the coterminous West. In the eastern half of the country, capitalization is not quite as low in many of the counties of little significant industrialization, although negative ratings are much more widespread; most of these areas are of more irregular terrain, but smaller farm sizes are also an impediment.

6
The Performance of Agricultural Industrialization

Although advanced agricultural industrialization correlates fairly well with areas of superior physical environment and market access, there is no reason to assume that it is equally successful throughout these areas in the achievement of economic goals. Physical conditions, even where they are better, vary greatly from place to place, and market centers vary even more in relationship of numbers and size to the pattern of high-quality land. Cost of inputs, quality of management, individual attitudes, and certainly the role of chance must also be added to the list of performance variegators both within and without the better farming areas. But knowing where and how well agricultural productivity and profitability covary with agricultural industrialization allows us to assess, at least spatially, how successful that industrialization has been in achieving its production objectives. And, success--even survival--being what it is, the covariation pattern also can offer clues as to where industrialization might increase in a major way.

Economic success, of course, should not be confused with farming efficiency. Productivity and profitability are only two aspects of farming efficiency, and even they have become increasingly associated with internal and external diseconomies. But personal gain has been a driving force behind agricultural industrialization, a stimulus firmly rooted in both economic necessity and the national ethic, and unless decided otherwise by society, it will continue to exert heavy influence. Thus the patterns of production and profit must be especially studied if not only fair but realizable policy decisions are to be made.

PRODUCTIVITY AND INDUSTRIALIZATION

National surveys of productivity distribution in American agriculture have usually used value of sales as the basic indicator. But as the farm has become more like a firm in the volume and variety of intermediate products that it uses, a productivity criterion commonly used by manufacturing analysts becomes more useful. This is value added, and it refers to what is left after the costs of purchases from other sources are subtracted from the payments and net profit of the firm. As such, it is the contribution to the national income or gross national product (GNP).[1] In agricultural terms, it is what remains of farm-related income after expenditures for plants, seeds, bulbs, livestock, poultry, fertilizers and other chemicals, machine hire and customwork, hand labor, fuel, and other farming inputs are deducted.

County census data are now available for computation of a national distribution pattern of value added by agriculture, although this opportunity by no means eliminates methodological and statistical problems, common afflictions of all productivity indicators. Expenditures for machine hire and customwork, for example, can be viewed either as wages, thus qualifying them for inclusion in the output of goods and services, or as expenditures primarily for machinery and equipment, thereby requiring them to be deducted as payments for products of other firms. I have chosen the latter interpretation, although it certainly denies the labor value inherent in these expenditures and consequently may distort regional relationships where areal distributions of mechanization and hand labor are fairly distinct from each other. Some economists have also questioned the continued usefulness of value added as a gauge of farm productivity, because off-farm manufacturing of agricultural inputs and off-farm processing of agricultural outputs keeps growing.[2] Presumably such a development would reinforce rather than diminish the leadership of the major areas of value added as now computed, but no firm evidence can be obtained until some means of extricating the information from the maze of input and output statistics can be found. Even the census data, as comprehensive as they are, are not beyond reservation; total production expenditures for 1969 (and 1974) are heavily weighted by the reporting of "all other production expenses," a category open enough to possible misinterpretation or underestimation by farmers that the Census Bureau has recommended caution in its use in any calculation.[3]

When value added is related to farm acreage and farm numbers, the distribution patterns that are produced bear out what one might expect from advanced agricultural capitalization: a correspondingly high level of productivity (Figs. 6.1 and 6.2). But the relationship is certainly not of a one-to-one order, and it is closer for the intensity of industrialization than it is for its scale (Table 6.1). Labor and land capitalization are also more important in productivity than they are in the industrialization structures for intensity and scale.

217

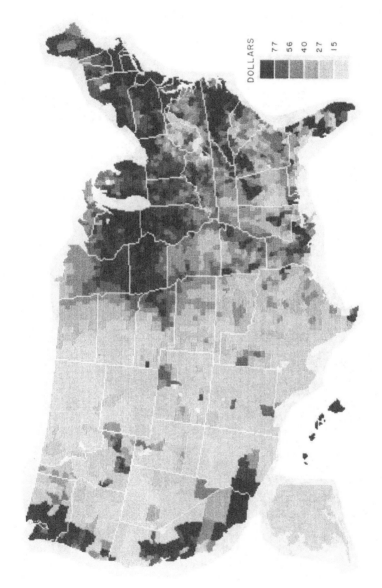

Figure 6.1. Value added per farm acre

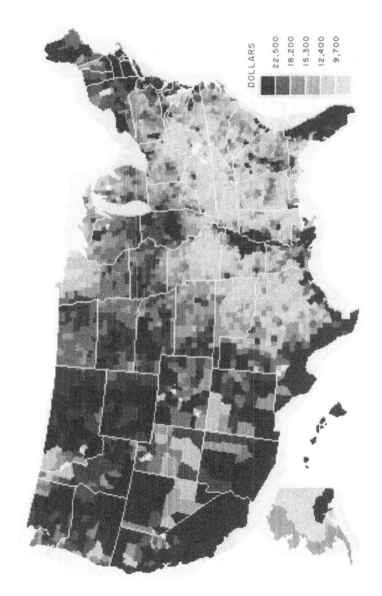

Figure 6.2. Value added per farm

Table 6.1. Correlations of productivity and profitability indicators with agricultural industrialization variables[a]

Industrialization Intensity

Indicators	LBINVA	LREXPA	MEINVA	MFEXPA	CRINVA	CREXPA	LVINVA	LVEXPA	Average
Value added/farm acre	.855	.973	.925	.916	.803	.839	.621	.666	.825
Net value of products sold/farm acre	.145	.152	.132	.174	.154	.144	.174	.136	.151

Industrialization Scale

Indicators	LBINVF	LREXPF	MEINVF	MFEXPF	CRINVF	CREXPF	LVINVF	LVEXPF	Average
Value added/farm	.675	.892	.715	.749	.602	.478	.273	.295	.585
Net value of products sold/farm	.097	.155	.194	.169	.247	.214	-.012	.149	.152
Net farm income/operator-equivalent	.354	.310	.500	.538	.475	.426	.041	.171	.352

[a]Key to the variables represented by the mnemonics is given in tables 4.1 and 4.8.

These modifications of the production-industrialization ratio are great enough to show up regionally. Above-median production intensity (over $40 per farm acre) in the interior and upper Northeast and in the upper Great Lakes area is clearly not as constrained by marginal physical conditions and by isolation as is industrialization intensity (Figs. 6.1 and 4.1). Production intensity also is somewhat more independent of industrialization even in a few favored cropping areas, most notably the tobacco and mixed crops area of Virginia and the Carolinas, the Sacramento Valley, and the Willamette Valley. The greater part of the southern croplands, however, displays the reverse of this production-industrialization ratio, with industrialization not even sufficient to maintain an equivalent measure of productivity. A similar deficit situation is to be found on the southern Plains.

With the added variable of farm size, areal correlations between the scales of production and general agricultural industrialization become even less powerful, though they remain statistically significant. Production scale in the Northeast that is above the median (more than $15,300 per farm) clearly surpasses the levels of large industrialization scale in areas of both economic disadvantage and advantage--including northern Megalopolis (Figs. 6.2 and 4.4). This also holds true, though to a lesser extent, in the Dairy Belt in Wisconsin and Minnesota. The scale of production is also slightly superior to that of industrialization on the northern Plains and even more so in the middle and lower Rio Grande Valley. But again, the ratio is reversed in the South, where the generally impressive scale of industrialization is not enough to remedy the low production volume of much of the Inner Coastal Plain. Again, too, the southern Plains share in this relatively lower ranking of production volume. Discrepancies like these, however, should not necessarily be accepted as evidence of overall industrialization diseconomies, as we shall see.

Because there is a generally good correlation between productivity and the intensity and scale of industrialization, we can expect a regional ranking of productivity similar to that constructed for the typologies of agricultural industrialization. Thus production is both extremely intensive (Class I: more than $77 per farm acre) and massive (Class I: more than $22,500 per farm) in the majority of counties representing the leading type of general agricultural industrialization. Similarly, insufficient production volume marks less industrialized types in the Middle West and Northeast, and inferior production intensity characterizes even less industrialized types in the South and West. Intraregional similarities also exist, as can be seen in a comparison of the twenty leading counties in production intensity and scale with those in the same two categories of industrialization; both production and industrialization intensities reach their peak in Megalopolis, whereas their scale peaks in the Pacific Southwest and Florida (Tables 6.2 and 4.3, and 6.3 and 4.10).

PROFITABILITY AND INDUSTRIALIZATION

Productivity is inseparable from profitability, but the variation between the two makes it wise to consider profits as well as production in evaluating the success of agricultural industrialization. However, as the restrictions and subsidies of government farm programs exert more influence on production decisions, and as farmers seek sources of farm income beyond their own farm in their efforts to maintain solvency, the difficulty of measuring monetarily the true extent of economic achievement in farm operations increases. Although there seems little chance that the problem--particularly the conceptual difficulty of differentiating crop control subsidies from profits--will be solved in the near future, census data make it possible to compute what the Census Bureau labels "net value of farm products sold." This form of net income is obtained by subtracting total farm production expenses (including here my estimated expenditures for operator labor)[4] from the estimated market value of all agricultural products sold. A small part of these expenditures, though, is for farming activities off the farm, and all expenditures are subject to the reservations already noted on possible reporting errors. The value of farm products consumed at home is not reported, and this statistic I have included through estimation.[5]

After dividing farm acreage and farm numbers into the net value of farm sales, it becomes quite obvious that profit making, in both intensity and scale, is much less a function of agricultural industrialization than is production. Its correlations with all the ratio variables for industrialization, though almost all positive and statistically significant, are considerably weaker (Table 6.1). Field labor and land capitalization, most important in both intensity and scale of production, no longer prevail. Yet there is no outstanding contribution by any of the capitalization inputs to either the intensity or scale of net sales income, although a slight tilt toward machine hire, mechanized labor, and livestock investment can be recognized for intensity, and a favoring of mechanization and cropping can be observed for scale.

Spatially, the result is a much more dispersed pattern for both intensity and scale of net sales yields. The East-West contrast so evident in the intensity of value added is now somewhat softened as large areas on

Table 6.2. The twenty leading counties in value added per farm acre[a]

	Dollars		Dollars
1. Queens, N.Y. (C)	27,771	11. Hartford, Conn. (C,G)	533
2. Hudson, N.J.	6,632	12. Dade, Fla. (C,G)	521
3. Suffolk, Mass. (C,G)	5,939	13. Santa Cruz, Cal. (C,G)	505
4. Union, N.J. (C,G)	2,990	14. Hood River, Ore. (C,G)	487
5. Nassau, N.Y. (C,G)	2,169	15. Summit, O. (C,G)	467
6. Cuyahoga, O. (C,G)	1,228	16. Middlesex, Conn. (C,L,G)	452
7. Passaic, N.J.	1,085	17. Honolulu, Haw.(C,L,G)	444
8. Bergen, N.J. (C,G)	839	18. Middlesex, Mass. (C,G)	436
9. Suffolk, N.Y. (C,G)	563	19. Atlantic, N.J. (C,G)	424
10. Lake, O. (C,G)	557	20. Ramsey, Minn. (C,G)	408

[a]Counties with some significant agricultural industrialization are coded for the particular industrialization emphasis: C = cropping; L = livestock and poultry raising; G = general.

Table 6.3. The twenty leading counties in value added per farm[a]

	Dollars		Dollars
1. Maui, Haw. (C,G)	247,720	11. Yuma, Ariz. (C,L,G)	96,212
2. Hendry, Fla. (C)	238,624	12. Martin, Fla. (C,G)	91,606
3. Palm Beach, Fla. (C,G)	223,043	13. Maricopa, Ariz. (L,G)	85,949
4. Kauai, Haw. (C,G)	185,629	14. Ventura, Cal. (C,G)	84,805
5. Imperial, Cal. (C,L,G)	140,983	15. Dade, Fla. (C,G)	81,593
6. Collier, Fla. (C)	140,785	16. Okeechobee, Fla. (L)	80,693
7. Kern, Cal.	130,356	17. Yolo, Cal. (C,G)	76,863
8. Monterey, Cal. (C,G)	115,495	18. Lee, Fla. (C,G)	76,648
9. Pinal, Ariz.	113,537	19. Gadsden, Fla. (C,G)	72,949
10. Honolulu, Haw. (C,L,G)	111,712	20. Colusa, Cal. (C,G)	72,922

[a]Counties with some significant agricultural industrialization are coded for the particular industrialization emphasis: C = cropping; L = livestock and poultry raising; G = general.

the Plains and in the Intermountain area improve their position; nevertheless, except for favored areas like the Red River Valley, Platte Valley, High Plains, and the smaller oases, intensity still is not sufficient to surpass the national median of $1 per farm acre (Fig. 6.3). The modification is even more for scale, for it is almost impossible to determine which half of the country is areally superior in above-median value (more than $700 per farm) (Fig. 6.4). Differences between the northeastern quarter and the South also are narrowed in both intensity and scale of net sales, although there is no doubt about the location of the largest Class I area in both categories (more than $10 per farm acre and more than $2,800 per farm): the Corn Belt and an offshoot into the dairy state of Wisconsin. Nevertheless, profits from poultry, tobacco, rice, sugarcane, citrus, vegetables, and other specialty crops have been great enough to give the South the preponderant share of the twenty leading counties for both intensity and scale; only two Corn Belt counties are included (Tables 6.4 and 6.5). Differences in cropping emphasis and in wage levels especially account for this southern advantage.

Such regional variations suggest more profitable agricultural industrialization in the West and South than elsewhere, but there are other spatial discrepancies between net sales indicators and industrialization that suggest even more an inefficiency of industrialization. Though on a smaller areal scale, these discrepancies occur in sections with some of the highest capitalization inputs in the nation. Most visible on both maps are large sections of the mid-Atlantic Seaboard and Mississippi bottomlands and the heart of the San Joaquin Valley; smaller examples of this disparity include parts of the Inner Coastal Plain in South Carolina and Georgia, the Texas High Plains in the vicinity of Lubbock, and southernmost Michigan and parts of the Western Michigan Fruit Belt. All of these productive agricultural areas rank with little-industrialized counties in such places as the Ozark Highlands, Great Lakes Cutover, and deserts and mountains of the West in having the greatest net sales deficits--more than a $2 loss per farm acre and more than $900 per farm. The especially large divergence of net sales from agricultural industrialization in the Megalopolis region suggests a number of possible causes. With the heaviest farming inputs per acre in the nation, operational costs are placing the region at an increasing disadvantage compared with other areas where better growing conditions and more land make it possible to produce more cheaply. Much of the farming in the Megalopolis area is also by its very nature expensive, for farms emphasizing fruit and truck, poultry, and dairy products have high expense turnovers, i.e., high ratios of short-period expenditures to output for harvesting

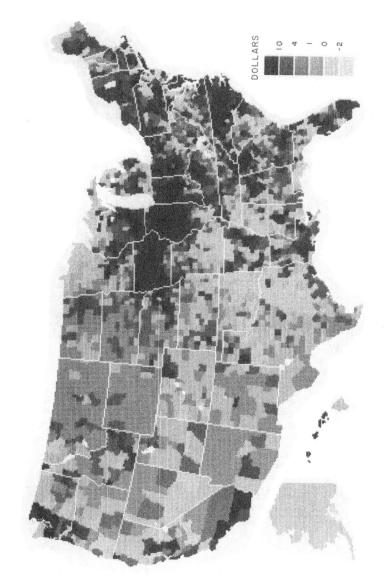

Figure 6.3. Net Value of farm products sold per farm acre

Table 6.4. The twenty leading counties in net value of farm products sold per farm acre[a]

	Dollars		Dollars
1. Queens, N.Y. (C)	3,528	11. Orange, Fla. (C,G)	56
2. Suffolk, Mass. (C,G)	764	12. Multnomah, Ore.	55
3. Cuyahoga, O. (C,G)	226	13. Simpson, Miss. (L)	50
4. Union, N.J. (C,G)	212	14. Gadsden, Fla. (C,G)	48
5. Summit, O. (C,G)	137	15. Cullman, Ala. (L)	48
6. Dade, Fla. (C,G)	99	16. Lake, Fla. (C,G)	48
7. Nassau, N.Y. (C,G)	89	17. Wilson, N.C.	47
8. Honolulu, Haw. (C,L,G)	75	18. Hall, Ga. (L)	45
9. Union, Ga.	61	19. Delaware, Pa. (C,G)	45
10. Merrick, Neb. (L,G)	60	20. Sarpy, Neb. (L,G)	45

[a] Counties with some significant agricultural industrialization are coded for the particular industrialization emphasis: C = cropping; L = livestock and poultry raising; G = general.

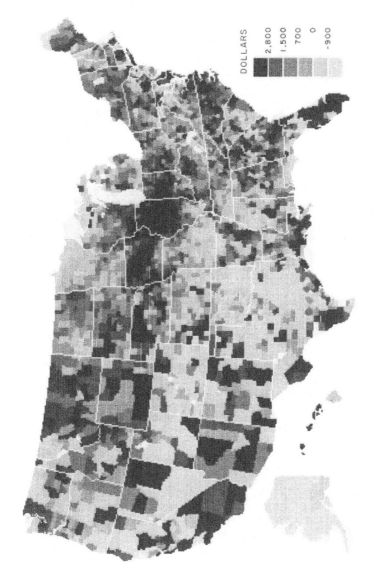

Figure 6.4. Net value of farm products sold per farm

Table 6.5. The twenty leading counties in net value of farm products sold per farm[a]

	Dollars		Dollars
1. Hendry, Fla. (C)	56,074	11. Pershing, Nev.	17,193
2. Maui, Haw. (C,G)	47,401	12. Orange, Fla. (C,G)	16,435
3. Palm Beach, Fla. (C,G)	26,790	13. Collier, Fla. (C)	15,909
4. Merrick, Neb. (L,G)	23,125	14. Dade, Fla. (C,G)	15,537
5. Deaf Smith, Tex. (L)	23,078	15. Arkansas, Ark. (C)	15,164
6. Gadsden, Fla. (C,G)	19,918	16. Highlands, Fla.	14,377
7. Colusa, Cal. (C,G)	18,916	17. Lake, Fla. (C,G)	14,030
8. Honolulu, Haw. (C,L,G)	18,742	18. Grant, Neb.	13,803
9. Jeff Davis, Tex.	17,713	19. Haskell, Kan.	13,769
10. Summit, O. (C,G)	17,436	20. Imperial, Cal.(C,L,G)	13,450

[a]Counties with some significant agricultural industrialization are coded for the particular industrialization emphasis: C = cropping; L = livestock and poultry raising; G = general.

labor, sprays, boxes and crates, and the like. Higher land costs, particularly close to the cities, add to the burden, though horticulture, with its especially large returns and smaller off-farm inputs, may still overcome the heavy expense. This would seem to be at least part of the explanation for the maintenance of high national rankings for counties in southeastern Pennsylvania and in the New York metropolitan area; the five leading counties in intensity of net sales are still in the heavily urbanized Northeast (Table 6.4).

We can also assume that the margin of sales efficiency is being reduced on the production end by the shift to part-time farming, a national phenomenon amplified in this area by the "pull" of many cities, which offer additional income attractions, and the "push" of many small farms, which handicap operators trying to cope with changing technologies that put a premium on larger units.[6] Land speculation, in which farming is used only as a holding action in order to capitalize on rising land values, also degrades production nearer urban areas. But whether part-time farming and speculation have reduced product-sales efficiency as much as operational costs have may be open to doubt, if one can judge by the almost uniform distribution of counties with above-median value added (Figs. 6.1 and 6.2) in comparison to the fragmented pattern for net sales (Figs. 6.3 and 6.4). Not all part-time farmers are less efficient than full-time operators, and a more intensive but also more flexible crop can be substituted for one whose capital is more immobile, such as a vegetable for a tree fruit. The answer obviously must come from studies of less aggregated data.[7]

Urban influences fail to explain the large net sales deficits in most areas beyond Megalopolis and its margins. Lower cotton production, caused by sluggish prices, reduced price-support loans, and smaller yields, appears most responsible for the losses in much of the lower Mississippi Valley and on the Inner Coastal Plain and South Texas High Plains. The poor position of the San Joaquin Valley core comes from a combination of the unfavorable cotton situation, widespread tax-loss farming, and possible irrigation inefficiency.[8] The tax-sheltering effects of capital gains provisions in the federal tax laws have contributed to a rapid expansion of fruit and vegetable farming, which was already well established and has always required large cash turnovers. "Wall Street" farming of this kind has also greatly stimulated investments in cattle feeding operations. Profit in these types of operations becomes secondary, because the emphasis must be on investment in order to take advantage of the tax loopholes that were created to encourage that investment; artificial losses can thus be generated, and are then used to offset or shelter nonfarm income from taxes. Substantial overplanting and overproduction, with its negative income effects, may well have resulted, not to mention the depressing effects on the operations of the smaller operators who cannot take advantage of such loopholes.[9] Since the time of this mapping, tax provisions of this kind have been somewhat reduced. The possibility of significant irrigation inefficiencies may also have at least a partial explanation in governmental influence, if one accepts the arguments of those who say that prices charged for water by state irrigation districts and the Bureau of Reclamation have been too low and thus have discouraged more efficient watering practices.[10]

Because government subsidies have stimulated capitalization by favoring those with larger capital resources, their effects on the spatial distribution of industrialization should be noted. Other sources of farm-related income, including customwork and recreational services, should also be accounted for, since it is the total farm returns of the operator that affect decisions on the amount and direction of capitalization. Whether these additional income sources, with the inclusion of sizable government payments, also give us a better indication of the financial success of industrialization is more debatable. There is no doubt, though, that despite certain unfavorable cropping conditions in several sections, subsidies in 1969 did discourage planting, at least of the main money crops of many areas, and to this extent represent income that would otherwise have been produced by farming. I have therefore added all of these supplementary moneys to the net value of farm products sold and, in order to obtain an estimate of operator efficiency, have divided the total by the number of "operator-equivalents," a unit that incorporates the contribution of part-time operators.[10] The resulting quotient thus also approximates net farm income.

Net farm income clearly correlates more closely with the individual variables of agricultural industrialization than do net sales, though not as much as does value added, and the large coefficients for mechanization and cropping reflect the favoring of crops by customwork and price supports (Table 6.1). National distribution of above-median income (more than $1,800 per operator-equivalent) is also more similar to the overall areal outline of general agricultural industrialization than is net sales, yet regional rankings are in some instances decidedly different from those of general industrialization (Figs. 6.5 and 5.1). The most obvious of these disparities appear on the Great Plains and along the seaboard in the Northeast. Operator profit on the Plains clearly surpasses the level of industrialization, the region having the largest share of counties with Class I net farm income (more than $4,200 per operator-equivalent). For large sections of Megalopolis beyond

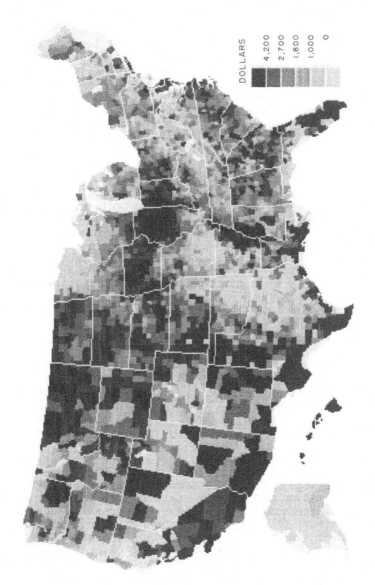

Figure 6.5. Net farm income per operator-equivalent

the margins of the metropolitan centers, however, the ratio is reversed--many counties even record a loss. Here small farms, the smaller amount of customwork, and an emphasis on crops that did not qualify for government payments can be held responsible. Both crop payments and customwork receipts, in contrast, now wipe out the deficit positions of the San Joaquin and lower Mississippi valleys, and put those two regions in the top classes. Other major areas of advanced agricultural industrialization, such as the cash-grain centers of the Corn Belt in Illinois and Iowa and the specialty farmlands of the Pacific Southwest, Gulf Coast, and Florida, retain their status. Operator profit actually reaches its peak in the subtropical areas, with Florida, Hawaii, California, and Arizona claiming fourteen of the twenty leading counties (Table 6.6), thus reemphasizing the particular importance of those states already indicated for value added and net value of products sold (Tables 6.3 and 6.5). The uniformly high achievement of farming operations in these subtropical and Middle Western areas therefore agrees fairly well with their leading positions in overall agricultural industrialization; only Megalopolis falls short, an exception highlighted even more by the generally excellent ratings of much of the Great Plains, where significant industrialization in most of the region is at minimum levels.

THE FUTURE SPATIAL PATTERN

Predicting the future areal expansion of so dynamic a process as agricultural industrialization is hazardous at best, yet this very dynamism of such a critical economic and social development demands at least a brief contemplation of possible trends. The productivity and profitability patterns suggest both barriers to and openings for further industrialization. It apparently has most closely approximated its limits on much of the Great Plains, where even excellent rewards cannot guarantee the survival of any but the least important industrialization type. Nor does industrialization of the most intensive kind appear capable of resisting the worsening competitive position of the Northeast as urban demands take away land and raise its costs and as comparative advantage increasingly favors the better-endowed farming areas. None of this rules out further growth in place; further farm amalgamation, continuing mechanization, more contract farming, and increasing fuel costs with their effects on transportation are some of the forces that will ensure additional industrialization. Nevertheless, these means must be weighed against their greater promise of success in less impacted areas. The consistently high efficiency ratings of the Pacific Southwest and Florida seem to portend a continuing rapid growth of agricultural

Table 6.6. The twenty leading counties in net farm income per operator-equivalent[a]

	Dollars		Dollars
1. Hendry, Fla. (C)	63,821	11. Colusa, Cal. (C,G)	18,177
2. Maui, Haw. (C,G)	57,052	12. Maricopa, Ariz. (L,G)	17,153
3. Deaf Smith, Tex. (L)	30,517	13. Orange, Fla. (C,G)	16,967
4. Pinal, Ariz.	28,553	14. Kern, Cal.	16,950
5. Palm Beach, Fla. (C,G)	27,747	15. Summit, O. (C,G)	16,668
6. Kauai, Haw. (C,G)	25,622	16. Pershing, Nev.	16,288
7. Imperial, Cal. (C,L,G)	23,375	17. Moore, Tex.	16,159
8. Merrick, Neb. (L,G)	20,383	18. Haskell, Kan.	16,005
9. Honolulu, Haw. (C,L,G)	19,849	19. Highlands, Fla.	15,919
10. Gadsden, Fla. (C,G)	19,177	20. Lake, Fla. (C,G)	15,493

[a]Counties with some significant agricultural industrialization are coded for the particular industrialization emphasis: C = cropping; L = livestock and poultry raising; G = general.

industrialization in the subtropical portions of the country, though not necessarily in all areas now having the highest ranks. Agriculture in many parts of the Southwest is facing heavy competition from expanding cities for land and, critically, water, and both urban expansion and deteriorating soil conditions are exacting ever larger duties from farming in southern Florida. Other parts of the South, then, might well furnish the most impressive scene in the subtropics as capital investors continue to seek areas with cheaper land, adequate water, and less expensive labor.

More intriguing, however, is the well-proven potential for further major industrialization in the principal center of American agriculture, the Middle West, and particularly its core, the Corn Belt, for there capitalization, with its great intensiveness and technical efficiency, involves more farmers than any other region of similarly advanced industrialization. It is an achievement that will be hailed by those who maintain that agricultural industrialization need not bring with it the demise of the family farm and widespread "corporate takeover." But industrialization continues to be an ongoing process, with farms becoming ever larger at the expense of other operators, the same as has occurred in the often-criticized "factory farm" areas. Here, then, is posed most starkly what is becoming one of the most severe economic and cultural dilemmas in American agriculture: how to preserve freedom and equality of opportunity without discouraging the initiative that is also esteemed and has done so much to promote agricultural progress. Whatever the eventual solution, it will most certainly, and appropriately, come from this midwestern "heartland."

NOTES

1. Lawrence Abbott presents a particularly clear and instructive explanation of value added in the context of national output and income in Economics and the Modern World, 2d ed. (New York: Harcourt, Brace & World, 1967), Ch. 11.

2. Laurits R. Christensen, "Concepts and Measurement of Agricultural Productivity," American Journal of Agricultural Economics, Vol. 57 (1975), pp. 912-913.

3. U.S., Bureau of the Census, 1974 Census of Agriculture. Vol. IV, Special Reports. Part 5, Corporations in Agricultural Production, p. 4. A source of possible local distortion of areal distribution may also be the instruction of the bureau to farmers reporting this item not to include the value of a landlord's share of crops in crop-share or livestock in livestock-share rental arrangements (U.S., Bureau of the Census, 1969

Census of Agriculture. Vol. V., Special Reports. Part 13, Data-Collection Forms and Procedures, p. 87.). The effects would probably be greatest in the Middle West, where the percentage of part-owners with crop-share contracts is the largest of any major U.S. region.

4. For the manner of computation, see Chapter 2.

5. Value of home consumption by states for 1969 was taken from Table 675, p. 475, of Agricultural Statistics 1970, U.S., Department of Agriculture (Washington, D.C.: Government Printing Office, 1970). This figure was then divided by the total number of farms in each state and the result was multiplied by the number of farms in each county selling at least $2,500 worth of products.

6. Howard F. Gregor, "Farm Structure in Regional Comparison: California and New Jersey Vegetable Farms," Economic Geography, Vol. 45 (1969), pp. 212-213.

7. In a study of part-time farmers in Waterloo County on the edges of the Toronto-Hamilton agglomeration in Ontario, Mage found that efficiency varied widely among his five types of part-time farming "situations" (Julius A. Mage, "Guelph Report 1--A Typology of Part-Time Farming," Part-Time Farming--Problems of Resource in Rural Development, ed. Anthony M. Fuller and Julius A. Mage [Norwich, England: Geo Abstracts Ltd., 1976], pp. 20-29). Ruth Gasson found in her sampling of farmers in Kent and Sussex counties southeast of London "surprisingly" little variation between full-time and part-time operators in land use intensity or labor efficiency (The Influence of Urbanization on Farm Ownership and Practice, Studies in Rural Land Use, Report No. 7, Department of Agricultural Economics, Wye College, University of London [London: Headley Brothers Ltd., 1966]).

8. Howard F. Gregor, "The Large Farm as a Stereotype: A Look at the Pacific Southwest," Economic Geography, Vol. 53 (1979), pp. 78-79.

9. Comprehensively and succinctly described in: Ingolf Vogeler, The Myth of the Family Farm: Agribusiness Dominance of U.S. Agriculture (Boulder, Colo.: Westview Press, 1981), pp. 163-194.

10. Robert C. Fellmeth, Politics of Land (New York: Grossman Publishers, 1973), pp. 56-60.

11. For the computation formula, see Chapter 2, Footnote 20.

Index

Absentee ownership, 8
Acidity, 68
Acreage controls, 69, 126. See also Farm programs, federal
"Acreage history," 63
Africa, East, 95
Agglomeration advantages, 83
Agglomerative tendencies, 78
Aggregated data, 16, 229
Agricultural industrialization, 48, 58, 88, 112, 123, 126; basic dimensions, 10; on better farmland, 13-21; capital demands, 83; concentration nearer cities, 21-24; conceptualization, 1-10; criticism, 1-2; cropping and general types, 192, 196, 198; cropping intensity and general intensity, 166, 169; cropping scale and cropping intensity, 177, 180; cropping scale and general scale, 180; cropping types, 192-198; definition, 1-2; disturbing effects, 1-2; future areal expansion, 232, 234; general, 230; general intensity structure, 159-165; general scale and general intensity, 173, 177; general scale structure, 173-177; general types, 189-192; human problems, 10n.4, 11n.11; inefficiency of, 224, 229-230; intensity, 10, 13-104; intensity substructures, 166-173; limited and significant, 204; livestock and cropping types, 198, 201; livestock and general types, 198, 201; livestock intensity and general intensity, 169; livestock scale and livestock intensity, 180; livestock types, 198-203; mechanization and, 132; and net farm income, 230, 232; pressures, 66; and productivity, 215-221; and profitability, 221-232; reaction to, 2; scale, 10, 105-157; scale substructures, 177-180; summary distribution, 44; types and productivity types, 220-221; types of, in cropping, 192-198; types of, in livestock-poultry raising, 198-203; types of general, 189-192; types of limited, in cropping, 207-209; types of limited, in general agriculture, 204-207; types of limited, in livestock raising, 209-213. See also Capitalization intensity; Capitalization scale; Industrialization
Agricultural officials, 83
Agricultural service man, 126
Aircraft, 121
Airplane seeding, 39, 121
Airplane spraying, 39, 121
Alabama, 19, 83-84, 95, 209; Black Belt, 19, 55, 84, 93, 108, 115, 130, 147, 150, 177, 196; central, 19; Coastal Plain, 150; Gulf Coast, 66,

109; Mobile Bay area, 36, 89, 115; northeastern, 19; northern, 29, 35-36, 42, 82, 150, 164, 177; southern, 84, 89, 138, 142
Alaska, 3, 48, 97n.3, 112, 196, 201; central, 151; coastal lands, 209; Fairbanks area, 204; Kenai Peninsula, 3; Matanuska Valley, 130; Tanana Valley, 151
Alfalfa, 52, 59, 62-63, 65, 75, 95, 136; green chopped, 154; hay, 145
Allegheny-Cumberland Plateau, 19
Allegheny Plateau, 17, 148
Alluvial fan slopes, 61
Almonds, 62
Anhydrous ammonia, 94
Animals, 153; soil, 70; purchases, 153. See also individual types
Appalachia, 35, 66, 207; northern, 26, 39; southern, 6, 18, 129, 208
Appalachian fringes, 53
Appalachian "fruit counties," 58
Appalachian Highlands, 3, 20, 148, 173
Appalachian hinterlands, 41
Appalachian valleys, 19, 84, 93
Apple graders, 37
Apples, 61
Arizona, 3, 24, 31, 64, 71, 127, 146, 232; Gila Basin, 138, 196, 201; Salt River Valley, 86, 137, 196, 201; southern, 16-17, 86-87, 95, 150, 198, 209; southwestern, 24, 30, 43, 61, 86, 89, 97, 108-109, 131, 164, 201; Yuma Valley, 86. See also Pacific Southwest
Arkansas, 21, 207; "Delta," 122; Grand Prairie, 55; northeastern, 55; northwestern, 42, 82; southeastern, 55; southwestern, 42, 82; St. Francis Basin, 55; Valley, 19. See also Lower Alluvial Valley
Artificial insemination, 76
Atlantic Coastal Plain, 80, 151; South, 21, 36, 46, 53, 58, 66, 68, 81-82, 88, 94, 106, 108, 115, 121-122, 129-130, 135, 138, 141-142, 166, 191, 209. See also Inner Coastal Plain
Atlantic Seaboard, North, 31, 70, 131, 136, 198. See also Megalopolis; Mid-Atlantic Seaboard
Aureomycin, 72
Automatic feeding, 35
Avocados, 61-62

Bacon, 50
Bankouts, 121
Barley, 59, 62-63, 95, 136, 145
Barns, 79
Bean threshers, 37
Beans, 65, 118; dry, 59
Bedders, 34
Beef, 50, 76-77, 86; consumption, 73; demands, 84; -hog-dairy area, 97; production, 47. See also Meat
Beef cattle, 75, 79, 84, 86-87, 94, 146-150; economy, 80; farms, 19; raising, 89, 93, 147. See also Cattle
Beef cows, 73, 77, 88, 146. See also Cattle, beef
Berry, D., 79
Bieri, K., 79
Biocides, 70
Black Belt, 19, 55, 84, 93, 108, 115, 127, 130, 147, 177, 196
Bottling plants, 148
Boxes, 227
Bracero program, 30
Breeding, 46; herds, 73
"Broiler factories," 72
Broiler industry, 93
Broiler prices, 103n.62
Broiler production, 82, 92
Buildings, 82, 87; average farm value, 110; on cotton farms, 110. See also Land and building capitalization
Bulk milk tanks, 33
Bulldozers, 121
Bulls, 153
Bureau of Reclamation, 230
Businessmen, 94

California, 4, 8, 18, 24, 30-31, 38, 53, 55, 62-63, 66, 71, 86,

95-96, 109-110, 127, 130, 132, 134, 146, 148, 177, 192, 209, 232; central, 61, 150-151, 169, 198; central coastal, 63; Central Valley, 3-4, 17, 63, 109, 131, 164, 196; Coachella-Imperial Trough, 17; Coachella Valley, 86; coastal, 64; Fresno County, 37; Imperial County, 24, 192; Imperial Valley, 62, 86-87, 136-137; Kern County, 64; Los Angeles area, 63; Los Angeles Basin, 63; Los Angeles County, 95; Marin County, 151; northern, 21; northern coastal, 131; Sacramento Valley, 21, 37, 43, 55, 88, 95, 120, 132, 137-138, 209; San Francisco Bay Area, 63, 87, 89, 150; San Joaquin Valley, 21, 37, 43, 45, 61, 63, 87-89, 95-97, 110-111, 121, 129, 201, 224, 229, 232; Santa Cruz County, 37; southern, 16-17, 24, 61, 86-87, 89, 95, 97, 108, 150, 169, 192, 196, 198; southern coastal, 43, 62, 131; southeastern, 43, 86, 109, 131, 164, 201; Tulare County, 88; Water Project, 63. See also Pacific Southwest; Pacific States
Calves, 93-94, 147
Canada, 92, 95; Prairie Provinces, 126; Waterloo County, Ont., 235n.7
Capital, 69, 137, 173; flexibility, 149; forms of farm, 9, 13; gains, 229; greater supplies, 28, 126; intensification and cities, 21; investors, 234; limits, 85; money, 9; outside, 82; real, 9, 72; relative prices, 1; resources, 230; supply, 70; working, 136
Capitalization intensity: of cropping, 46-72; higher-order patterns, 44-46, 65-72, 96-97; of labor, 24-31; of land and buildings, 13-24; of livestock and poultry raising, 72-97; of mechanization, 31-46. See also individual intensity types
Capitalization scale: of cropping, 132-142; higher-order patterns, 128-132, 138-142, 154-155; of labor, 111-116; of land and buildings, 106-111; of livestock and poultry raising, 142-155; of mechanization, 116-132. See also individual scale types
Carnegie, A., 83
Carrots, 62
Cash corn farming system, 114
Cash crop enterprises, 51
Cash cropping, 17, 78, 82, 91, 146, 198-199
Cash crops, 56, 66, 68-69, 78, 135-136, 209. See also Money crops
Cash grain, 50, 52; areas, 69, 191, 209, 232; farming, 52-53; production, 51, 140. See also specific grain areas
Cattle, 52, 73, 87, 89, 93-94, 96, 136, 147, 153, 177; beef, farmers, 93, 229; corn-, -hog economy, 145; crop-, farmers, 229; feed, 85; feeders, 73; feeding, 86, 91, 94, 96, 130, 148, 209, 229; growth of, population, 73, 91; -hog area, 79, 115; -hog farms, 114; industry, 86; operations, 36; pasturing, 75; purchases, 91, 94; raisers, 95; raising, 76, 82, 84, 92-94, 147, 180; ranches, 38, 142, 144, 146-148; revolution, 84; smaller, farms, 201; trailing, 144. See also individual types; Livestock; Livestock raising
Celery, 62
Center pivot irrigation, 43, 120, 126-127
Central America, 95
Chance, 213
Chemicals, 47, 50, 65-66, 70-71, 102n.58, 141, 215. See also Fertilizers
Cherries, 63
Chicken houses, 39
Chicken prices, 103n.62
Chickens, 75. See also Poultry
Cities, 22, 41, 53, 60, 71, 79,

86, 135, 229; advantage of northern, 99n.15; competition from expanding, 234; dairy areas incorporated as, 87; feedlots supplying, 73. See also Industrial centers; Urban areas; Urban centers
Citrus: farms, 29; fruit, 4, 56-57, 61, 66; production, 57. See also individual crops
Climate, contradictory nature, 66
Climates: cool, temperate, 61; hot desert, 61; subtropical, 61
Climatic advantages, 22, 56, 60
Climatic influences, micro-, 62
Climatic variations, 61
Clover, -timothy, 52
Coffee, 120; farms, 38
Collective farms: Soviet, 110; State, 12n.16
Colorado, 17, 134; Grand Valley, 65; northeastern, 38, 58, 84-85, 94, 163; Piedmont, 44, 129, 145, 154, 164, 196; Rocky Mountain Front, 17, 58; San Luis Valley, 30, 65, 129, 134; South Platte Basin, 44, 84, 89, 94, 145; southern, 30; Western Slope, 38, 65, 201
Colorado Plateaus, 129, 196, 207
Columbia Plateau, 134, 191; western, 64
Combines, 35, 46, 118, 121, 126; custom, 126; self-propelled, 121
Combining, 39; custom, 126; mass-, 39
Communication problems, 111
Community attitudes, 79
Comparative advantage, 232
Components analysis, 159; as factor analysis, 187n.2, 187n.5; and rotation, 187n.5
Concentrates, 93, 95; per milk cow, 91
Connecticut: eastern, 81
Contract farming, 42, 72, 122, 232
Contractual arrangements, 72, 80, 82
Cooperatives, growers', 29

Copra meal, 95
Corn, 10, 17, 35-36, 43, 45, 47-48, 51, 54, 56, 59-61, 63, 66, 73, 78-80, 93, 119, 121-122, 128, 136, 145, 154; cash grain, 51, 79, 128; -cattle-hog economy, 145; grain, 53; hybrid, 50; -oats-hay rotation, 50; pickers, 35, 46, 118; picking, 39; planter, 33; silage, 119, 145; -Soy Belt, 50; yields, 50-51, 93
Corn Belt, 4, 17-18, 21, 23-24, 26, 31, 34-36, 41, 46, 48, 50-53, 56, 58-59, 68, 73, 75, 77-79, 82, 84, 91, 93-94, 105-106, 108-109, 112, 114, 132, 135-138, 145-146, 148, 192, 224, 234; eastern, 45, 78-79, 91, 114, 129, 140, 142; farm, 73; western, 18, 41, 45-46, 73, 76, 79, 89, 91, 109, 115, 122-123, 128-132, 140, 148, 150-151, 154-155, 164, 169, 177, 196, 209
Corporate farming, 65
Corporate farms, 7-8, 11n.11, 12n.16, 121. See also Factory farms; Industrial farms
Corporate takeover, 234
Corporations, 7; capitalist, 12n.16; farm, 44, 111; feeder-pig, 75
Corrals, 87
"Cost-price squeeze," 41, 122
Costs, 232; dealer, 141; distributor, 141; of inputs, 215; irrigation, 63, 65, 71, 119; labor, 25, 28, 43, 82, 119, 136, 144; land, 53, 63, 80, 83, 87, 140, 146, 229; machine, 119, 136; machine repair, 39; machine write-off, 33, 136; middleman, 137; operational, 38-44, 46, 224, 229; production, 81; pumping, 121; water, 71
Cotton, 9-10, 19-20, 35-38, 47, 55-56, 60, 62-63, 66, 121-122, 127, 136, 147, 151; acreage, 63; pickers, 35, 46, 121; production, 56, 229; sugarcane-rice-soybean-, areas, 45

Cotton Belt, 55
Cotton farms: in Oklahoma, 137; large, 110, 121; mechanized, 44
Cottonseed, 95; cake, 146; hulls, 145
Cows, 148; brood, 153; densities, 87; Holstein, 76; populations, 77, 95. See also Beef cows; Dairy cows
Crates, 229
Crop-cattle farmers, 85
Crop competition, 80
Crop diversity, 63
Crop enterprises, 48
Crop farmer-cattle feeder, 85
Crop farmers, 30
Crop farms, 31, 136; large, 141
Crop income, 69
Crop investment intensity, 47-65; and crop investment scale, 137-138, 142, 154-155; and cropping expenditure intensity, 65-72, 97, 142, 154-155; and cropping expenditure scale, 142, 154-155; and livestock-poultry expenditure intensity, 97, 154-155; and livestock-poultry expenditure scale, 154-155; and livestock-poultry investment intensity, 97, 154-155; and livestock-poultry investment scale, 154-155
Crop investment scale: and crop investment intensity, 137-138, 142, 154-155; and cropping expenditure scale, 140-142, 154-155; and cropping intensity scale, 142, 154-155; and farm size, 132, 134-138, 140-141; and livestock-poultry expenditure intensity, 154-155; and livestock-poultry expenditure scale, 154-155; and livestock-poultry investment intensity, 154-155; and livestock-poultry investment scale, 150-151, 154-155
Crop-livestock dichotomy, 180
Crop payments, 232. See also Subsidies

Crop production, 95
Crop agents, 141. See also Fungicides; Herbicides; Parasite control; Pesticides; Sprays
Crop quotas, 57. See also Farm programs; Government policies
Crop residues, 95
Crop-share rental, 234, 235n.3
Crop specialization, 48
Crop specialty areas, 45, 122, 127, 134, 191
Crop specialty farms, 3
Crop surpluses, 14
Crop variety, 52, 62-63
Cropland, 16, 76, 91, 116, 127; change in, harvested, 21; decline, 56; in eastern United States, 63; expansion, 21, 55, 60; as farm size indicator, 3, 5-6; gains in the West, 21; in Idaho, 64; irrigated, 21; in Washington, 64
Cropland Adjustment Program, 14. See also Farm programs, federal; Government policies
Cropping, 66, 70, 72, 80, 97, 135, 140, 146, 159, 166, 173, 180, 192, 196, 201, 221, 230; cash, 17, 78, 82, 91, 146, 198-199; demands, 73; differences in, emphasis, 224; enterprises, 144, 147; intensification, 55, 60, 64; intensity of capitalization, 46-72; irrigation, 145; rainfed, 145; row, 82; scale of capitalization, 132-142; specialty, 34, 53, 112, 135; systems, 51; unfavorable, conditions, 230
Cropping expenditure intensity: and crop investment intensity, 65-72, 97, 142, 154-155; and crop investment scale, 142, 154-155; and cropping expenditure scale, 141-142; 154-155; and livestock-poultry expenditure intensity, 96-97, 154-155; and livestock-poultry expenditure scale, 154-155; and livestock-poultry investment intensity, 88-89, 97, 154-155; and livestock-poultry investment scale, 154-155. See also individual enterprises

Cropping expenditure scale: and crop investment intensity, 142, 154-155; and crop investment scale, 140-142, 154-155; and cropping expenditure intensity, 141-142, 154-155; and farm size, 138, 140-141; and livestock-poultry expenditure intensity, 154-155; and livestock-poultry expenditure scale, 154-155; and livestock-poultry investment intensity, 154-155; and livestock-poultry investment scale, 154-155
Crops, 46, 135, 145, 230; cash, 56, 66, 68-69, 78, 135-136, 209; contracting, 66; "defensive," 64; emphasis on, 232; expanding, 66; failed, 47; grain, 38, 50, 62, 92-93, 95; intensive, 48, 50; irrigated, 119; machine, 122; money, 52, 135-136, 230; price attractiveness, 48; specialty, 19, 42-43, 45, 52, 78, 80, 115, 118, 135, 137, 141, 146, 191, 224; subtropical, 127; tree, 63; truck, 52, 60, 135, 222; value, harvested, 47-65; value sold, 47; value, unharvested, 47; vegetable, 62, 87. See also individual crops
Cummins, D. E., 149
Custom cutters, 126
Customwork, 46, 130, 216, 230, 232; expenditure intensity, 38-44; expenditure intensity and major cropping areas, 42-43. See also Labor; Machine hire
Cutover, Great Lakes, 4, 26, 34, 39, 48, 77, 208, 224; in Michigan, 48, 78, 224; in Minnesota, 78; in Wisconsin, 48, 71

Dairy areas, 45, 69, 76, 78, 87, 112, 191, 207. See also specific areas
Dairy Belt, 26, 51-53, 68-69, 73, 76-77, 80-81, 89, 91, 106, 108-109, 122-123, 131, 135-136, 138, 140, 142, 177; western, 105, 115, 148, 150, 169, 198, 220
Dairy cattle, 78-79, 84, 88, 91, 147-148
Dairy cows, 77, 79-81, 92, 150
Dairy enterprises, 85, 91. See also Dairying; Drylot dairying
Dairy farmers, 28, 33, 52, 79, 81, 91-93, 95-96
Dairy farms, 3, 19, 28, 30, 33-34, 37, 53, 76-77, 114, 148-149; large-scale, 148; smaller, 201
Dairy-fruit-vegetable areas, 45
Dairy herd replacements, 77
Dairy herds, 77, 88; feed rations, 91; increase in, 91; larger, 76
Dairy operations, 36, 80, 148
Dairy products, 222
Dairy specialization, 80
Dairy specialty areas, 38, 45
Dairy-specialty crop complex, 53
Dairy-vegetable lowlands, 45
Dairying, 28, 52-53, 68, 79-81, 83-84, 86, 89, 92-94, 112, 147, 149, 191; intensiveness of, 123. See also Dairy enterprises; Drylot dairying
Dairying industry, 78
Data transformation, 179n.1, 186n.1
Dates, 61
Defoliants, 65. See also Herbicides
Delmarva Peninsula, 28, 53, 80-81, 92
"Delta," 21, 56, 58, 122, 130. See also Lower Alluvial Valley; Lower Mississippi Valley; Mississippi bottomlands; Mississippi lowlands
Deltapine plantation, 147
Diminishing returns, 70
Discounts, volume, 141
Discs, 37
Disease: control, 46; organisms, 70
Diseases, 71
Diseconomies, 215, 220
Disk harrows, 121
Ditchers, 121
Drainage: ditch-and-tile, 20; land, 111; reclamation, 21,

53-54
Drained areas, 66
Driftless Area, 17, 41, 69, 151
Drought: damage, 47; and farm size, 119; in the West, 119
Dry-farming rotations, 64
Dryland farming, 60
Drylot dairies, 72, 87
Drylot dairying, 31, 80, 87, 92, 94, 96, 146; semi-, 94
Drylot dairymen, 95-96
Dusters, 34

Earth movers, 121
East, U.S., 3, 16, 43, 62, 106, 123, 130, 132, 135, 138, 142, 146, 149-151, 154, 164, 180, 192, 196, 198, 201, 204, 207, 213; -West contrasts, 173, 221; -West disparity, 137, 141. See also United States, eastern
Economies of scale, 75-76, 85, 95, 119
Efficiency: farming, 215; labor, 235n.7; mechanization, 45; operator, 230; product-sales, 229; ratings, 232; sales, 229; superior, 46; technical, 234. See also Profitability
"Egg factories," 72, 87
Energy: costs, 81, 110; shortages, 43. See also Fuel; Oil
Entrepreneur: local, 83; smaller, 82
Environmental regulations, 79
Eutrophication, 68

Factor analysis, 159, 166, 187n.2
Factory farms, 8, 28, 189, 234. See also Corporate farms; Industrial farms
Factory system, 72
Factory-type operations, 55
Family farms, 7, 11n.11, 12n.16, 26, 234
Farm consolidation, 18, 54, 232
Farm expansion, 110-111
Farm income, 114. See also Income
Farm programs, federal, 14, 48, 56, 221; corn, 93; cotton, 63; wheat acreage controls, 126. See also Crop quotas; Government policies; Tax policies
Farm scale, 2. See also Farm size; Farms; Large farms
Farm schedules, 149
Farm size, 2, 82, 91, 137, 148, 154, 220; constraints, 128; and crop investment scale, 132, 134-138, 140-141; and cropping expenditure scale, 138, 140-141; disparity between, and intensity, 3-6; implications for capitalization, 105; and land and building investment intensity, 108-111; and land and building investment scale, 109-111; large, 130, 153; and livestock-poultry expenditure scale, 153-154; and livestock-poultry investment scale, 144-149; and mechanization investment scale, 118, 120-124, 126; small, 153, 207, 213. See also Farm scale; Farms; Large farms
Farm workers, 129, 207; hiring, 126; male, 28; migratory, 30, 207; part-time summer, 28; resident, 136; for sheep operations, 86. See also Labor
Farmers, 12n.16, 69, 91-92, 94, 126, 198, 207, 221, 234; Corn Belt, 50, 77; drylot, 95; entrepreneurial spirit, 12n.17; family, 48; full-time, 235n.7; income expectations, 14; irrigation, 127; marginal, 82; Megalopolitan, 81; Middle Western, 92; northern, 69; part-time, 235n.7; Piedmont, 54; Shenandoah Valley, 83; southern, 66, 69; using fertilizers, 69; western, 69. See also specialization types; Growers; Operators
Farmland: concentration on the better, 13-14, 39; good, 69; idling of, 23; share of, in pasture and marginal land, 14; specialty, 232. See also Land
Farms, 144, 232; annual sales of $100,000 or more, 4; business organization, 4; corporate, 7-8, 11n.11, 12n.16, 121;

distribution, 3; eastern, 135, 140; factory, 8, 28, 189, 234; family, 7, 11n.11, 12n.16, 26, 234; fragmented, 41, 110-111, 126; heavily capitalized, 106, 137; in the Imperial Valley, 136; irrigated, 71, 118; large crop, 141; large industrialized, 109-111; large landed, 111; more diversified, 110; more mechanized, 101n.34; "1-5," 47, 97n.3, 105; poorer, 26; state collective, 12n.16; statistical representation, 3; subsistence, 3; very large, 123. See also individual types
Farmsteads, 110
Feed, 73, 81-82, 89, 154; base, 149; cattle, 85; companies, 82; concentrate, 93, 95; conditions, 153; corn gluten, 95; crop mix, 52; crops, 52, 73, 77, 118, 130, 144-147; diffusion of, 93; expenditures, 73, 96, 153; flow, 93; formula, 93; grains, 9, 80, 92, 96; -handling equipment, 144; processors, 82; production, 76, 95, 144; purchases, 91, 94-95, 153; requirements, 92; sources, 81; storage facilities, 76; supplemental, 85; supplements, 1; supplies, 92, 201; surplus area, 93; wheat-mixed, 95. See also individual crops; Forage crops
Feeder cattle, 76, 79, 91, 96
Feeder-pig corporations, 75
Feeder pigs, 77; sales, 75
Feeders, 91, 93, 95-96. See also individual types
Feeding, 46, 77, 86, 93, 96; conditions, 147; livestock, 17, 73
Feeding systems: mechanical, 76
Feedlot areas, 91
Feedlot Belt, 86-87
Feedlot facilities, 144
Feedlot fattening, 144, 146
Feedlot industry, 88; success, 84
Feedlot operators, 85-87, 96, 147
Feedlot operations, 31, 86, 153; economies of scale, 75; large-scale, 85, 94; water in, 84; westward expansion, 85
Feedlots, 72-73, 87, 93, 147, 153; concentration of cattle in, 85; Montfort, 153
Fertilization, 59-60; heavy, 66, 70; of newly drained areas, 66
Fertilizer residues, 68
Fertilizers, 1, 13-14, 25, 47, 50-51, 65-71, 75, 94, 136, 141, 216; residual efforts, 147. See also Chemicals
Field crops, 51, 62, 64, 121, 127, 137. See also individual types
Field graders, 37
Field stubble, 146
Financial institutions, 137
Flash freezing, 34
Flatwoods, 57
Flax, 59, 62, 136
Flint Hills, 20, 94, 145, 154, 201
Florida, 4, 8, 18, 30-31, 37, 53, 57, 94, 110, 122, 177, 192, 196, 198, 221, 232; central, 6, 21, 29, 66, 108, 115, 127-129, 131, 142, 150, 155, 166, 191, 209; Central Lake District, 30, 57; eastern coastal, 57; Everglades, 57, 111; Gadsden County, 224; "Gold Coast," 83, 89, 132, 148; Indian River District, 57; Interior District, 57; Jacksonville area, 83, 148, 150; Lake Okeechobee area, 148; Miami area, 150; middle, 46, 137; Nassau county, 151; northeastern, 115, 151; northern, 150; Panhandle, 36, 58, 82, 115, 142, 166; peninsular, 23, 36, 45, 56, 82, 88, 106, 108-109, 115, 122, 129-130, 135, 140, 147, 150, 154, 164, 177; southeast coast, 97; southeastern, 45, 108, 132, 191, 209; southern, 19, 21, 29, 42, 46, 57, 66, 109, 115, 122, 127-128, 131, 135, 137, 142, 150-151, 155, 166, 177, 192, 234; St. Johns County, 115; Tampa-St. Petersburg area, 83, 89, 97, 148, 150

Flowers, 57
Fodder crops. See Feed; Forage crops
Food, 2; demands, 83; surpluses, 1-2
Forage crops, 66, 79, 86. See also Feed
Forage harvester, 33
Forage yields, 75
Ford, H., 83
Fragmented farm, 41, 126; expansion, 110-111
Fragmented plots, 64, 110
Frost, 56-57, 61, 127
Fruit, 26, 28, 30, 37, 52, 58, 61, 63, 71, 78, 224; deciduous stone, 61; fresh, 57; -and-potato belt, 136; production, 191; small, 64; tree, 229
Fruit areas, 61, 112. See also specific areas
"Fruit counties," 58
Fruit-dairy-poultry areas, 45
Fruit enterprises, 53, 123
Fruit farming, 229
Fruit farms, 124
Fruit growers, 61
Fruit, truck, and dairy region, N.Y., 112
Fuel, 1, 45-46, 121, 127, 216; companies, 137; expenditure intensity, 38-44, 128-132; expenditure scale, 126-132; in greenhouse agriculture, 128; increasing costs, 232; for pumping, 42; shortage, 127; worsening, situation, 144. See also Energy; Natural Gas; Oil
Fungicides, 65, 70. See also Crop-protection agents; Herbicides; Parasite control; Pesticides; Sprays

Gasson, R., 235n.7
Georgia, 19, 83-84, 122, 196, 209; Chattahoochee Valley, 19, 35; Coastal Plain, 42, 109, 135, 141; Inner Coastal Plain, 127, 129-130, 224; Lower Piedmont, 147, 150; northern, 19, 29, 35-36, 42, 82, 150, 164, 173, 177, 192; Piedmont, 23; -South Carolina Piedmont, 55; southern, 19, 45-46; southwestern, 58, 108, 122, 142, 166
Gins, 110
Government payments, 230, 232. See also Price-support loans
Government policies, 14, 42, 51, 81; influence, 230; on storage, 93. See also Crop quotas; Farm programs; Policy Decisions; Price-support loans; Tax policies
Grain: areas, 153; corn, 51, 53, 79, 128; crops, 38, 50, 62, 92-93, 95; drill, 33; farmers, 127; production, 94; small, 118; sorghum, 20, 51-52, 59-60, 63, 85, 94, 118-119, 145; stubble, 95; surpluses, 94; trucks, 126. See also individual crops
Grainlands, 58
Grape growers, 61
Grapefruit, 57
Grapes, 62-63, 65
Grass, 68; brome, 75; short and mid-, 145; tall, 145
Grasslands, 145
Grazing: fenced, 144; lands, 20; rotational, 86; stocker-, 147
Great Basin, 144
Great Lakes area, 3, 28, 30, 112, 192; eastern, 42; Lake Michigan littoral, 166; lower, 45-46, 52, 68-69, 78, 89, 115, 123, 131, 135, 137-138, 151, 164, 169, 198; upper, 219. See also Great Lakes states
Great Lakes states, 24, 34, 114, 149. See also individual states
Great Plains, 4, 20, 39, 58, 70-71, 84-85, 91, 94, 108, 112, 116, 118, 127, 132, 138-140, 144-146, 150-151, 153, 169, 177, 191, 196, 207, 224, 230, 232; megalophilia on the, 126; northern, 20, 58-59, 118, 129-130, 134, 144-145, 153, 180, 220; southern, 20, 39, 43, 45, 51, 59, 86, 89, 93-96, 119-120, 134, 151, 153-154, 169, 198, 220; western, 106, 127.

See also High Plains; Spring
  Wheat Belt; Winter Wheat Belt
"Green chopping," 76
Green feeding, 76
Greenhouse agriculture, 128
Greenhouse industry, 42
Greenhouses, 42
Gross farm product, 4
Gross national product (GNP),
  216
Gross sales, 4
Gross value, 7
Growers, 52, 63; fruit, 61;
  grape, 61; plum, 62. See also
  Farmers; Operators
Gulf Coast, 88, 122, 166, 177,
  191, 209, 232; Prairies, 3-4,
  19, 23, 55, 57, 82; south
  Texas, 19; Texas, 19, 115,
  150, 192, 196; Texas-Louisi-
  ana, 122, 135; western, 21,
  106, 108-109, 127, 129-130,
  135, 141, 151, 191. See also
  Gulf Coastal Plain
Gulf Coastal Plain, 66, 68, 82,
  115, 141; western, 150.
  See also Gulf Coast; Louisiana-Texas Coastal Prairies

Harrows, 34
Hart, J. F., 19
Hawaii, 17, 30-31, 43, 45, 61,
  71, 88, 95, 109-110, 112, 115,
  120, 132, 134, 146, 164, 196,
  232; fruit areas, 61; Hawaii
  County, 38, 138; Honolulu
  County, 17, 24, 38, 138;
  Kauai, 17, 45, 131; Kona
  Coast, 38; Oahu, 45, 88-89,
  95, 97, 131, 150
Hay, 38, 51, 76, 80, 92;
  alfalfa, 145; balers, 46, 118;
  corn-oats-, rotation, 50;
  legume, 145; production, 92,
  118
Haying enterprise, 92
Heady, E. O., 136
Heaters, 127
Heifers, 88; dairy, 148
Herbicides, 50, 65, 121. See
  also Crop protection agents;
  Defoliants; Fungicides;
  Pesticides; Sprays

Herd quality, 76
Herd size, 146, 148
Herdsmen, 148
High Plains, 43, 58-60, 119, 129-
  130, 134, 138, 140-141, 145-
  146, 151, 154, 161, 169, 177,
  191, 196, 198, 224; South
  Texas, 71, 109, 129, 131-132,
  138, 141, 145, 154, 164, 196,
  229; Texas, 20, 30, 38, 43, 58,
  60, 89, 155, 209, 224. See
  also Great Plains; Winter Wheat
  Belt
Highland Rim, 19
Hog farming, 75, 81; corn-
  cattle-, 145. See also Hog
  raising; Swine enterprises
Hog feeders, 75
Hog feeding, 130, 209
Hog prices, 103n.62
Hog raising, 75-76. See also Hog
  farming; Swine enterprises
Hogs, 75, 77, 79; market, 75;
  pasturing, 75. See also Pigs
Hop pickers, 37
Horticultural belt, 136
Horticultural farms, 110, 137
Horticultural production, 57
Horticultural products, 56-57,
  63-64, 136. See also individ-
  ual products; Nursery products
Horticultural sales, 64
Horticulture, 53, 229
Hybridization, 50, 59-60
Hydroelectric power, 127

Idaho, 64, 96, 134, 137; interior, 191; lower Snake River
  Plains, 30, 38, 64, 89, 96,
  131, 154; middle Snake River
  Plains, 38, 64, 89, 131, 154;
  northern, 86, 145; Payette
  County, 115; Snake River
  Plains, 17, 44, 65, 71, 97,
  121, 129, 141, 155, 164, 169,
  191, 201; southeastern, 38;
  southern, 30, 86
Illinois, 4, 41, 45-46, 51, 56,
  110, 128-129, 132, 148, 177,
  180, 191-192, 232; central, 69,
  78, 129, 132, 180; drainage in,
  21; Driftless Area, 151; east-
  central, 17, 50, 88, 106,

108-109, 123, 140, 142; eastern, 78; Grand Prairie, 17, 20-21, 50, 69, 123, 151, 166, 173, 196, 209; northeastern, 51, 108, 192, 196; northern, 52, 73, 109, 129, 140, 142, 153, 164; northwestern, 17, 150; southern, 18, 51, 56; western, 153. See also Corn Belt

Income, 221, 230; above-median, 230; farm-related, 114, 230; livestock, 69; net farm, 230, 232; nonfarm, 229. See also Profit; Profits

Incorporated farms: see Corporate farms

Incorporation, 8

Indiana, 45, 51, 77, 106, 114, 140; drainage in, 21; northeastern, 79; southern, 18, 79. See also Corn Belt, eastern

Industrial centers, 48, 112; See also Cities; Urban areas; Urban centers

Industrial farms, 2, 26, 109-111. See also Corporate farms; Factory farms

Industrial inputs, 25

Industrialization, 88; importance of capital, 8-9; and incorporation laws, 8; political measures and pressures of, 14; of small farms, 7; typologies, 10, 189-213. See also Agricultural industrialization; Capitalization intensity; Capitalization scale

Industrialized operations, 57. See also Industrialization

Inner Coastal Plain, 4, 45, 127, 129-130, 177, 192, 220, 224, 229. See also Atlantic Coastal Plain

Insects, 68, 71. See also Pests

Intermountain area, 85-86, 106, 108, 120, 138, 144, 164, 169, 192, 198, 201, 224; southern, 138

Intermountain oases, 70-71, 89, 169

Intermountain states, 44. See also individual states

Intermountain West. See Intermountain area

Iowa, 41, 45-46, 56, 73, 75, 80, 97, 148, 151, 164, 177, 180, 191-192, 232; Driftless Area, 151; eastern, 150; north-central, 17, 50, 209; northeastern, 17, 91; northern, 114, 128; northwest, 150; Prairie, 17, 20-21, 69, 166, 196; western, 114, 198, 201. See also Corn Belt

Irrigated areas, 60, 65, 85, 120, 129, 149, 169; yields in, 119

Irrigated cropland, 21

Irrigated crops, 119

Irrigated farms, 71, 118

Irrigated feed crops, 130

Irrigated land, 17, 63, 118, 126-127, 144, 198, 209; in California and southern Arizona, 209; distance from, 198; on the Great Plains, 126; production on, 118. See also Cropland, irrigated

Irrigation, 16, 21, 39, 42-43, 58-60, 63-65, 71, 87, 111, 119, 121-122, 130, 132, 140, 145, 149, 153; center-pivot, 43, 120, 126-127; costs, 63, 65, 71; cropping, 145; deep-well, 63; districts, 230; expansion, 65, 71; farmers, 127; farming, 16, 60; and fertilization, 71; flood, 122; inefficiency, 229-230; in the Pacific Southwest, 71; of rice, 42; role in the West, 85-86; sprinkler, 43, 65, 119, 121-122; supplemental, 64; supplies, 84; systems, 71; technology, 119; water, 60, 140

Isolation, 207, 220

Jewell, J. D., 83
Jobbers, 141
Joint product, 161

Kansas, 30, 43, 59-60, 119, 126, 145; central, 20; eastern, 94, 209; Flint Hills, 20, 94, 145, 154, 201; northeastern, 84; western, 20; Wyandotte County,

115. See also High Plains;
Winter Wheat Belt
Kentucky, 3, 89, 93, 122, 177;
Blue Grass Basin, 19, 24, 58,
68, 84, 93, 207; central, 36,
201; eastern, 19; middle, 84,
150; western, 36
Kiwi, 63
Korb, K. W., 33

Labor, 7, 13, 46, 91, 115, 136,
159, 166; "captive," 114;
cash-wage, 111; concentration,
12; contract, 25; costs, 25,
28, 43, 82, 119, 136, 144;
demand, 130; economies, 25;
family, 25-26, 29; farm, 52,
114; field, 164, 221; hand,
46, 130-131, 161, 166, 173,
180, 216; harvesting, 224;
hired farm, 25, 29-31, 42; as
industrialized farm indicator,
111; inputs, 25, 46, 54;
investments, 31-38; and land
capitalization, 216, 221; less
expensive, 234; less unionized, 82; markets, 112;
mechanization and, 173; mechanized, 46, 130-131, 161, 164,
221; migratory crews, 126;
multiple tenant, 111; operator, 25; peaks, 126, 161;
productivity, 1, 25; relative
prices, 1; share-cropper, 29;
shortages, 48, 69-70; theoretical problems of, inputs, 25;
underemployed, 93; work gangs,
114; "worker-equivalents," 25,
29; year-round, 161. See also
Customwork; Farm workers;
Machine hire
Labor capitalization scale: and
labor capitalization intensity, 111, 115-116; and land
and building capitalization
scale, 112, 114-115
Labor capitalization intensity,
24-31
Labor expenditure intensity, 24-
31; and labor expenditure
scale, 111, 115-116, 130-132;
and mechanization expenditure
intensity, 46, 130-132; and

mechanization expenditure
scale, 130-132
Labor expenditure scale: and
labor expenditure intensity,
111, 115-116, 130-132; and land
and building investment scale,
112, 114-115; and mechanization
expenditure intensity, 130-
132; and mechanization expenditure scale, 130-132
Lake Champlain-St. Lawrence
Plain, 148
Land, 30, 64, 78, 83, 92, 126,
138, 159, 166, 173, 207, 209,
224, 234; and building capitalization, 13-24, 106-111; and
building investments, 13-24;
carrying capacity, 86; cheaper,
148; Class I and II, 24; clearing, 111; costs, 53, 63, 80,
83, 87, 140, 146, 229; drainage, 111; good agricultural,
87; irrigated, 17, 63, 118,
126-127, 144, 198, 209; labor
and, capitalization, 216, 221;
lesser showing, 180; logged
over, 88; marginal, 73, 121;
midwestern agricultural, 18;
poorer, in the South, 82;
poorly drained, 73; purchases,
144; quality, 69; reclamation,
111, 121; rising, values, 229;
rough, 73; speculation, 229;
transactions, 41; unirrigated,
118; near urban centers, 13-
14, 16; urban pressures on,
79; U.S. agricultural, 154; use
by livestock operators, 87;
values, 14, 16, 19, 23
Land and building capitalization
intensity: concentration nearer
cities, 21-24; concentration on
better land, 13-21; and farm
size, 109-111; and land and
building capitalization scale,
108-111
Land and building capitalization
scale: and farm size, 109-111;
and land and building capitalization intensity, 108-111
Land and building investment
intensity, 13-24; and farm
size, 109-111; and land and

building investment scale, 106-111
Land and building investment scale: and farm size, 109-111; and land and building investment intensity, 106-111
Land input intensity, 13-24
Land planes, 121
Large farms, 43, 109-111, 141; industrialization indicator, 2-8; and irrigation, 43. See also Farm scale; Farm size
Leaching, 71
Leasing, 111
Legume silage, 145
Lemons, 61-63
Leonardo, E., 79
Lime, 65, 75
Listers, 34
Livestock, 64, 89, 145, 159; county values, 72; -crop economy, 209; enterprises, 33, 48, 51, 77, 79, 81, 87, 144, 149; farming, 83, 146; farms, 4, 31, 153; feeding, 17, 73; income, 69; industry, 145; inventories, 148; investment, 221; operations, 130; operators, 87; production, 89, 146; products, 30, 64, 146; purchases, 94; raising, 19, 68, 72, 79, 82, 84, 88, 96-97, 144, 146-147, 166, 173, 180, 191-192, 198, 201, 209; ranches, 142, 144, 146; revolution, 93, 147; -share rental, 234n.3; systems, 146; transportation of, 96, 144; variables, 161. See also individual animals and systems
Livestock-poultry capitalization: intensity, 72-104; scale, 142-157
Livestock-poultry expenditure intensity, 89-96, 164; and crop investment intensity, 97, 154-155; and crop investment scale, 154-155; and cropping expenditure intensity, 96-97, 154-155; and cropping expenditure scale, 154-155; and livestock-poultry expenditure scale, 154-155; and livestock-poultry investment intensity, 89-97, 154-155; and livestock-poultry investment scale, 154-155
Livestock-poultry expenditure scale, 151-155; and crop investment intensity, 154-155; and crop investment scale, 154-155; and cropping expenditure intensity, 154-155; and cropping expenditure scale, 154-155; and large farm size, 153-154; and livestock-poultry expenditure intensity, 154-155; and livestock-poultry investment intensity, 154-155; and livestock-poultry investment scale, 154-155; and small farm size, 153
Livestock-poultry investment intensity, 72-88, 164; and crop investment intensity, 88-89, 97, 154-155; and crop investment scale, 154-155; and cropping expenditure intensity, 97, 154-155; and cropping expenditure scale, 154-155; and livestock-poultry expenditure intensity, 89-97, 154-155; and livestock-poultry expenditure scale, 149-150, 154-155; and livestock-poultry investment scale, 149-150, 154-155
Livestock-poultry investment scale, 142-151; and crop investment intensity, 154-155; and crop investment scale, 150-151, 154-155; and cropping expenditure intensity, 154-155; and cropping expenditure scale, 154-155; and large farms, 144-149; and livestock-poultry expenditure intensity, 154-155; and livestock-poultry expenditure scale, 154-155; and livestock-poultry investment intensity, 149-150, 154-155; and smaller farms, 145-146, 148-149
Loess: Bluffs, 66; soils, 17
Long-term investments, 46-47, 79
Long-term financing, 75
Louisiana, 35, 45, 57, 95, 177;

Acadian Prairies, 57, 109; New Orleans area, 115; southern, 46, 57-58, 122-123, 132; -Texas border area, 82; -Texas Coastal Prairies, 55, 81, 83, 135, 138, 140; Texas-, Gulf Coast, 122, 150. See also Lower Alluvial Valley; Mississippi Delta

Lower Alluvial Valley, 21, 24, 42, 55, 82, 108, 141, 151, 177, 192, 209. See also "Delta"; Lower Mississippi Valley; Mississippi bottomlands; Mississippi lowlands

Lower Mississippi Valley, 4, 21, 35-36, 42, 45-47, 66, 68, 81, 88, 106, 108-109, 115-116, 121, 127-132, 135, 137-138, 140, 142, 166, 191, 198, 209, 229, 232; land clearing in the, 111. See also "Delta"; Lower Alluvial Valley; Mississippi bottomlands; Mississippi lowlands

Machine costs, 119, 136
Machine crops, 122
Machine depreciation, 39
Machine harvesting, 126
Machine hire, 37-39, 42-43, 216, 221. See also Customwork; Labor
Machine inventories, 37, 119-121, 124, 137
Machine repair: costs, 39
Machine work, 128
Machinery, 1, 8, 25, 33, 36-37, 39, 45, 110-111, 114, 126, 136, 216; buildings housing, 110; companies, 137; and equipment investment intensity, 31-38; facilities, 76; fueling, 127; industry, 116; large, 48; lines, 116; manufacturers, 46; -operating firms, 36; operation, 50. See also Machines
Machines, 44, 46, 48; digging, 37; field, 120; harvesting, 33; hired, 130; hiring of, 126; larger, 123; smaller, 116; wind, 127. See also individual types; Machinery

Mage, J. A., 235n.7
Maine, 80, 92, 149, 154; Androscoggin County, 151; Aroostook County, 132, 209; northern, 114, 128, 130, 151, 191; southern, 28; southwestern, 81, 151
Man-equivalent values, 99n.20
Management, 7; communication problems, 111; firms, 44; good, 68; quality, 215; systems, 1, 43
Manufacturers, 141
Manure, 70, 84, 96; feedlot, 85; spreader, 33
Market atraction, 22, 52, 60-61
Market conditions, 149, 151, 204
Market connections, 86
Market demands, 78, 80, 95; Eastern, 62
Market distance, 92
Market gardening, 53, 114, 149. See also Truck farming
Market inelasticity, 13
Markets, 64, 78-79, 82, 96, 146, 192, 201, 215; access to, 144, 215; competition on world, 64; growth, 56; in home building, 57; isolation from major, 204; labor, 112; large, 86, 122, 136; local, 64; in Megalopolis, 80; national, 64; in the Northeast, 80; in northern United States, 56; profitability of the, 128; in the South, 82, 93-94; urban, 69, 77-78, 136, 148; wheat, 56. See also Population
Maryland, 30, 53; Peninsula, 54, 68
Massachusetts: eastern, 81
Mather, E. C., 126, 153
Meadows, 86
Meat, 75. See also Beef
Mechanization, 43, 119, 132, 136, 159, 161, 166, 180, 216, 221, 230; agricultural, 132; in American agriculture, 161; capitalization intensity, 31-46; capitalization scale, 116-132; continuing, 232; -crop linkage, 54; efficiency, 45; farming, 44, 116; in harvesting and feeding roughages, 76;

higher-order patterns, 44-46,
128-132; and labor, 173; and
large-scale farming, 116-132;
over-, 34, 123; of peanut
harvesting, 122; relationship
to agricultural industrialization, 132; scale, 116-132;
of specialty-crop operations,
128; yields and, 136
Mechanization expenditure intensity, 38-44; and labor expenditure intensity, 130-132;
and labor expenditure scale,
130-132; and labor investment
intensity, 46; and mechanization expenditure scale, 128-
132; and mechanization
investment intensity, 44-46
Mechanization expenditure
scale: and labor expenditure
intensity, 130-132; and labor
expenditure scale, 130-132;
and mechanization expenditure
intensity, 128-132; and
mechanization investment
scale, 126-128
Mechanization intensity, 31, 34,
38; dilution of, 37; expenditure, 38-44; investment, 31-
38, 44-46, 123-124; and labor
intensity, 31-38; and land
quality, 34; patterns compared, 44-46
Mechanization investment intensity, 31-38; and mechanization
expenditure intensity, 44-46;
and mechanization investment
scale, 123-124
Mechanization investment scale,
116-124; and farm size, 118,
120-124, 126; and land and
building capitalization scale,
120-124; and mechanization
expenditure scale, 126-128;
and mechanization investment
intensity, 123-124
Mechanization operational
expenditures: intensity, 38-
44; intensity and labor expenditure intensity, 46; scale,
124-128
Mechanized labor, 46, 130-131,
161, 164, 221

Mechanized operations, 48
Megalophilia, 126
Megalopolis, 23-24, 28, 31, 34,
41-42, 45, 53, 66, 70-71, 80-
81, 83, 87-89, 91-92, 97, 106,
108-110, 115, 123, 128-132,
135, 137, 140, 142, 148, 153,
164, 169, 177, 191, 198, 201,
221, 224, 230, 232; northern,
92, 220; southern, 92. See
also Mid-Atlantic Seaboard;
North Atlantic Seaboard; Northeast
Melons, 62
Metropolitanization, 164. See
also Urban influence; Urbanization
Mexico, 95
Michigan, 17, 22, 31, 41, 77-78,
81, 106; Alleghan-Ottawa-Kent
counties, 79, 89; central, 52;
Cutover, 48, 78, 224; Lower
Peninsula, 41, 78, 108; northern, 6; Saginaw Plain, 22, 41,
78, 166; southern, 18, 51, 224;
Upper Peninsula, 28, 78; western, 79, 89; Western, Fruit
Belt, 28, 41, 69, 78, 112, 224
Mid-Atlantic Seaboard, 3, 18, 28,
30, 79-81, 92, 129, 138, 149,
164, 224, 230. See also
Megalopolis; North Atlantic
Seaboard
Middle Atlantic states, 24. See
also individual states; Northeast, U.S.
Middle West, 4, 8-9, 17-18, 20,
22-23, 29, 34, 39, 41, 45, 48,
51-53, 55-56, 61, 66, 69-70,
73, 78-81, 85-86, 88, 91-95,
106, 108, 123, 130-131, 135,
140-142, 164, 166, 177, 180,
189, 191, 196, 220, 234,
235n.3; drainage in the, 20;
eastern, 77, 198, 209; western,
80, 89, 92, 97
Migrants, 31
Migration patterns (crops), 62-
63
Migrations: seasonal sheep, 144.
See also Transhumance
Milk, 76, 80, 92; hauling, 148;
prices, 92; reconstituted, 81;

sales, 81
Milkers, 148
Milking, 80; machine, 33; parlors, 33; systems, 33
Milksheds, 77
Milo, 51, 59, 95
Minerals, 50
Minnesota, 17, 21, 30, 41, 73, 81, 91, 198, 220; Cutover, 78; Valley, 80, 123, 151, 166; northern, 69; Ramsey County, 115; southeastern, 73; southern, 39, 51-53, 114, 128, 209; southwestern, 153. See also Corn Belt, western; Dairy Belt, western; Red River Valley
Mint, 64
Mississippi, 19, 21; Black Belt, 19, 55, 84, 93, 127, 130; "Delta," 122; Gulf Coast, 109; Loess Bluffs, 147; northern, 19, 36; northwestern, 147; Pine Hills, 42, 147, 150; southern, 42, 55, 66, 82-83; Yazoo Basin, 55. See also Lower Alluvial Valley
Mississippi alluvial lands. See Lower Alluvial Valley
Mississippi bottomlands, 19, 42, 56, 66, 224. See also "Delta"; Lower Alluvial Valley; Lower Mississippi Valley; Mississippi lowlands
Mississippi Delta, 23, 29-30, 57, 108, 115, 131-132, 164
Mississippi lowlands, 56, 122. See also "Delta"; Lower Alluvial Valley; Lower Mississippi Valley; Mississippi bottomlands
Missouri, 77, 207; "boot heel," 55; northern, 34, 209; southeastern, 55; southern, 18-19; southwestern, 83; Valley, 17
Mixed crop area, 36, 42
Mixed farming, 48, 164; tobacco-, 192
Molasses, 95
Money crops, 52, 135-136, 230. See also Cash crops
Monmonier, M. S., 34
Mono-enterprise, 77. See also Single-crop cultivation
Monoculture. See Single-crop cultivation
Montana, 58-59, 118, 126, 129; Bitterroot lowlands, 86; Flathead Lake lowlands, 86; Salmon lowlands, 86; western, 86

National ethic, 215
Natural gas, 43, 70. See also Fuel
Nebraska, 43, 59, 73, 75, 85, 108, 120, 126, 146, 198; eastern, 58, 84, 198, 201; northeast, 150; Sand Hills, 145; Scotts Bluff area, 30, 44; south-central, 58-59; southeastern, 17, 58, 94; southern, 161; southwestern, 20, 60; western, 30, 38. See also Corn Belt; Platte Valley; Winter Wheat Belt
Net farm income, 7
Nevada, 17, 86, 120, 134; Clark County, 115; Humboldt Valley, 134; southern, 65; Virgin Valley, 65
New England, 3; northern, 80, 115; southern, 22, 53, 68, 80, 164; states, 24
New Hampshire, 92; southeastern, 81
New Jersey, 21, 80, 110; northern, 81; southern, 81
New Mexico, 17, 44, 180. See also Rio Grande Valley, middle
New York, 28, 34, 122; Black River Valley, 148; City metropolitan area, 192, 229; Finger Lakes Region, 80, 112, 115; Hudson Valley, 28, 123; Lake Champlain-St. Lawrence Plain, 148; Mohawk Valley, 28, 148; northern, 80; Ontario-Mohawk Plain, 123, 129-131, 191; Ontario Plain, 112, 115; southeastern, 149, 151; southern, 154; Sullivan County, 151; western, 41, 112, 128, 132
Nitrogen, 50, 68, 70; fertilizer, 70
North Carolina, 24, 35-36, 42, 45, 54, 58, 108, 123, 164, 177,

191-192, 196, 209, 220;
central, 29; coastal, 66;
Coastal Plain, 83, 166; Duplin
County, 83; eastern, 19, 29,
54, 115, 164; Piedmont, 84,
196; "Urban Crescent," 28, 84;
Virginia-, boundary, 55;
western, 29, 177, 192
North Dakota, 30, 118, 126, 137,
145; southeastern, 84. See
also Red River Valley; Spring
Wheat Belt
North, U.S., 29, 35, 69, 82,
115, 121-123, 127, 129, 141,
148, 177, 198
Northeast, U.S., 18, 20, 22-23,
29, 34, 39, 44-46, 70-71,
78, 80-81, 89, 92, 94, 108,
112, 114-115, 122, 135-136,
148-150, 153-154, 164, 173,
177, 180, 189, 191, 196, 198,
220, 229-230, 232; dairy
areas of the, 154; interior,
220; upper, 220
Northeastern quarter (U.S.), 44,
108, 224. See also Middle
West; Northeast, U.S.
Nursery products, 57. See also
Horticultural products
Nut harvesting equipment, 37
Nut hulling equipment, 37
Nuts, 61, 64

Oats, 51, 59, 80; corn-, -hay
rotation, 50
Ogallala Formation, 20, 60, 119
Ohio, 51, 77, 106, 114; Cleveland area, 128; drainage in,
21; eastern, 17; Maumee
Valley, 78, 88, 166, 173, 209;
northeastern, 201; northwestern, 78; southeastern, 34;
southwestern, 79. See also
Corn Belt, eastern
Oil, 127. See also Energy;
Fuel; Petroleum industry
Oklahoma, 30, 43, 47, 126, 137,
145, 207; central, 20; Crosstimbers, 20; Osage Hills, 145;
southeastern, 19
Olives, 62
Omaha-Amarillo Beef Belt, 94
Onion field graders, 37

Onion planters, 37
Onion sackers, 37
Onion toppers, 37
Operator-equivalents, 99n.20, 230
Operators, 53, 69, 92, 95, 128,
144, 207, 229; Corn Belt, 52;
custom, 126; expanding, 41;
feedlot, 85-87, 96, 147; fulltime, 99n.20, 229; larger, 25,
48, 75, 95, 116, 119, 126-127,
135-137; machinery, 46, 127; of
machines, 46; nonfarm, 39;
part-time, 230; poultry, in
Megalopolis, 81; smaller, 25,
48, 76, 95, 127, 135-136, 229;
smaller, in Florida, 110;
specialized, 44; struggling,
82. See also individual types;
Farmers; Growers
Opportunity, 234
Orange areas, 52
Oranges, 57, 61-63; Navel, 61;
Valencia, 61
Orchard crops, 38. See also
individual crops
Orchardists, 36
Orchids, 120
Oregon, 16, 24, 64, 134; Hood
River Valley, 16; interior,
129; northeastern, 120; northwestern, 87; western, 46, 95,
146; Willamette Valley, 16, 29,
38, 44-45, 64, 71, 88-89, 96,
108, 115, 130-131, 134, 142,
164, 169, 191, 209, 220.
See also Columbia Plateau;
Pacific Northwest; Pacific
states
Organic material, 66; depletion,
70
Osage Hills, 145.
Overplanting, 229
Ozark-Ouachita Highlands, 3-4,
18, 77, 205. See also Springfield Plateau

Pacific Coast, 20, 24, 46, 68,
71, 89, 144, 169. See also
West, U.S., Far
Pacific Northwest, 68, 112, 115,
138, 191; Trans-Cascade, 29,
38, 44, 88, 164; urbanized
counties, 89

Pacific Southwest, 31, 37-39,
    43-46, 60, 62-64, 68, 71, 92,
    94-95, 106, 108, 115, 120,
    122-123, 127-128, 130-131,
    134-135, 137-138, 141-142,
    146-147, 151, 153-155, 164,
    177, 180, 191, 221, 232.
    See also Southwest, U.S.
Pacific States, 89, 112. See
    also individual states; West,
    U.S., Far West
Packing companies, 29
Packing operations, 85
Packing plants, 87
Parasite control, 46. See also
    Crop-protection agents;
    Fungicides; Herbicides;
    Pesticides; Sprays
Part-time farming, 84, 91, 149,
    198, 229
Pasture, 16, 50, 80, 93, 144,
    147; cropland, 52; improvement, 73; mountain, 96
Pea harvesters, 37
Peanut-cotton farms, 42
Peanut harvesting, 121
Peanuts, 36, 54-55, 58; drying,
    42; harvesting, 122
Pears, 63
Pearson correlation coefficient,
    161
Peas, 34
Pennsylvania, 28, 34, 122;
    southeastern, 53, 80-81, 229;
    western, 80, 192, 201
Pesticides, 1, 25, 65, 70, 121.
    See also Crop-protection
    agents; Fungicides; Herbicides; Parasite control;
    Sprays
Pests, 70-71. See also Insects
Petroleum industry, 23. See
    also Oil
Philippines, 95
Phosphorus, 68
Pickup baler, 33
Piedmont, 4, 66, 106, 141, 207;
    Georgia, 23, 150; lower, 53,
    150; North Carolina, 84, 196;
    northern, 45, 82; South
    Carolina, 55, 150; "Urban
    Crescent," 28, 84; Virginia,
    149, 196

Pig feeders, 73
Pigs, 75, 77, 79, 91. See also
    Hogs
Pineapple: sugarcane-, lands, 45
Pineapple plantations, 110, 120
Pineapples, 61
Pipe: companies, 137; gated, 120;
    irrigation, 122
Plains states, 106. See also
    individual states; Great Plains
Plant populations, 50, 71
Plantation system, 82; legacy in
    the South, 121-122
Plantations: conversion of, 147;
    industrialized, 12n.16; pineapple, 110, 120; Southern, 136;
    sugarcane, 110, 120
Planters, 121
Plants: expenditures for, 216
Platte Valley, 196, 224; lower,
    145; lower middle, 58; middle,
    38, 71, 84, 108, 132, 138, 142,
    161, 169; South, 44, 84, 89,
    94, 145, 154, 164; upper, 38,
    58
Plowing, 39
Plows, 34, 37; contour, 121
Plum growers, 62
Policy decisions, 215. See also
    Government policies
Political pressures, 25
Pollution, 1; air, 85; soil, 85;
    water, 85
Pond construction, 42
Population, 149. See also
    Markets
Population centers. See Urban
    centers
Pork, 50
Potato farms, 137; sprinkler-
    irrigated, 137
Potato harvesters, 118
Potatoes, 37-38, 53, 59, 65, 80
Poultry, 28-30, 42, 45, 77,
    79-81, 83, 89, 92-94, 115, 149-
    150, 159, 177, 216, 224; areas,
    42, 46, 82-83, 89, 153-154,
    207, 209; county values, 72;
    enterprises, 85; farmers, 72,
    96; farms, 19, 26, 29, 35, 87;
    feed purchases, 92; investment,
    83; producers, 93; production,
    89; profits from, 224; and

255

tobacco areas, 39; -tobacco belt, 35; -tobacco-mixed crop area, 36, 42, 46. See also individual types; Livestock; Livestock-Poultry
Poultry raising, 31, 36, 42, 81-85, 87-89, 94, 97, 146-148, 164, 166, 180, 192, 198, 201; intensity in the South, 173; intensive industrialization of, 177; in Megalopolis, 81; similarity to industry, 72
Power: hydroelectric, 127; resources, 43; sources, 123
Prairie Provinces, 126
Precision planters, 34
Price-support loans, 229. See also Farm programs; Government payments
Price supports, 228
Pricing mechanisms, 73
Processing, 62
Processors, 52
Product standardization, 72
Production, 55; areal intensification, 25; costs of, 13, 81; crop, 95; expenses, 65; and fertilizer consumption, 71; and general agricultural industrialization, 215-221; insufficient, 220; more intensive, 118; and mechanization, 119; scale of, 13; volume, 116. See also individual products
Productivity: and agricultural industrialization, 215-221; intensity and scale, 216-221; pressures for, 91; problems of, indicators, 216; and profitability, 221, 224, 229-230, 232; regional ranking, 220-221; types and agricultural industrialization types, 220-221
Profit: making, 221-232; net, 216; operator, 230, 232. See also Income; Profits
Profitability: and agricultural industrialization, 221-232; intensity and scale, 221-232; and productivity, 221, 224, 229-230, 232. See also Efficiency
Profits, 33, 52-53, 82, 96, 137, 221, 224; and bigness, 116; squeeze, 144. See also Income; Profit
Protein, 50
Prunes, 63
Pulpwood, 136
Pumping, 43; costs, 121; equipment, 121; fuel for, 42; installations, 63
Pumps, 65, 121-122

Radios: two-way, 110
Rainfed cropping, 145
Ranchers, 86, 94, 144; smaller, 85
Ranches, 38, 142, 144, 146-148
Ranching areas, 153; more intensive, 130. See also specific areas
Ranching "peninsula," 146
Range, 16, 86
Real estate values, 14
Reclamation: drainage, 21, 53-54; land, 111, 121
Recreational services, 230
Red River Valley, 20, 30, 38, 48, 58-59, 71, 88, 108, 118, 134, 138, 140, 142, 151, 169, 191, 196, 224
Refineries, 120
Rent, 81
Renting, 111
Repair shops, 120. See also Tractor stations
Replacement stock, 95
Resource depletion, 59
Retail chains, 82
Rhode Island, 81
Rice, 21, 35, 39, 55-56, 66, 121-122, 136, 147, 224; "core," 45; farming, 95; farms, 37, 55, 120; irrigation of, 42; production, 55; sugarcane-, -soybean-cotton areas, 45
Rio Grande Valley, 129, 131, 149; lower, 30, 38, 44, 58, 115, 129, 134, 142, 164, 166, 220; middle, 38, 65, 134, 220
Risks, 137
Rocky Mountain area, 85, 106; northern, 96

Root crops, 37. See also
 specific types
Rotations, 62; dry-farming, 64
Roughage, 93
Row cropping, 82
Row spacing, 50
Rural ethic, 26
Rural exodus, 114

Safflower, 63
Sales: efficiency, 229; gross, 4; net, 230; value of, 215
Salinization, 21
Schnell, G. A., 34
Sea Islands, 115
Seasonal movements (crops), 62
Seed companies, 137
Seeds, 13, 25, 47, 65, 136, 216
Sheep, 77, 86, 88; farmers, 96; operations, 86; prices, 103n.62
Sheepherding, 144
Sheepmen, 144
Shenandoah Valley, 83
Shrubbery, 57
Silage, 76, 153; corn, 119, 145; legume, 145; sorghum, 145
Silo-filling, 39
Silo unloaders, 33
Single-crop cultivation, 136. See also Mono-enterprise
Siphon tubes, 119
Smith, D. L., 121
Soil animals, 70
Soil Bank Program, 14
Soils: alluvial, 17, 66; Coastal Plain, 68; Dairy Belt, 77; deteriorating conditions, 234; in dryland areas, 71; grassland, 84; loess, 17; midwest, 70; organic, 57, 66; peat and muck, 57; prairie, 17; sandy, 57; southern, 141
Sorghum silage, 145
South America, 95
South Atlantic states, 3. See also individual states; Southeast, U.S.
South Carolina, 24, 36, 42, 45, 94, 108, 141-142, 177, 192, 196, 220; Coastal Plain, 109, 135, 166; eastern, 19, 115; Georgia-, Piedmont, 55; Inner Coastal Plain, 127, 129-130, 224; lower Piedmont, 147, 150; northeastern, 54; Sea Islands, 115; southern, 45-46
South Dakota, 30, 118, 126, 137, 146, 198; central, 129. See also Red River Valley; Spring Wheat Belt
South, U.S., 4, 9, 14, 18-21, 23-24, 29, 35-36, 39, 42-43, 46, 53-58, 61, 63, 66, 68-70, 73, 81-85, 92-94, 105-106, 108-109, 111, 114, 121-123, 127, 129, 140-142, 146-147, 150, 153-154, 164, 166, 169, 173, 177, 180, 189, 191, 196, 198, 209, 220, 224, 234
Southeast, U.S., 4, 91, 95. See also South, U.S.; Southeastern states
Southeastern states, 95. See also individual states; Southeast, U.S.
Southwest, U.S., 3, 55, 63, 96, 153, 234. See also Pacific Southwest
"Soybean revolution," 50
Soybeans, 17, 19, 35-36, 45, 50-55, 59, 61, 66, 73, 78-79, 93, 111, 119, 121, 136; expansion in the South, 55-56; meal, 95; oil, 50; sugarcane-rice-, -cotton areas, 45
Specialization, 48, 50, 52, 75-76, 88, 126; areal, 61-62; dairy, 80; increasing, 146; operational, 76; by regions, 52; spatial, 76; varietal, 62
Specialty crop areas, 45, 122, 127, 134, 191. See also individual-crop areas
Specialty cropping, 34, 53, 112, 135
Specialty crops, 19, 42-43, 45, 52, 78, 80, 115, 118, 135, 137, 141, 146, 224; production, 191
Spinach, 136; cutters, 37; loaders, 37
Sprayers, 34
Spraying, 127
Sprays, 227. See also Crop-protection agents; Fungicides; Parasite control; Pesticides;

Herbicides
Spring Wheat Belt, 118, 136, 145, 151, 209; western, 118-119
Springfield Plateau, 83. See also Ozark-Ouachita Highlands
Springfield Prairies, 19
Stock dams, 145
Stocker calves, 147
Stocker-grazing, 147
Stockers, 93
Storage cellars, 137
Subsidies, 230; agricultural, 48; crop control, 221. See also Crop payments
Subsistence farms, 3
Success: economic, 215
Sugar beet harvesters, 118
Sugar beet pulp, 95, 145
Sugar beet tops, 95, 146
Sugar beets, 38, 59, 62, 65, 136
Sugar plantations, 38
Sugarcane, 35, 56-57, 61, 66, 120-122, 224; farming, 57; farms, 30; lands, 57; -pineapple lands, 45; plantations, 110, 120; -rice-soybean-cotton areas, 45; vegetable-, areas, 45
Suppliers, 141
Swine enterprises, 79. See also Hog farming; Hog raising

Tax laws, federal, 229
Tax loopholes, 229-230
Tax-loss farming, 227. See also "Wall Street" farming
Tax policies, 111. See also Farm programs; Government policies; Price-support loans
Tax situations, 79
Taxes, 229; rising, 87
Technological pressures, 25, 96
Technologies, 60, 73, 76; changing, 229; industrialization, 80
Technology, 1, 13, 116; advancing, 2, 12n.16; agricultural, 142; communication, 110; irrigation, 119; pressures of, 120
Telephones, 110
Television: closed-circuit, 110

Tenant: multiple, 111
Tennessee, 68, 93, 177; eastern, 19, 35-36, 84, 192, 201; middle, 84, 150; Nashville Basin, 19, 24, 84, 93, 207; north central, 58; northeastern, 58, 89; western, 19
Texas, 43, 47, 59, 94-95, 147, 207, 209; Blackland Prairie, 4, 19, 23, 30, 55, 66, 94, 109, 127, 207; central, 20, 201, 204; Coastal Prairies, 84, 147, 151; Corpus Christi Plains, 19; Cross Timbers, 20, 147, 204; eastern, 30, 42, 201; Edwards Plateau, 147; Grand Prairie, 23, 207; Gulf Coast, 19, 115, 150, 192, 196; Louisiana-, Coastal Prairies, 55, 81, 83, 135, 138, 140; -Louisiana Gulf Coast, 122; northwestern, 94; Panhandle, 60, 84-85, 94, 97; Post Oak Strip (Belt), 84, 94, 147, 204; Rio Grande Delta, 19; southernmost, 30; western, 180. See also High Plains; Rio Grande Valley
Tidewater, 54
Timothy: clover-, 52
Tobacco, 45, 53, 55, 58, 61, 66, 82, 224; air-cured, 68; allotments, 54; areas, 19, 29, 36, 42, 45-46, 68, 122, 177, 196; "belts," 29; brightleaf, 54; burley, areas, 89; burley, belts, 58; curing, 39, 42, 45; enterprise, 35, 84; farms, 29; flue-cured, 54, 68, 196; harvester, 35-36; larger, farms, 36; -mixed crop farming, 192; and mixed crops area, 220; operations, 164; poultry and, areas, 39; poultry-, belts, 35
Tomato picker, 37
Tomatoes, 62
Tractor stations, 121. See also Repair shops
Tractors, 33-34, 37, 46, 121
Transhumance, 144. See also Migrations
Transportation, 81, 85, 93, 144, 232
Tree crop shifts, 63

Tree crops, 63. See also
 specific crops
Truck crops, 52, 60, 135, 224
Truck enterprises, 123
Truck farming, 53, 57, 114, 135;
 centers, 115. See also Market
 gardening
Trucks, 120-121, 144, 147;
 grain, 126; refrigerated, 148
Turkey prices, 103n.62
Turnovers: expense, 224, 229
Two-row transplanter, 35

Unemployment: rural, 207
United States, 68, 95, 115, 147;
 eastern, 57, 63, 108, 148;
 northeastern, 191; northern,
 56, 150; southern, 45, 201;
 western, 106, 180
Urban annexation, 87
Urban areas, 88, 229; accessi-
 bility to, 63; coalescence,
 64; competition from, 71; milk
 sales in, 81. See also
 Cities; Industrial centers;
 Urban centers
Urban influence, 22, 45, 63, 89,
 164, 196, 229. See also
 Metropolitanization; Urbani-
 zation
Urban markets, 69, 77-78, 136,
 148; milk needs, 77
Urban pressures, 25, 79, 87
Urban-rural competition, 87
Urbanization, 30, 149, 232; loss
 of citrus land to, 57; pres-
 sures of, 198. See also
 Metropolitanization; Urban
 influence
Urea, 72
Utah, 17, 96, 134; basin lands,
 201; Salt Lake Oasis, 65;
 Sevier lowland, 86; Wasatch
 Oasis, 17, 38, 86

Value added, 216, 230, 232,
 234n.1
Value of farm products sold:
 net, 221, 232
Varimax rotation, 166, 187n.5
Vegetable crops, 62, 87. See
 also individual crops; Vegetables

Vegetable enterprises, 123
Vegetable farmers, 36
Vegetable farming, 227
Vegetable farms, 37, 137; large,
 111
Vegetable growers, 37
Vegetable production, 57, 137
Vegetable raising, 34
Vegetable residues, 145
Vegetable-sugarcane areas, 45
Vegetables, 26, 28, 30, 37,
 52-54, 56, 61-66, 71, 79, 122,
 137, 224, 229. See also
 individual crops; Vegetable
 crops
Vermont, 122, 154
Vertical integration, 7, 72,
 82-83, 85, 137
Vertical zonation, 61
Vertically-integrated farm, 83
Virginia, 22, 36, 42, 122, 138,
 177, 220; coastal, 66; eastern,
 54; -North Carolina boundary,
 55; Piedmont, 149, 196; Ridge-
 and-Valley area, 149; Shenandoah Valley, 83; southwestern,
 201; western, 19, 84

Wage competition, 28
Wage rates, 99-100n.21, 112, 114-
 115, 224
Wages, 218; cash, 29
"Wall Street" farming, 229. See
 also Tax-loss farming
Walnuts, 61
Warehouses, 137
Washington, 16, 24; Big Bend
 area, 65; central, 30, 44,
 64-65; Columbia Basin, 169,
 196; Columbia Basin Project,
 44, 65; eastern, 44, 88, 120,
 140; interior, 129, 191;
 Palouse, 65, 88, 120, 140, 142,
 145, 209; Puget Sound Lowland,
 16, 38, 44-45, 64, 72, 88-89,
 97, 108, 115, 131, 150; southeastern, 64; Walla Walla
 Valley, 44; Wenatchee Valley,
 16, 30, 44, 64; west-central,
 164; western, 46, 87, 96, 146,
 153-154, 169, 191, 198; Yakima
 Valley, 16, 30, 38, 44, 64, 96.
 See also Columbia Plateau;

Pacific states
Water, 234; competition for, 87; costs, 71; in feedlot operations, 84; irrigation, 60, 140; pumping, 63; resources, 43, 58; shortages, 43, 60; struggle for, 64; supplies, 63-64, 84
Water projects: federal, 118
Weeds, 39, 68
Wells: deep, 121
West, U.S., 3-4, 14, 16, 38-39, 43, 46, 48, 69, 71, 73, 84-85, 95, 106, 108, 112, 115, 120-121, 123, 127, 129-130, 132, 134-135, 138, 140, 142, 144, 146, 149, 151, 153-154, 177, 180, 192, 198, 204, 207, 213, 220, 224; drought in the, 119; East-, contrasts, 173, 221; East-, disparity, 137, 141; Far West, 24, 53, 142; poor showing, 138. See also United States, western
West Virginia, 3, 19
Western states, 73, 89. See also individual states; West, U.S.
Wheat, 38-39, 54, 59, 80, 118, 136; acreage controls, 126; areas, 65, 191; California, 63; farming, 118; farms, 119, 191; Mexican, 62; spring, 126; winter, 56, 59, 126
Wind machines, 127
Winter Wheat Belt, 59, 71, 108, 126, 136; "new," 119; "old," 119; subhumid, 30, 38, 43, 58, 108-109, 119, 138, 145, 161, 207, 209
Wisconsin, 17, 41, 51-52, 73, 76-78, 91, 106, 110, 114, 148, 164, 180, 198, 220, 224; Cutover, 48, 71; Driftless Area, 151; eastern, 28, 33, 77, 148, 192; northern, 52, 114; potato and cranberry section, 112; southeastern, 18, 39, 41, 51, 77, 89, 108, 164; southern, 91; western, 69, 78. See also Dairy Belt
"Worker-equivalents," 25, 29. See also Labor
Wyoming, 58-59, 118; Big Horn Basin, 58; northwestern, 86; Basin, 201

Yearlings, 153